To Felicity

Contents

❖

Introduction

THESE days, when you get fed up sitting in Dublin Castle listening to businessmen explain why they gave bundles of cash to a senior politician, you can slip down to the Lower Yard, out the gate opposite the Olympia Theatre, and up the lane to your right. There's a door there leading into the back of number 13 Dame Street, and when you go through you find yourself in Café Rio, a large, long room with wooden floors, mustard-coloured walls, and table service. The waiting staff are young and mostly foreign, from continental Europe, Australia, North America. You can have a latte, a cappuccino, a macchiato, a café mocha, an espresso, a double espresso, an ordinary coffee, a hot chocolate, tea even. It's like so many of the new cafés which opened in the mid-1990s when, for the first time since the Act of Union, Dublin experienced a sustained and substantial economic boom. You can sit there and try to remember, or imagine, what it used to be like: the capital of a failed economy, a failed political entity; a large town, half empty, populated with those fortunate enough not to have had to leave, or who were too indolent to do so.

Back in the 1950s the room occupied by the café was a shop, Callaghan's, a supplier of clothes and equipment to people who kept and rode horses, people who were, as often as not, descendants of the ruling and upper classes who ran Ireland prior to the creation of the Free State. Customers might drive in from large houses in the surrounding counties or even north, south or west

1

Co. Dublin, make some purchases, and then go for a drink in the Shelbourne or Hibernian hotels. In the shop they might rub shoulders with representatives of the Irish Catholic or nationalist bourgeoisie, lawyers and doctors and businessmen, people who shared many characteristics with them: people who went to university at a time when the vast majority didn't attend second-level school; people who travelled abroad for pleasure, sometimes had wine with their dinner, rode horses. If they got into conversation they might touch on politics, de Valera's policy of protectionism, the truly awful state of the country.

Up on the top floor in a few dusty rooms looking out over the city's rooftops, an impatient young man who had just set up an accountancy practice spent much of his free time discussing the state of the new republic's economy, what needed to be done, and why it was Fianna Fáil which was best equipped to carry out this programme. Charles Haughey was twenty-five years old. He and his partner, Harry Boland, were Fianna Fáil activists who, over the coming years, would build a very successful accountancy practice on the back of business done with men who were going to make money in the new, post de Valera republic. What the State needed, Haughey believed, was tough, able, aggressive men who would make lots of money and thereby be able to compete in the tough world of free-market capitalism. The opposite of protectionism.

Although obsessed with politics, Haughey wanted to share with these imagined entrepreneurs the material pleasures which would come with money. He was interested in cars, wanted to drive something luxurious and expensive, like a Jaguar. He wanted to live in a grand house. He liked to eat and drink in the good restaurants which, in those days, were found in the city's more expensive and well-established hotels. He liked horses, galloping across open spaces in the Phoenix Park early in the morning, the exhilaration involved. He was ambitious and able, aggressive and daring, wild even. He believed he could have it all. He was one of life's superior beings.

There was something else too, something which might initially seem contradictory but was more likely a key element of his ambition: he suffered from great insecurity. He wanted the rich and the posh, the people who stood comfortably in Callaghan's buying riding-boots for their children, to accept him as one of their class. It was something that would eat at him all his life, this desire to be accepted in what some people call the top levels of society. He would never gain acceptance, but for some reason always continued to care.

As well as the respect of the established and privileged, he wanted general adulation. He would come to see himself in terms of pre-colonial Irish history, the King of All Ireland to whom other, lesser chieftains should pay homage and offer gifts in thanks for being allowed operate in a blessed and well-run kingdom. He would gather around him people who shared this high opinion of him, people who would in turn benefit from their closeness to the king. It seems he believed the greater good was always served by his getting what he desired. It is absurd, difficult to believe, yet it would seem to be true.

When you finish your coffee you get into a car, drive down Dame Street towards Trinity College, follow the traffic down Westmoreland Street and over O'Connell Bridge, turn right onto the quays. How many hundreds and thousands of times did Haughey make this journey? Through the 1950s, 1960s, 1970s, 1980s, 1990s, the new century. The city changed and stayed the same. He'd turn to the left at Liberty Hall, drive around the Custom House and left into Amiens Street. Later, in the 1960s, this journey would take him past the offices of Haughey Boland, the building his company moved to as it expanded and became a force in the Dublin accountancy world. Many of the people who will feature in this book worked in these offices or employed the services of the accountants who worked there. A company called Amiens Securities became familiar to all those who, during Haughey's nadir, made a good living for a few years prying into his personal financial affairs, searching in vain for nuggets of pure, uncontestable corruption.

He'd pass the Five Lamps, cross the humped bridges over the canal and railway, come to Fairview and his former secondary school, St Joseph's Christian Brothers' School. In the early years, and then again later in his life, he would turn left soon after the school onto the Malahide Road, drive north away from the estuary, past the Casino at Marino and up to the Catholic church at Donnycarney. When he was young he would turn left here, into Collins Avenue, and then left again, into Belton Park. He grew up in number 12, a corner house with a small front garden and a garage. A comfortable, lower middle class home in an old estate of identical houses. The day I went to see it a man stopped beside me and confirmed that I was looking at Haughey's childhood home. "His mother lived there up until she died a few years ago," he said. "His two sisters still live there." An old friend of Haughey's said to me on another occasion that Haughey had a happy childhood, but a poor one.

After he got married he bought a house in Raheny, another corner house, slightly larger, with a bigger garden. Number 490 Howth Road, on the left just before you come to Raheny when you are driving out of town. This was home when a lot of the big connections were being made, when money was really starting to come in and Haughey was a young buck taking a city by storm. It was when he was living in this house that he first got elected.

His children were born when he was in this house. They called him "Da". So did his wife, Maureen.

It was when he was in this house that one of his rich clients came up with a proposal which made him rich. He sold his Raheny home and bought a large Georgian house on forty-five acres called Grangemore. To get to where that house used to stand you drive to the Donaghmede shopping centre and turn to the left just past it. There is a housing estate where the streets are Grangemore this and Grangemore that. The houses were built by the client who suggested Haughey buy the land and then later bought it from him at a hugely increased price. There are cars in the driveways of semi-detached, three-bedroomed houses, children playing on the streets. No-one you ask knows where the big house used to stand.

Later again, when he'd made his killing on the Grangemore land, he moved to Abbeville, Kinsealy. Once this was an attractive estate, well outside the city, walled along the Malahide Road, the big house set well back and out of view. These days, however, from the outside it appears under siege. The road to Malahide is busy with traffic. The country lanes on both sides of the estate are also busy. The nearer lane on the city side is filling up with new houses, including two new bright-coloured houses built for two of Haughey's sons and which are situated off the road, in fields, not far from each other, bare-looking. The lane on the far side of the estate leads to a Cement Roadstone (CRH) plant, site of a land deal between Haughey and CRH a few years after he bought the estate. Perhaps inside, in the house or in the fields in from the roads, all these encroachments, all this ugliness is invisible, inaudible, difficult to imagine.

One day I met a friend of Haughey's for lunch in a Dublin restaurant so we could discuss what he was like. I mentioned how a taxi driver had once said to me, as we drove past the gates to Abbeville, that it was a proper house to have the Taoiseach living in. My lunch companion responded that Haughey too always felt image was important. He liked, when senior politicians or bankers or industrialists were visiting Ireland from abroad, to invite them to Kinsealy, where they would be confronted by a house comparable to those they themselves might live in, and where they would be fed good meals and offered fine wines. He liked to be able to counter any impression the visitors might have about Ireland being an economic basket case. He wanted to represent the state well, and did so by owning a mansion and keeping a well-stocked cellar.

It was the same with his own appearance, and hence the Charvet shirts and tailored suits. He didn't want to appear before them with the arse out of his trousers. He didn't want to present the visitors with anything that would allow them to look down on the State and its people. He had strong national feelings, and it meant a lot to him when on visits abroad to be the leader of one free country meeting another such leader. He was proud to represent the Irish as a free nation, owners of their own destiny, something which most of its citizens now take for granted.

When Haughey began his career in Fianna Fáil de Valera was still the party president. Haughey attended meetings where the old revolutionary sat in the chair. Seán Lemass, Haughey's father-in-law, had also taken part in the 1916 Rising and the struggle for independence. Haughey is a transitional figure, someone who has seen huge change and has been an architect of much of that change during the thirty-five odd years of his political career. He once said in an interview that politics would have had less attraction for him if the State had not needed to be developed, created almost. To be a politician who simply administered a fully developed western democracy, he said, would have been far less interesting.

From the purchase of the house in 1969 Abbeville became the centre of the Haughey legend. How he came to afford such a home and how he could afford its upkeep remained a mystery for thirty years. He filled the house with antiques and works of art. Its walls are heavy with portraits of its owner. His egotism and desire to avoid dislike were to be his Achilles heel, the personality trait which would prevent him living up to the potential those who observed him believed he most definitely had. He could cut through red tape, ignore advice, get things done. But he worried too much about being unpopular.

During his last governments, circumstances contrived to force him to make the necessary decisions. Many of the difficulties the regimes faced were sorted out during half-social meetings in Kinsealy at the weekends. Likewise with Haughey's personal finances. From 1969 to his death in May 1994, Haughey's close associate Des Traynor would visit Haughey on Saturday mornings and they would go to the Abbeville library and discuss their secret dealings. Other members of Haughey's inner circle attended for similar encounters. The most controversial and secretive dealings of the latter half of the twentieth century in Ireland were discussed in the room. It was also in the Abbeville library that Haughey held meetings in early 1997, during which he realised that the secret he had kept for so long concerning his personal finances was now about to be disclosed. If walls had ears, the walls of Charles Haughey's library would have better tales to tell than most.

He suffered periods of melancholy and had fits of panic and doubt. When he was having really bad times senior party figures, such as Brian Lenihan, would travel to Kinsealy and pick him up off the floor. People wondered how a man who was so aggressive and decisive during crises could then fall apart when times were less taxing. Booze was probably part of the answer, with restraint during the periods of crisis being followed by binges which were in turn followed by depression and paralysis.

He ran himself hard. The stress of high office was combined with carousing, womanising, dealing in horses, betting at the races, and the high life generally. We now know that for Haughey political survival was always necessary for personal financial reasons as well as for reasons of political ambition. All along there was the tension created by his massive overheads, his lack of adequate income, the threat of being exposed.

All his political life he performed a high-wire act, and he almost made it safely to the other side. Terry Keane, the social diarist who had an affair with him for thirty years, has recorded one of her early impressions of him, that he was, like her, a chancer. He wanted power, wealth, the pleasures of life. He admired Napoleon, it is said, not a particularly attractive figure. He admired Mitterand, whose reputation is now in tatters, much like Haughey's, and surely much more deservedly so. You wonder whether it was what they got away with, rather than what they achieved, which won his admiration.

He paid a price for his greed. In the end the reputation he cared so much about was destroyed. He had to suffer huge, continuous ignominy at a time when he might otherwise have been assessing his accomplishments. Keane dumped on him when he was down, by selling her story to *The Sunday Times* and then going on television. His years since 1997 were a misery, filled with tribunals, criminal hearings, and tax bills. He never expressed remorse, or chose to explain how he came to act in the way he did. He never came clean. And so, in the end, the State which he set out to serve came to view him as one of its enemies.

Yet he made a significant contribution. Many insiders credit him, rather than Albert Reynolds, with having played the key Dublin role in setting the Northern peace process in motion. Many of the decisions made by his last two governments undoubtedly laid the foundations for the prosperity which came in their wake. He could have done more, if the suspicion which always surrounded him had not existed, if his work had not been hampered by the tension and complications caused by his constant need for money. The time he spent in power would have been longer if his personal financial dealings had been honest.

His desire to devote his life to politics but also live like a lord caused huge damage to political and public life in the Republic. It is at least fair to put the question whether the bad done outweighs the good. However, perhaps it was never possible to separate political and personal ambition. Perhaps for Haughey they were both part of the same need.

In the end the truth about his life was disclosed because of a fall-out inside one of the State's richest families. He got caught in the crossfire. It emerged that for years, decades, a large number of people at a certain level in Irish society had known the truth about a dangerous figure at the heart of Irish politics, but kept their counsel.

This book concentrates on the subject which Charles Haughey wanted all his life to keep secret and which has been missing from earlier works about him: the truth about his money. It tells its story chronologically up to 1987 when, having spent five years in opposition, Haughey finally got his hands back on the reins of power. For the period 1987, to 1992, when Haughey was Taoiseach, the story is structured thematically. This is because during that period the truth about his personal finances is particularly chaotic. It seems he recognised he had only so much time left to gather enough money to see him through his retirement years, and acted accordingly. Large amounts of money which had been donated to the party during this period were taken by Haughey. The third part of this book, dealing with his retirement years, returns to a chronological structure.

A final point which deserves mention is that this book does not tell the whole truth about who gave money to Haughey and what, if anything, they got for it in return. Only some of the details are known. For instance, despite its years of inquiry, the Moriarty Tribunal never found out where the money to fund Haughey's bills for the year 1988 came from. It did not come from the usual bank accounts in Guinness & Mahon. Haughey could be of no assistance.

Haughey's sworn evidence to the McCracken and Moriarty Tribunals was that for most of his political life he did not know where his money was coming from, and so couldn't have done favours for his benefactors. It followed that he could not assist anyone making inquiries into his affairs. It is unlikely that the full truth will ever now emerge. Readers are offered what follows as an outline of what occurred. The rest can be imagined.

Part One

1925–1987

1

A Descendant of Kings

I N 1986, during Haughey's long period as leader of the opposition, a large hard-backed collection of his speeches was published. It was called *The Spirit of the Nation*, and it was edited by Martin Mansergh, a senior Fianna Fáil party adviser and specialist on Irish-British relations. In his introduction Mansergh wrote: "Charles Haughey's political career and achievements are unmatched among his contemporaries and he is the outstanding parliamentarian in the independent Ireland of the late 20th century." Mansergh wrote that Haughey had no input into what was contained in the book other than with the earlier part of the book's opening biographical note.

That note informed readers that Charles James Haughey was born on 16 September 1925 at "Mountain View", Castlebar, Co. Mayo, the third of seven children and second son of Seán Haughey, Commandant, 4th Battalion, Western Command, 2nd Brigade, and his wife, Sarah, née McWilliams. Both parents came from Swatragh, Co. Derry, where their families had lived for generations. Descent "can be traced back to the Uí Neill, the Kings of Ulster." The note continued: "In Irish 'Haughey' means a horseman or knight as the Irish version Eochaidh is derived from the word *each*, meaning a steed. The numerous Ó hEochaidh clan inhabited a wide area of Mid-Ulster and were Kings of Ulidia up to the end of the 12th century. One of the Ó hEochaidh Kings fought and fell with Brian Boru at Clontarf. Haughey's Fort is part of the Emhain Macha (Navan Fort) site near Armagh."

Haughey's father, Seán, was active in the War of Independence in Co. Derry, joined the Free State army upon its establishment, and served as a battalion OC in Ballina and Castlebar. Because of bad health he resigned his commission in March 1928, when aged only twenty-nine years, and settled with his family in Burrow Road, Sutton, Co. Dublin. The following year the family moved to a farm in Dunshaughlin, Co. Meath, and in 1933 moved to 12 Belton Park, Donnycarney. The family there "kept open house for friends and visitors from the North," according to the biographical note. Seán Haughey suffered from multiple sclerosis, and the family of nine survived on his small army pension. They were poor.

Haughey attended the Christian Brothers' primary school at Marino and secondary school at Fairview. He was a bright pupil, took first place in the Dublin Corporation Scholarship examinations, and won a scholarship to University College, Dublin. He joined the Local Defence Force in 1940 when he was fifteen years old and transferred to the FCA upon its formation. He studied commerce in university, won a bursary, and graduated with an honours B.Comm in 1946. In college he took an active interest in politics and debating, interests he shared with a contemporary, Garret FitzGerald, who was to be a lifelong political opponent. After graduating he was articled to Michael J. Bourke of Boland, Bourke & Company. In 1948 he won the Institute of Chartered Accountants John Mackie Memorial Prize. He became an associate member of the institute in 1949, and a fellow in

1955. In 1949 he succeeded in the then unusual achievement of being called to the bar while working as an accountant. He was impatient, energetic, and very able.

Haughey had a strong interest in Ireland's relationship with its nearest neighbour. While still in university he took part in a demonstration outside Trinity College, provoked by the college's hoisting of a Union Jack to mark VE Day. He was part of a group which pulled down the flag and burned it in front of the college gates, a fact alluded to in the biographical notes which introduce *The Spirit of the Nation*. When Haughey's father died in 1947, former IRA comrades provided a guard of honour at the funeral.

That same year Haughey joined Fianna Fáil, signing up for the Tomás Ó Cléirigh Cumann, Dublin North-East, where his friends from St Joseph's, Marino, George Colley and Harry Boland, were already members. Both his friends' families were part of the Fianna Fáil establishment. Boland was the son of Gerry Boland TD, Minister for Justice in the period 1932 to 1948. His brother Kevin was to serve in cabinet with Haughey. Colley was the son of Harry Colley TD. Soon after joining the party Haughey was elected secretary of his cumann and then of the Comhairle Dáilcheantair, Dublin North-East. He was an active and valuable party member.

In 1950 Haughey and Harry Boland set up their accountancy practice, a sister of Boland's who worked as a secretary being the firm's only employee. The two accountants and party activists had studied commerce together in UCD. Their rented offices at 13 Dame Street were next to the Dame Street branch of the Munster and Leinster bank, now part of AIB. They conducted the firm's banking in the branch, and Haughey became a valued personal customer.

Haughey Boland & Co. took on its first articled clerk in 1951, a 20-year-old man called John Joseph (Des) Traynor. He was six years younger than Haughey and a little bit shorter in height. The son of a garage owner from Grand Canal Street, Dublin, he was five foot five and already on the way to developing his distinctive double chin. Educated in the Christian Brothers' school, Westland Row, and later St Mary's College, Rathmines, he had not attended university and so served a longer apprenticeship than would otherwise have been the case. He was articled to Haughey, and the two men quickly became friends.

The next person to join the firm was Maurice O'Kelly. Like Haughey, O'Kelly was a first-class honours commerce graduate from UCD. He and Traynor shared a room, and Haughey and Boland each had a room of their own. Traynor and O'Kelly became lifelong friends, but O'Kelly and Haughey never hit it off.

In those days articled clerks paid a fee to the firm they were working for. O'Kelly, because he was a university graduate, finished his apprenticeship before Traynor. A sportsman who played rugby and League of Ireland football, O'Kelly developed an interest in venture capital, the funding of businesses in the hope that they would grow and provide a sound return. Soon after completing his time with Haughey Boland he went to work in Hong Kong, where he stayed for a number of years before returning to Dublin and setting up the first venture capital business in the city.

Boland had no particular speciality or area of expertise as an accountant, according to associates. What he liked most was the detailed dogwork rather than the wide picture, preferring tasks such as the sorting out of specific complicated problems to, say, reviewing the overall financial health of a particular enterprise. That said, he was comfortable mixing with big business. He was to be one of the founding members of Taca, the controversial Fianna Fáil fund-raising organisation, and served as secretary of the organisation. He never made the move into full-time politics and spent his career working with the accountancy firm.

Like his partner, Haughey never developed a speciality as an accountant. He was not particularly driven, his all-consuming interests being politics, the debating of political issues, and socialising. He used his combination of interests and talents to bring business to the fledgling accountancy firm. He was expert in what three decades later would be termed networking. This interfacing between the worlds of business and politics was at the core of the growth of the fledgling accountancy firm.

Traynor was smart, discreet, humorous, meticulous, tough, determined, and very interested in money. He worked hard and he prospered. In time he found he enjoyed the challenge and stress that came with deal-making and major business transactions, a combination which, along with his smoking habit, was to have serious repercussions for his health. One of his specialities was taxation, and according to one former associate he was obsessed with devices for lowering people's liabilities. "He got a thrill out of tax schemes. He loved them."

Traynor became a partner in Haughey Boland and played a central role in developing the firm into a significant force. In time his business career expanded to include new roles, and as a tax expert and adviser he played an important part in the affairs of some of the largest companies in the State, saving them millions of pounds in Revenue bills. He provided a similar service to the rich and powerful men who owned and ran these companies. When he died in 1994 he was one of the most highly respected "blue chip" businessmen in the State, an expert deal maker and chairman, a rich and able man who had done very well. His reputation has since been destroyed.

Like Traynor, Haughey had an interest in taxation. He believed the greater the amount of profit business people were able to retain, the greater would be their enthusiasm for business activity, a view shared by the clients he introduced to Haughey Boland. The revolutionary generation which had established the Republic were being succeeded by a generation motivated by materialism rather than ideas of independence and moral asceticism. A patriotism which had almost been defined by its anti-materialism was being replaced by a materialism which was clothed, with varying degrees of sincerity, with patriotism. Haughey became the public face of this new, brash and impatient Irish republic.

Less publicly, he and Traynor were together forming the core of a secret "golden circle" which was to exist for the thirty-year span of Haughey's political career and was itself to form a crucial component of the new Ireland.

Other early employees of Haughey Boland will feature in this book. Jack Stakelum was articled to Haughey and became a very close friend of Traynor's. He subsequently left the firm and set up Business Enterprises Ltd, a company which provided financial services and which, from the early 1990s, played a key role in the month-to-month administration of Haughey's finances. Stakelum carried out the liquidation of Abbeyville Ltd, a company used by Haughey when he was buying his estate and mansion in Kinsealy, north Co. Dublin. He also provided other business services to the Haughey family.

Another former employee of Haughey Boland, Sam Field-Corbett, specialised in providing secretarial services to clients, such as establishing companies, presenting documents to the Companies Office on their behalf, and keeping shareholdings on behalf of unidentified beneficial owners. Field-Corbett acted as a director of Larchfield Securities, a company owned by the Haughey children which held a number of the Haughey family assets. On Traynor's suggestion Field-Corbett left Haughey Boland in the 1970s and established his own secretarial services company, Management Investment Services. Traynor told Field-Corbett he'd send business his way, and proved true to his word.

Another person who will feature in this book, Paul Carty, joined Haughey Boland in 1967 and rose to become a managing partner in 1980. Carty was born in 1940 and attended the O'Connell Christian Brothers' school in North Richmond Street in Dublin. He became a partner in Deloitte Touche when that company absorbed Haughey Boland in the early 1990s. Carty played a role in the management of the Haughey family's financial affairs.

In 1951 Haughey stood as a Fianna Fáil candidate for Dublin North-East alongside Oscar Traynor TD, Harry Colley TD, and Eugene Timmons. He was not elected. Two years later he was co-opted onto Dublin Corporation on the death of Senator Michael Colgan, but he lost the seat in the 1955 local elections. In the May 1954 general election he again failed to win a seat.

He stood in April 1956 in a by-election caused by the death of the former Lord Mayor of Dublin Alfie Byrne and again was not successful. In March the following year he was rewarded for his persistence when he was elected in the last general election of the pre-television age. He got 4,168 first-preference votes. His win, however, was at the cost of his friend George Colley's father, Harry Colley. When the Dáil reconvened after the election Éamon de Valera, then seventy-five years old, was elected Taoiseach for what was to be his last term of office.

Haughey had married Maureen Lemass in 1951. His father-in-law, Seán Lemass, was Minister for Industry and Commerce in the de Valera government. It was a time when morale in the

State was particularly low, with boats to England carrying both the economy's chief export, live cattle, and the most visible sign of the economy's inadequacy, young emigrants. Lemass was at the forefront of Fianna Fáil's efforts to jump-start economic life in the State. As Minister for Industry and Commerce he came into contact with many of the business people who were to prosper in the coming decades, people such as the hotelier P. V. Doyle and property developers Matt Gallagher and John Byrne. Haughey, through his relationship with Lemass and his involvement with Fianna Fáil, also got to know these men, some of whom began to use the services of the Haughey Boland firm and, in particular, of Des Traynor.

In his first speech to the Dáil in May 1957, during the budget debate, Haughey concentrated on the need for economic development. What was needed, he said, were industrialists who were making profits and who would in turn make investments in pursuit of further profit. "I should like to put forward the proposition that the trouble with this country is that too many people are making insufficient profits. Too many people are actually making losses. The trouble is not that our bloated industrialists make too much profit but that too few of our industrialists are able to carry on at all."

He argued that the profit motive would fuel the State's economic development, and that the State should be ready and willing to support industrialists in their pursuit of profit. It would be of benefit to the State from every point of view, and particularly from the point of view of the weaker sections of the community, if industrialists were put in a position where they could make profits adequate to ensure their continuation in business and their ability to finance further expansion. What was needed, he said, was a "tremendous national crusade" for economic development.

Over the following few years Haughey made a number of unsuccessful proposals for the reduction or elimination of taxes on specific activities in order to stimulate growth, at one stage suggesting, for example, tax exemptions for market gardening in Irish-speaking areas. In a speech on the budget in 1961 Haughey told the Dáil: "Since I have interested myself in economic affairs I have always been aware of the fact that the greatest single stimulus one can give to an economy is to reduce direct taxation."

Two years after Haughey's first electoral success, de Valera resigned as Taoiseach and was replaced by Lemass. In May 1960 Haughey was appointed parliamentary secretary to the Minister for Justice, Oscar Traynor.

In offering Haughey the post of parliamentary secretary Lemass said: "As Taoiseach it is my duty to offer you the post of parliamentary secretary, and as your father-in-law I am advising you not to take it." Lemass must have known that giving this advice was a pointless exercise. Haughey was patently a political animal and had already publicly expressed his desire to become leader of Fianna Fáil within ten years.

He was already showing signs of personal wealth. A year before the offer from Lemass he had moved with his family from their semi-detached house in Raheny to nearby Grangemore. The large Georgian house was on 45 acres and was a long way in size and luxury from his childhood home. As the 1950s came to a close Haughey must have viewed his progress with some satisfaction. The pleasure must have been all the greater for being mixed, as it presumably was, with the conviction that the adventure had only just begun.

2

The Tax Commissioner's Residence

PEOPLE who knew Haughey in the 1950s say he was such an able young man, so driven and so involved in politics, that they have no doubt he would one day have become Taoiseach, whether or not he'd married Maureen Lemass. Whatever the truth or otherwise of that, there can be little doubt that his marriage put him on the inside track, knocking years off the time it took him to become a recognised contestant for the party leadership.

When he married Maureen Lemass on 18 September 1951, the ceremony was attended not only by her father, Seán Lemass, then Minister for Industry and Commerce, but also by the then Taoiseach, Éamon de Valera. Haughey was just two days past his twenty-sixth birthday. The couple had met at university, where Maureen had, like her husband, read commerce. Haughey had at the time of his marriage established his accoutancy firm with his friend Harry Boland. The young couple moved into 490 Howth Road, a comfortable, middle-class semi-detached house.

During the following ten years the couple had four children: Eimear, born in 1955; Conor, born in 1957; Ciarán, born in 1960; and Seán, born in 1961. It must have been a busy decade, with Haughey establishing himself in business and politics and at the same time being father to four young children. His talent and promise were widely recognised. In 1961 the then leader of Fine Gael, John Dillon, praised his "exceptional and outstanding ability".

He made sure of his hold over his Dáil seat. In the general election in October 1961 he topped the poll in Dublin North-East, more than doubling his first-preference vote from the 4,168 which had seen him elected for the first time in 1957, to 8,566. He was appointed Minister for Justice.

As well as being an able politician he was a high-profile one. His ability and impatience combined with his extravagance meant he made excellent copy. In 1962 he became the only member of cabinet to own a racehorse when he acquired a five-year-old bay mare called Miss Cossie. The purchase of the horse received a large amount of media coverage, including an "interview" with the horse carried in the *Sunday Review*. "I'm now a status symbol," the horse said. "In fact, I might start a whole new fashion among successful young men. I'm like a Mercedes, though perhaps not quite as fast."

Over the coming years Haughey dealt heavily in horses, some of which won races in Ireland and the UK. The dealings were recorded by the press, and especially the sums involved. His racing colours were black and blue. One of his horses was called Aristocracy.

He liked to hunt and was often pictured in the newspapers in full hunting gear, complete with top hat, riding out with the

Ward Union staghounds. On one occasion he was returning from a hunt when a stag jumped over him and his horse, knocking off his top hat. The incident received extensive media coverage. Some of the older and more republican members of Fianna Fáil disliked what they considered Haughey's flashiness, his Jaguar and Mercedes cars and his involvements with horses and hunts. They regarded hunting as an Ascendancy pastime.

However, there was no doubting his ability. Haughey was seen as one of the most able, if not *the* most able of the younger breed of politician then in Fianna Fáil. Along with George Colley, Donogh O'Malley and Brian Lenihan, all now deceased, he was part of a movement for the reform and limited liberalisation of southern Irish society. As minister Haughey supervised a busy programme of new legislation and impressed his colleagues with both his energy and his ability. He also displayed an interest in the arts during the early 1960s, making speeches illustrating support for a broad range of cultural activities.

In October 1964, following the resignation of the Minister for Agriculture, Paddy Smith, Haughey was appointed in his place. Smith had resigned over what he saw as the favouring of industrial development over agriculture. The emphasis on industrial development during the era of Lemass's leadership was creating very real tensions and led to significant confrontation between the farmers and Haughey. There were criticisms of the way Haughey handled the crisis, though the bruising did him no damage in his home constituency.

He again topped the poll in the general election in April 1965, winning 12,415 first-preference votes and being elected on the first count with 3,500 votes over the quota. He continued in office in the Department of Agriculture and continued to preside over difficult relations with the well-organised farmers. In November

1966, when Lemass decided he should resign to allow someone younger to take his place, Haughey, then forty-one years old, was one of those who was considered a possible successor.

However, many had already changed their opinion of Haughey and had come to view him with suspicion. Fine Gael's James Dillon said of him: "He stinks, politically, of course." George Colley, who was also considered a possible successor to Lemass, spoke about "low standards in high places." When the then Minister for Industry and Commerce, Jack Lynch, reconsidered an earlier decision not to go for the position, Haughey withdrew from the contest. He gave his support to Lynch, who defeated Colley by fifty-two votes to nineteen.

Haughey was appointed Minister for Finance. The position was seen as more suitable to Haughey's talents than that of agriculture, and his opportunity to shine was enhanced by the fact that he was to hold the position during a period of relative prosperity. He helped old-age pensioners with the introduction of schemes for free electricity and free public transport, as well as free radio and television licences. He gave more money to the arts, to sports and to youth projects, made special tax provisions for the disabled, and improved the working conditions of civil servants. He introduced tax exemption for artists in his 1969 budget. His ability and his decisions made him an admired and popular figure, though, as already noted, he was not without his critics. A British Embassy note sent to London around this time described him as "shrewd, tough, ruthless and ambitious" but also as tending towards caution and being unimaginative in his brief. It noted the fact that Haughey was subject to criticism for "aping the ways of the English ascendancy."

Part of Haughey's allure at the time was not just the fact that he was able but also that he was wild. The journalist Terry

Keane, in her memoirs published by the *Sunday Times* in May 1999, said she first met Haughey in 1964, when as fashion correspondent with *The Irish Times* she was attending a function in Iveagh House. She viewed him as a "bit of a wide boy". He had a reputation for womanising and there were many stories doing the rounds about him, she wrote, some false and some true.

His wildness was not just a youthful trait. Someone who worked closely with Haughey more than a quarter of a century later held a similar view: "The thing about Charlie is that he has this really wild side to him. We've had some great craic working together. Great fun."

Grangemore and the forty-five acres that came with it cost Haughey in the region of £10,000, a large amount of money in 1959, when £10 per week was a decent wage. A TD's salary was less than £1,500, making Haughey's new home worth seven to nine times his income from politics. His income from his accountancy firm is not known but would have been greater than his income from politics. However, when, a year after the purchase of Grangemore, Haughey was appointed parliamentary secretary to the Minister for Justice, he retired as an active partner with Haughey Boland. Within a few years his main declared income would be his salary from politics.

In an interview in the *Sunday Business Post* in 1998, Patrick Gallagher, former head of the Gallagher Group and son of the group's founder, Matt Gallagher, said his father urged Haughey to buy Grangemore, telling him that in time the group would buy it back for a substantially increased sum.

That is in fact what happened. During Haughey's ownership of Grangemore the lands were rezoned, with permission for up to 386 houses, and the value of the property soared. Haughey sold it to Gallagher Group Ltd in 1969, when he was Minister for Finance. A minister's salary at the time was £3,500. The Gallagher Group, via Merchant Banking, paid Haughey £204,000. The sum involved was enormous and constituted a huge financial windfall for Haughey. During the lead up to the 1969 general election the Fine Gael director of elections, Gerald Sweetman, made much of the sale, claiming Haughey had avoided paying tax on his windfall as a result of provisions included in the Finance Act (1968) by Haughey. Haughey issued a "categorical denial" that he used his position as minister for his own benefit. Lynch defended his minister in the Dáil, saying Haughey was "a well-off man before he became a minister in our Government, and he would be a far better off man if he never took office in Government." It is possible that Lynch was right.

In the decades that followed it was believed by many that the huge profit he made from the Grangemore sale was the source of Haughey's otherwise unexplained wealth; that he had been living ever since off the proceeds, wisely invested.

The sale of Grangemore in 1969, however, could not explain how Haughey managed to buy a 127-acre stud farm at Ratoath, Co. Meath, in March 1968. He bought the property without taking out a mortgage. According to Haughey's file with AIB bank, which was read into the public record by the Moriarty Tribunal in 1998, Ratoath was bought for £30,000. At the time, as we have already seen, Haughey's salary as a minister was £3,500. In 1969 a further thirty acres adjoining the stud farm were bought by a company Haughey had had established for tax reasons, Abbeyville Ltd.

The Gallagher Group knocked down Grangemore and built a housing estate on the lands. The company was part of a huge land, housing, property development, pub and banking business run by Matt Gallagher, a Fianna Fáil supporter and friend of Haughey. Gallagher came from a small farm in Tobercurry, Co. Sligo. He emigrated to Britain in 1932 and made money in building and property development. He returned to Ireland in 1949 and with his brothers took over a company called Paramount Builders Ltd, later to change its name to Gallagher Group Ltd. The business expanded rapidly and Gallagher became an extremely wealthy man. His brother James was Fianna Fáil TD for Sligo-Leitrim and chairman of the Abbey Group. Matthew was interested in horses and after he became successful lived with his family in Hollywood Rath, a stud farm and mansion near Mulhuddart, in north Co. Dublin. His children went to the State's most elite schools.

Gallagher was one of the group of successful business figures who associated themselves with Fianna Fáil and in particular Lemass and Haughey in the 1950s and 1960s. At the time the financial viability of the State was dependent on excise duty from sales of alcohol and tobacco, "a very undesirable and unhealthy position," as Haughey was later to put it. The programme Lemass introduced saw a period of growth which led to the rapid expansion of Dublin, creating huge opportunities for property developers. In the rush to develop, much of the city's architectural heritage was knocked down and replaced by often ugly office blocks, many of which were then leased to the State.

The Fianna Fáil fund-raising group Taca, with which Haughey was closely associated, served as a focal point around which many of the wealthy figures from this period congregated. Matt Gallagher gave one day per month towards Taca. Property developers featured heavily in the group, members of which dined in the Russell Hotel, St Stephen's Green, since demolished, and the Gresham Hotel in O'Connell Street. After dinner in the Gresham some of the group would move to Groome's Hotel in Cavendish Row, the short street between O'Connell Street and Parnell Square. Groome's was then owned by Joe Groome, an honorary secretary of Fianna Fáil who had lived on the premises since he was three years of age. His mother had sheltered people there during the War of Independence and the Civil War. The bar was popular with Fianna Fáil deputies, senators and ministers but was also frequented by journalists and actors appearing in the Gate Theatre opposite. Drinking in the hotel bar would often continue, contrary to the licensing laws, until well into the early hours.

According to Patrick Gallagher, the group his father belonged to had dreams of building a more prosperous Ireland. They saw their businesses and their growing accumulation of wealth as part of a patriotic programme associated with Lemass and, more directly, with Haughey. Gallagher's version has it that the group accumulated wealth while sponsoring Haughey as he made his way up the political ladder. It was a planned programme for the transformation of the State.

"Haughey was financed in order to create the environment which the Anglo-Irish had enjoyed and that we as a people could never aspire to," he told the *Sunday Business Post*. The new Ireland and the new, more prosperous Irish would take the place of the Anglo-Irish, moving into their mansions and their country estates. Gallagher described the renovation by the State of the Royal Hospital, Kilmainham, Government Buildings and Dublin Castle, and his own group's contribution towards the Royal Hibernian Academy art gallery in Ely Place, as being part of this process.

"Everything was planned. Somebody had to live in the big house and Haughey created a marvellous situation with these projects at Kilmainham, Dublin Castle and the Taoiseach's office. Our contribution was the RHA."

Gallagher said that when he took control of the family group after his father's death, he thought at first that Haughey might give favours in return for the support he was given. "But not a thing. You might be introduced to people who could help but he was not slow to tell you to go and sort out your own business."

Patrick Gallagher was only twenty-two years of age when his father died in 1974. According to Gallagher, his father called him to his house and when he came over poured him a glass of whiskey. Sitting in a Queen Anne chair, Matt Gallagher raised an arm and said: "I love Napoleon. This is my Waterloo," and died.

Within days young Gallagher found himself at the head of the huge family enterprise, which he set about expanding. He told the Moriarty Tribunal he had had a long-standing friendship with Haughey and was "somewhat in awe" of him in his youth. He said his father had been a supporter of Fianna Fáil and of Haughey and that he pledged to continue to support him after his father's death. Haughey would sometimes invite him to Abbeville, he said, to shoot pheasant on the estate and be entertained afterwards in the house. Between 1974 and 1979 he gave £15,000 in political contributions to Haughey.

According to Gallagher's *Sunday Business Post* interview, it was part of the plan that Des Traynor would look after Haughey's personal finances while Haughey looked after affairs of state. Traynor became a director and small shareholder in Gallagher Group Ltd and other Gallagher companies and provided tax advice both to the company and its owners. He joined Gallagher Group Ltd as a director in 1961, acquiring 100 of the company's 10,420 issued shares. He was by this time a partner with Haughey Boland. He lived at 12 Raheny Park, Howth Road, close to

Haughey's first family home and not too distant from Grangemore. The house was part of a development built by the Gallaghers. Neil Blaney, another figure associated with Taca, lived in another house in the same development.

Christopher Gore-Grimes, a solicitor with Gore & Grimes, who had their offices in Cavendish Row next door to Groome's Hotel, was also appointed a director of the Gallagher Group that year. Members of the Gore-Grimes family lived in Howth and were associated with the Howth Yacht Club, which Haughey would later join. John Gore-Grimes was well known for the trips he made in his yacht to inhospitable locations in the Arctic and Antarctic, adventures which he recorded in long-hand in journals he kept. Another family which lived in Howth and were associated with the yacht club were the Guinness family, relatives of the brewers and descendants of the founders of Guinness & Mahon bank.

Changes in the structures of Gallagher Group Ltd from around this time, which can be seen from its records in the Companies Office, involved measures that have become associated with Traynor, namely the creation of trusts and the use of offshore companies. There were various changes in the shareholding structure during the 1960s, with, in 1967, the bulk of the allotted shares, including 300 then belonging to Traynor, being assigned to Gallagher Trusts Ltd. In April 1972 the Gallagher Group shares which had previously been held by Gallagher Trusts Ltd were transferred to a holding company in the Cayman Islands. That company was called Bering Estates Ltd, and it had an address at Bank of Nova Scotia Trust Company (Cayman) Ltd, PO Box 501, Georgetown, Grand Cayman, Cayman Islands.

Traynor resigned as a Gallagher director on 12 December 1969, the day after he had moved from Haughey Boland to take up a new position on the board of Guinness & Mahon bank. Soon after this appointment Traynor and John Guinness became involved in the establishment of a subsidiary of the Dublin bank in the Cayman Islands. The subsidiary was named Guinness Mahon Cayman Trust Ltd. The Guinness & Mahon operation established by Traynor was initially run by two executives from Bank of Nova Scotia Trust Company (Cayman) Ltd. Their names were John Collins and John Furze.

Bering acted as the holding company for the range of companies run in Ireland by the Gallaghers, including Merchant Banking Ltd, of which Traynor had also been a director. Profits received by the Gallagher family from the activities of their various companies apparently came from Bering rather than from any of the Irish-resident companies. Evidence of the close relationship between Haughey and the Gallagher Group emerged in the wake of the liquidation of Merchant Banking Ltd in 1982, the year when most of the Gallagher companies were placed in receivership. The liquidator of the bank discovered that Haughey had loans of more than £15,000 outstanding. He also discovered that some of the bank's loans were in fact gifts and were not expected to be repaid, though he never confirmed that Haughey's loans fell within this category. Haughey repaid the money when asked to do so by the liquidator.

John Byrne was another property developer associated with Haughey who made money in Dublin during the 1960s. The two men have been friends for forty years, and some friends of Haughey's said Byrne knows Haughey as well as anyone and better than most. He was not one of the figures who would drink into the night in Groome's Hotel in the 1960s and was a careful and guarded man who liked to keep other people's knowledge of his affairs to a minimum. During his evidence to the Moriarty Tribunal, Byrne said that he had never given a penny to Haughey. Asked why, he said he just hadn't. Haughey in his evidence indicated that it was his opinion also that he had never received money from Byrne.

Byrne, the son of a small farmer from Co. Kerry, prospered in the UK, where he established himself as a dance hall owner and property developer. He opened and ran the Galtimore, a large night club in London which booked some of the big names in the Irish showband world and was a popular venue with the Irish in London. (The club is still in existence and still owned by the Byrne family.) He repeated the Galtimore formula in other English locations and followed it again in his native Kerry when he returned to Ireland. He returned around the time Lemass was overseeing the opening up of the Irish economy. When Byrne built the Mount Brandon Hotel in Tralee, Co. Kerry, Lemass performed the official opening. The hotel had a large ballroom and night club, and still has.

One of Dublin's better-known and perhaps more regrettable office blocks, O'Connell Bridge House on Burgh Quay, was built by one of Byrne's companies, Carlisle Trust. The office block was built on the site of the former Carlisle Building before the introduction of the planning permission laws. It was leased to the State in 1965 for thirty-five years. Other office blocks around the city were also built by Byrne and leased to the State. Born in March 1920, Byrne was still involved in property development in 2000 and was still knocking down Georgian buildings and building office blocks in their place. He was behind the demolition of the building at the corner of Parnell Square and Gardiner Row in 1998. An office block was constructed on the site.

There was a political row in the early 1980s concerning a deal that Byrne was involved in in Baldoyle, north of Dublin. One of Byrne's companies, Endcamp, took out a number of mortgages on property in Baldoyle and Portmarnock in the mid to late 1970s. Endcamp, which numbered Traynor among its directors, planned to build two thousand houses between Baldoyle and Portmarnock, but there was a lot of local opposition. There was talk about the fact that Byrne and Haughey were friends, and the political controversy became so intense that Byrne's solicitors issued a statement denying that Haughey had "any direct or indirect interest, beneficial or otherwise," in the project.

Carlisle Trust Ltd was established in January 1958. In 1961, the year Traynor and Christopher Gore-Grimes joined the board of Gallagher Group Ltd, the two men also joined the board of Carlisle Trust. The registered office of the company was changed to 6 Cavendish Row, Dublin, the address of Gore & Grimes, solicitors. Anthony Gore-Grimes became company secretary.

The initial directors were John Byrne, described in the company documents at the time as a dance hall proprietor, with an address in Bayswater, London; his brother Thomas Byrne, described as a farmer, from Kilflynn, Co. Kerry; and a Michael Harnett, who acted as a solicitor for the company and soon afterwards resigned from the board.

The annual returns for the year to March 1962 showed Traynor and Thomas Byrne owning one A share each, and Christopher Gore-Grimes owning the other eight. Gore-Grimes was also shown as owning a further 990 B shares. John Byrne was recorded as not directly owning any shareholding in the company, having transferred his two A shares to Gore-Grimes during the year.

The B shares, of course, were being held by Gore-Grimes on behalf of the true beneficial owner or owners. In July 1972 the 990 B shares were shifted to the Cayman Islands. The change occurred three months after the similar move involving the Gallagher shares, though in this instance the structure used was different. No holding company was created, and the shares were held by Guinness Mahon Cayman Trust Ltd, the Cayman company established by Traynor. A trust was established in the Cayman Islands, and Guinness Mahon Cayman Trust Ltd acted as the trustee.

In August there was a change in the status of the A and B shares, and the owners had to sign a document consenting to the change. Traynor signed the document twice: once as the holder of one A share, and again on behalf of Guinness Mahon Cayman Trust, the holder of the 990 B shares.

Carlisle sometimes loaned money from Guinness & Mahon bank, Dublin. The files in the Companies Office show that in September 1975 a charge for £490,000 was taken out against O'Connell Bridge House, St Anne's, Anglesea Road, Donnybrook, Dublin 4, and 157–164 Townsend Street. Two years later another charge was taken out with Guinness & Mahon. The file does not reveal the amount, though the annual returns show that the company's indebtedness rose that year from £1.05 million to £2.2 million. The company often had significant debts, registering debts of £3.1 million in its returns for 1977 and £6.29 million in the 1982 returns. For earlier years the returns do not give profit and loss figures, though more recent filings do and often show substantial losses.

In the mid-1970s, secretarial services for the company were moved, with Sam Field-Corbett's Management Investment Services (MIS) taking over from the service offered by Gore & Grimes, solicitors. MIS was originally based at 3 Trinity Street, a property owned by Guinness & Mahon bank and just around the corner from that bank's premises. The company later moved to

Winetavern Street, Dublin 8, the sloping street that goes from Christ Church Cathedral down to the River Liffey.

Byrne and Gallagher did at least do some business together. In 1978 one of Byrne's companies was having difficulty getting a tenant for a Dublin building. The company was called Breldorm Ltd and the directors were Byrne, Traynor, and Anthony Gore-Grimes. Eventually the building, Seán Lemass House in St Stephen's Green, near Leeson Street, was sold on by Byrne. It was bought by Patrick Gallagher, whose father had died four years earlier and who was now head of the Gallagher Group, with which again Traynor was involved. In a deal that received extensive media coverage at the time, Gallagher resold the building within two months for £7.5 million, making a profit of £2.1 million, while only ever having paid a deposit of £500,000. The Irish Permanent Building Society was the purchaser, and it was then the largest property deal ever negotiated between two Irish entities. The principal negotiators were Patrick and Paul Gallagher on one side and Edmund Farrell on the other. Farrell was managing director of the society, having essentially inherited the job from his father, after whom he immediately renamed the neo-Georgian office block Edmund Farrell House. Farrell junior will feature again in this book.

In 1969 Haughey bought Abbeville and 250 acres in Kinsealy, north Co. Dublin. The house, according to Mark Bence-Jones's *Guide to Irish Country Houses*, was built for the Rt Hon. John Beresford, Taster of the Wines in the Port of Dublin, Commissioner of the Revenue, brother of the first Marqui of Waterford and one of the most powerful men in Ireland at the end of the eighteenth century. Extension work was carried out about 1790 by James Gandon, the architect of Huguenot origins who designed the Custom House and the Four Courts. The name of the house commemorates the fact that Beresford's first wife came from Abbeville, in northern France. Former owners of the house included Professor James William Cusack, surgeon-in-ordinary to Queen Victoria in Ireland.

The twelve-bedroom house and 240 acres cost £145,977, substantially less than Haughey was paid for Grangemore. At the time of the purchase Haughey's political salary of £3,500 per annum was not nearly enough to pay for the upkeep of the house, even if no mortgage was involved. The house was sold by a company, Farm & General Equipment (Éire) Ltd, and bought by Abbeyville Ltd. A few years later Haughey was to value the contents of the house at £50,000. Abbeyville Ltd was owned by Charles and Maureen Haughey. In 1975, for tax reasons, the property was transferred to the names of Charles and Maureen Haughey.

The size of the house was such that Haughey would later use it on State occasions. He told the Moriarty Tribunal:

> When I came into office for the first time in 1979 there was a very live proposal on the table at that time to build a Taoiseach's residence in the Phoenix Park. I thought that was not a good idea. In fact I vetoed it because the Phoenix Park was sacrosanct and I didn't think the public at that time was ready to have a specially built Taoiseach's residence.
>
> I decided that at least for my time anyway in the office of Taoiseach, Abbeville would do perfectly well as a Taoiseach's residence. There was no particular need for any new sparkling armoured palace in the Phoenix Park, that Abbeville would fulfil the terms of whatever ancillary

things had to be done as party leader, as Taoiseach. And, as I say, Abbeville did fulfil that role from 1979 to 1991 in a major way.

Abbeville would be staffed, manned by people from the Taoiseach's office at weekends because we would be meeting people, receiving deputations, entertaining people and a whole variety of activities, all undertaken on behalf of either the Government or the party as such. Why would we do that? For reasons mainly of confidentiality in some cases, for reasons of convenience and certainly inso-far as outside people were concerned, foreign people, there was all the difference in the world – and this applied particularly to America – there was all the difference in the world in my giving a dinner party in an official building and at home in Abbeville. The idea of being brought to the Taoiseach's own home and entertained there was very, very important and significant from the point of view of public relations, diplomatic relations.

Some of the costs of running such meetings or events at Abbeville were met by the State. But that was all in the future. In the 1970s, Haughey employed a stud manager and other farm and domestic staff to run his new home and was soon paying an annual wages bill in excess of £30,000. He made no profit from the lands he owned and described himself at the time in documents as a "gentleman farmer". It was a grand life-style which cost thousands of pounds per month to maintain. He was living far beyond his means, but his situation was modest enough compared with those of John Byrne and the Gallaghers.

In 1959 Byrne switched address from London to Simmonscourt Castle, Simmonscourt Avenue, Dublin 4. Those who know the property say it is extremely grand and well maintained. It is now known as Simmonscourt Lodge and sits on some extremely valuable acres in the heart of Ballsbridge. Byrne lived in the property with his wife, Anne Ciara Byrne, twenty-four years his junior and a former Rose of Tralee, and their children. The large home was furnished with valuable antiques and artefacts from some of the Georgian houses he had knocked down to make way for office blocks. Byrne kept horses, was a regular attender at race meetings, and at one stage used to fly his own helicopter. He had an attractive old church in the midlands taken down and reconstructed in the grounds of his Ballsbridge home, and a bell specially made and engraved for the church's bell tower. After his move back to Dublin he kept an apartment in London, where his family retained its ownership of the Galtimore ballroom. According to Terry Keane, she and Haughey would sometimes make use of Byrne's apartment during trips to London. Byrne, who had extensive property holdings in both the UK and Ireland, was one of the richest men in the Republic.

The same was true in his time for Matt Gallagher. He died in 1974, at a time when estates worth more than £200,000 in value were subject to estate duty at 55 per cent. Although Gallagher, when he died, was at the head of a huge building and banking empire and owned vast amounts of property, his estate was valued at nil. This was because of the transfer to Cayman trusts of most of his property in the years before he died, and debts which he somehow managed to owe to these trusts. The documents filed in the Probate Office included details of his holdings at his home in Hollywood Rath, Co. Dublin, and Ballymacarney, Co. Meath. His home had four reception rooms, six double bedrooms and one single. It had a three-car garage, two lodges, and two stables. A second house, at Ballymacarney, had three reception rooms, five double bedrooms, and two single bedrooms. The servants' wing had another four bedrooms, and there were two three-bedroom lodges, two double garages, and outhouses. The estate included 784 acres, and the two houses and the stud farm offices were connected by an intercom system.

Gallagher's children lived in houses of even greater splendour. In the late 1970s Patrick Gallagher purchased Straffan House, Co. Kildare, the former residence of Farah Zangeneh Djanbani, widow of an Iranian air force general executed by the Khomeini regime in Iran. He had one half of the house, which had been demolished, rebuilt. A nineteenth-century house which, according to Bence-Jones, mixes Italianate and French château styles, it had a tall, slender campanile tower with two tiers of open belvederes and stood on an estate of 300 acres, which included formal gardens and an elaborate Victorian fountain.

The house and estate were bought by a Gallagher company with a £1 million loan from the Northern Bank Finance Corporation, and a further loan of £1 million was used to rebuild and refurbish the mansion. The purchase was made in this way so that Gallagher could avoid having to pay the taxes which would have fallen due if he had extracted the price of the property in earnings from one or a number of his companies. He saved himself a tax bill of almost £1 million. However, as a consequence of buying the property in this way, he and his family lost their home when the Gallagher Group collapsed. The Byrnes put them up for a time in Simmonscourt.

Patrick Gallagher's brother Paul bought Castle Howard, near Avoca, Co. Wicklow, when the brothers were at the height of their prosperity. The castle was built in 1811 for a Lt-Col Robert Howard and, according to Bence-Jones, combined the two archaic styles of a castle and an abbey. It boasted a large music room with Vienna chandeliers, a dining-room with seating for twenty, and staff quarters which included six bedrooms and an indoor riding arena. Again the property was bought by a Gallagher company as a tax-saving device.

As well as living in the large houses of the former gentry, the new rich also developed a taste for breeding horses and attending meets. As we have already seen, Haughey developed similar interests. During his time as Minister for Finance, Haughey had introduced a special measure making income from horse breeding free from tax. When he was later in difficulty with AIB Bank, Haughey for some time resisted pressure that the bank put on him to sell his stud farm. It was, he said, his only tax outlet, though what exactly he meant by that is not clear from the bank records of the time. Haughey's tax measure led to the growth of the Irish bloodstock industry and provided the foundation for a number of very significant fortunes, most notably that of John Magnier, a multi-millionaire horse breeder whom Haughey was later to appoint to the Seanad.

Compared with Byrne and the Gallaghers and others he associated with then and in the future, Haughey's life-style after he moved into Kinsealy was not particularly lavish. He travelled in a Mercedes, furnished his house with antiques, and owned a stud farm; others travelled by Rolls-Royce, bought horses that cost as much as Haughey spent in a year, and owned racecourses. For the super-rich who set out in the 1960s to make fortunes which would allow them to move into the stately homes of the Anglo-Irish, Haughey's life in Abbeville with some horses and staff was not particularly impressive. Nevertheless, it was far beyond his means.

3

The Wilderness Years

IN 1969 Haughey was on top of the world. He had bought, for cash, an estate and mansion just a few miles north of his old Donnycarney home. He was Minister for Finance. Every weekday morning a Government Mercedes drove him from his eighteenth-century home to his office in Leinster House. On Saturday mornings, safe from the public's gaze, he, his friend Des Traynor and some of the richest businessmen in the State gathered in the library in Abbeville to discuss their secret affairs. Jack Lynch would not remain Taoiseach and president of Fianna Fáil for ever. And when he went, Haughey would seek to replace him. The best was yet to come.

In his budget that year Haughey introduced tax exemption for writers and artists. It added to his already considerable reputation and mystique. He was a rich and powerful man who, amidst all the pressures of political life at the highest level, could still find time to indulge an interest in the cultural life of the State. He was able, ruthless, and committed to public affairs: an aristocrat.

In the June 1969 election Haughey got 11,677 votes in Dublin North-East and was elected on the first count with more than 2,000 votes above the quota. Fianna Fáil won seventy-five seats or an overall working majority of five. He and Fianna Fáil were riding high; but for Haughey disaster was approaching, coming from the North.

During the summer of 1969 tension in Northern Ireland reached its climax with the Battle of the Bogside. Lynch made a speech in which he said the Irish Government "can no longer stand by and see innocent people injured." The British government sent in troops. The Government decided that a sum of money, the amount and channel of disbursement of which would be decided by Haughey, would be made available for the victims of the Northern violence. Within the Government Haughey and others were at odds with Lynch, in that they were presenting a more hardline view of what should be done. Fianna Fáil, the "slightly constitutional party", as Lemass had dubbed it, was in crisis. Discussion on Northern policy was complicated by the ever-present issue of who would succeed Lynch. Nationalist feeling was high. In 1970 Lynch said he had become aware of what he called an "attempt to unlawfully import arms from the Continent." On 6 May he sacked Haughey from his Government. Later that month Haughey was taken from his Kinsealy mansion in a Garda car and charged with conspiring to import arms. He was acquitted of the charge, but his political career was in ruins.

The disaster had financial as well as political repercussions. When moving to Kinsealy, Haughey was confident Traynor could organise sufficient income for the upkeep of the estate. However, Haughey's file with AIB Bank shows that as soon as he was sacked from cabinet, his finances began to spiral out of control. He later argued that his finances became such a mess during the 1970s because he was so busy restoring his political fortunes. However, there is a less innocent way of interpreting what happened. Developments in the 1970s fit a broad pattern which emerged from the Moriarty Tribunal's examination of his finances during the 1980s and 1990s. Put simply, the evidence supports the view that when Haughey was in power the money tended to flow in, and when he was out of power the money tended to dry up.

Haughey's first "drought" occurred in 1970 when he was sacked from the Government and his political prospects looked grim. Given the cost of maintaining Abbeville, whether he was on a Government minister's salary or that of a TD was not the issue: obviously his money came from elsewhere. When disaster struck, the money dried up.

Being the fighter that he was, Haughey saw his return to the back benches as a temporary setback. He set in train a programme of winning the hearts of the Fianna Fáil grass roots, touring the State by car at nights and weekends, attending party functions and shaking hands, the so-called chicken and chip circuit. The car used by Haughey was supplied by the Gallagher family. His driver was often Liam Lawlor, a Fianna Fáil supporter who was subsequently to be elected a TD and who was to end up wealthy and being investigated by a Dublin Castle tribunal. Lawlor was to make history, of a sort, by being the first politician jailed as a result of the tribunals.

Haughey continued to live an extravagant life. A system had been established for administering his finances, with staff and other bills incurred by him each month being sent by his secretary at Abbeville to Haughey Boland and Co., which then saw that they were settled. The company made the payments from a client account, that is, an account it kept for payments relating to its client. Two partners from the firm were authorised to sign cheques drawn on Haughey's own bank account whenever money was needed to replenish the balance in Haughey's client account with his former firm. The point of the system was that Haughey never had to be bothered with his everyday personal affairs. The problem in 1970 was that there were no longer any funds going into the personal account that the partners from Haughey Boland were writing cheques against.

Haughey's solution to the problem was to do nothing. He banked with AIB, Dame Street, where he had been considered a valued customer. In business circles in those days wealthy or famous clients were called KBIs, meaning key business influencers. Haughey was a KBI and the bank thought having him as a customer would bring more business its way. But then came the Arms Crisis and Haughey's sacking, and the dream customer became a banker's nightmare.

Within a year Haughey was hugely overdrawn on his account. The bank held some securities against Haughey's overdraft, but senior executives felt that such was Haughey's popularity among the Fianna Fáil faithful that any move against him could have negative repercussions for their overall business. People might withdraw from AIB or choose not to bank with it in the future if it became known that it was moving against Haughey. It was made very clear to the bank by him that he would not voluntarily dispose of assets, and that he would prove a very difficult adversary if it chose to take him on. In other words, the bank would have to have a public spat with him if it wanted to move on its securities. AIB was stuck.

Both Haughey and the bank were aware that if his financial difficulties became public knowledge, Haughey's political career could be fatally damaged. Part of his mystique with his public was that he seemed enormously wealthy but had no obvious means to support this life-style. All through the 1970s Haughey and AIB were locked in a game of dare, where the stakes were hundreds of thousands of pounds and the highest political office in the land. Quite a number of senior AIB executives were aware of what was happening.

Haughey's response to demands from the bank that he reduce his debt was to make promises and projections. As the decade went on the bank was to learn to think little of his promises and his often pie-in-the-sky schemes. Haughey, for his part, was to learn to think little of the bank's threats. The only currency which was to retain its value was the AIB money Haughey continued to spend.

By the summer of 1971 his personal overdraft was £244,000, or nearly thirty-five times his Dáil salary, which was £7,000. Haughey, described in bank documents as a "gentleman farmer and TD", ran a stud farm and cattle farm but made little money from either. The farms may even have incurred losses, and the stud farm's bank account was £11,000 overdrawn. His overdraft was extraordinary for a non-commercial account, particularly as the bank knew the customer was living far beyond his means.

In a meeting with the bank in September 1971 Haughey promised he would sell some assets: cattle worth £20,000; the shares held by the bank; an interest he held in Simmonstown Stud, which he said was worth £48,000; and "other odds and ends" which he said were worth a further £10,000. The total came to £101,000 and would equal less than half his debt. He also said he would pursue the sale of his Ashbourne lands by way of private treaty. The bank had the deeds for 154 acres at Ashbourne, and shares valued at £23,000.

Three months later the personal account was still overdrawn by £225,000. The bank reviewed the matter at senior regional level. Haughey said he was still trying to sell the lands at

Ashbourne and was negotiating with Cement Roadstone for the sale of forty to fifty acres of Abbeville land. At the time Lemass was chairman of Cement Roadstone. The bank's regional board expressed its "extreme dissatisfaction" with the situation, but Haughey kept his chequebooks.

One cheque from these chequebooks was written in a nightclub in Leeson Street, Dublin. In the early 1970s there was a nightclub there called Club Elizabeth, run by a Maurice Boland and considered fashionable. Terry Keane, then working as a fashion editor for the *Sunday Press*, was in the club on a night in January 1972 with a group which included Haughey. Others around her table included Lady Valerie Goulding, an advertising executive, Desmond O'Kennedy, and others. It was, according to Keane in her *Sunday Times* memoirs, a tense gathering, with Haughey feeling he was unwelcome. Haughey stood up and announced he was going to leave. Keane urged him not to and to dance with her instead.

The couple danced for a time and then sat at a table for two, the others having gone home. When they were leaving later Haughey, having paid the bill with a cheque, asked Keane to lunch with him in London the following day. She agreed to go with him on the day after that. They dined in Parks, then a fashionable London restaurant, and spent the night in the London apartment owned by John Byrne.

The affair lasted for thirty years, and friends of Haughey's who disliked Keane later said that it involved lavish expenditure. Keane recounted how during another lunch in London, Haughey ordered champagne so expensive that a murmur went through the restaurant. As the bottle was being brought to their table another customer stopped the sommelier to look at the label. Haughey said: "Who's that fucker, and what's he doing with my champagne?" Keane identified the moment as the one where she fell in love. She realised, she wrote, that she and Haughey looked at life the same way, that they were both "chancers".

Chancer was an assessment of Haughey that AIB would surely have agreed with by 1972. In March of that year the bank's advances committee fixed an outside limit of £250,000 on his overdraft, with the condition that it be "strictly subject to reduction by half that amount within three months, and be cleared within six." Haughey almost managed this. He lodged £100,000 in June and thereby reduced the overdraft to just £153,000. He got the money by borrowing it from the Northern Bank Finance Corporation, using the Ashbourne lands as collateral. The deeds of the land were released by AIB to allow the loan to go ahead. However, if AIB believed the development heralded a change in attitude on Haughey's part, it was to be sorely disappointed. The balance on the account almost immediately began to deteriorate again. By November the debt was back up to £183,000.

AIB pressed Haughey to deal with his finances. "He gave his firm undertaking to clear fully by end February 1973," an official noted in November 1972. Haughey said he was going to sell the Ashbourne lands, for which he had received an offer of £200,000, and thirty acres at Abbeville, for which he had an offer of £100,000. The Abbeville offer was from Cement Roadstone. Three years earlier Traynor had been at the heart of the creation of Cement Roadstone from two separate companies, Cement Ltd and Roadstone Ltd. He was a director of the new company. Lemass had been chairman of the board from 1970 to 1972, and Haughey had been suggested as his successor.

CRH bought seventeen-and-a-half acres in Kinsealy from

Haughey in December 1973. The price paid was £140,000, almost the full amount Haughey had paid for his Gandon mansion and estate four years earlier. CRH was to issue a press statement in March 1999 saying that Traynor played no role in this trans-action, and that the lands concerned were prime limestone-bearing lands. The quarry is in fact still in production, and, as was noted in the Introduction, an active CRH site still exists on the edge of the Abbeville estate.

There was an election in February 1973, and Fine Gael and the Labour Party formed a coalition under Liam Cosgrave. Haughey was re-elected with 4,500 votes over the quota. At the 1972 party ard fheis he had been re-elected party vice-president, and in July 1973 he was elected chairman of the Oireachtas Joint Committee on the Secondary Legislation of the European Communities. He was on his way back, much to the discomfort of some within the party who believed he constituted a sort of poison.

By April 1973 Haughey's debt to the bank totalled just over £230,000, and by December the debt had grown by another £65,000. At this point Haughey sold the seventeen-and-a-half acres of Abbeville land to Cement Roadstone for £140,000, in a deal by which he was to receive the money by instalment. Around the time of the sale, Haughey borrowed another £160,000 from Northern Bank Finance and further reduced his debt to AIB. By February 1974 the debt was down to just over £120,000.

The bank opened a "special" account in which it created a debt which it used to reduce Haughey's overdraft in his personal and stud accounts. This enabled it to rule off the amount which had been given to Haughey, despite any evident ability to repay it from his income, and start afresh with accounts which would in theory be kept in control henceforth.

Within a month of conducting the exercise the bank's Leinster board "reluctantly and with grave doubts" agreed to sanction some extra overdraft facilities on the personal and stud farm accounts. While considering the application the board noted "once more" the "difficulties, strain and embarrassment which had been suffered by the bank due to Mr Haughey's proclivity towards making arbitrary, unauthorised drawings on his accounts." The Dame Street manager, Tom Fitzgerald, was told that a "a clear and unequivocal understanding must now be come to with your client" that the new overdraft and associated terms "will be strictly adhered to and that he will so arrange his affairs that his accounts will never again occasion situations of confrontation or difficulty."

Within four months the two accounts were £41,000 in excess of the agreed limits. When informed, the regional manager, J. J. McAuliffe, was "appalled". He asked the Dame Street manager, Fitzgerald, to question Haughey about a number of matters and get back to him before he would bring the issue to the attention of the Dublin regional board. Fitzgerald, McAuliffe instructed, should "have a very firm talk with Mr Haughey." When Fitzgerald was writing again to the board about Haughey, McAuliffe added, "We trust you will be in a position to let us have his categorical assurance that his accounts will be operated in a strictly orthodox fashion henceforth."

Haughey was contacted by Fitzgerald and later wrote to him. The letter, dated 22 July 1974, was typed on an Abbeville letterheading.

Dear Tom,
I refer to our recent talk when you conveyed to me the views of the Regional General Manager and his anxiety that the limits be adhered to strictly.

These temporary excesses have arisen from a combination of circumstances outside my control and it is my intention that they be eliminated by 30th September at the very latest.

Among other sources available for these reductions are a large insurance claim the payment of which is awaited and the sale of my yearlings which this year represent a very valuable consignment indeed.

In the interim I will, if necessary, make additional securities along the lines we discussed available if this is considered necessary.

I shall call to see you as soon as possible. Please explain to the Regional General Manager that I am just at present particularly preoccupied with Dáil business and relative matters but will be much freer to attend to these matters after this week.

Yours sincerely

When Haughey did attend for a meeting with his bank manager a week later, in the Dame Street branch, McAuliffe also attended. McAuliffe pointed out that Haughey had accepted certain conditions the previous February before his new overdraft limits had been authorised, and had promised to supply a mortgage protection policy for £40,000 as security. However, Haughey had ignored these conditions and he, McAuliffe, would not be surprised if the bank decided that, should the situation not be rectified immediately, it could no longer do business with him. An AIB memorandum of the meeting continues:

Mr McAuliffe went on to say that he could understand the extraordinary circumstances in which Mr Haughey had been forced to seek a very temporary excess of £20,000 (to replace brood mare) to be quickly funded from proceeds of relative insurance claim but he was seriously disturbed to find that the other drawings had pushed up the excess to £46,585. An indebtedness on these accounts beyond the total figure of £40,000 could not and would not be tolerated and he called for immediate regularisation of the situation.

Mr Haughey acknowledged he had overstepped the bounds and, while "he had never let down the bank" and, in effect found any restraint on his accounts unnecessary and galling, he would clear the excess overdrafts from insurance claim money and sale in September of young bloodstock, value £100,000, and portion of cattle herd, value £40,000.

McAuliffe said the bank would not wait. He "wanted immediate steps to be taken and, having ascertained that, while surplus monies £70,000 had now been exhausted [payment of interest, purchase of Inishvickillane, living expenses, etc.] Mr Haughey had a sum of £30,000 in Deutsche Marks deposited in a bank in Switzerland (sale show jumper, reported in the press to have fetched £40,000)," he demanded that this money be repatriated and lodged in immediate reduction of the bank debts, leaving the balance of the excess indebtedness to be cleared from proceeds of the insurance claim, collection of which should be executed with the minimum of further delay.

Mr Haughey said he would give serious consideration to this and, having discussed the matter with his wife, would telephone Mr Fitzgerald on Thursday.

Turning to the security aspect of the accounts, Mr Haughey said he had been unable to trace an Insurance

Policy which he thought he had and which would meet the collateral arrangements. He wasn't anxious to take out a further policy at this time and asked the bank to accept instead

Deeds house in Sligo purchased for some £10,000

Deeds Innishvickillane Island (250) acres which he valued at £25,000 (cost £20,000?)

In the course of the interview Mr Haughey said: "I have no income" and this might be taken as support for the view held by the bank that his living expenses are huge and totally unrelated to his Dáil salary and to income from farming and bloodstock breeding. It also emerged that he has a building site in Wexford and other pieces of property elsewhere in family and Trust names and that he intends to build an elaborate house on Innishvickillane.

McAuliffe must have gone home feeling depressed.

Although the bank documents indicate that Haughey said the house in Co. Sligo was purchased for £10,000, this was not the case. The house, on Cloonagh beach near Lislary, Co. Sligo, came with thirteen acres when it was transferred from the ownership of John Andrew Currid in January 1972. At the time £10,000 would have been a very high price for the property. According to Thomas Currid, his late brother, John Andrew gave the house to Haughey "as a present." Local people say Haughey rarely used the house, though his brothers and sisters did.

John Andrew Currid was a successful and colourful business-man who operated Barney's amusement centre in Talbot Street, Dublin, as well as owning property in Dublin and London. Traders in Talbot Street remembered Currid as being fond of fedoras and linen suits. How he came to be friendly with Haughey is not known. He sold his arcade and moved to London some time in the 1970s.

Currid's mother died when he was young and he was raised by his grandmother and uncle, who left him the house in Co. Sligo. "There was some land and it is on the top of the shore," Thomas Currid told *The Irish Times* in March 1999. "A lovely place."

Tom Gilmartin, the Luton-based property developer who alleged he gave Pádraig Flynn £50,000 in 1989, is also a native of Lislary. A dispute between his family and the Haugheys led to a strip of land being transferred to his mother, Kathleen Gilmartin, in June 1986.

According to Gilmartin, the 1.7 acres "was a strip of land that adjoined our land and for the best part of forty years it was ours. It was just a sandbank really, but it became part of our land as part of a deal from about forty years ago. John Andrew was friendly with Charlie Haughey and he gave him the house and Charlie Haughey attempted to claim that piece of land as well."

Asked if he thought the spot was beautiful, Gilmartin said: "I spent twenty years dreaming of getting out of it. It is windy, wet and damp. Life is hard there."

Currid was a religious man. A Catholic, when starting out on his business career he was helped by a number of Jewish traders, and it was a kindness he never forgot. He never married, and when he died he left a considerable part of his £2 million fortune to charities. He gave £400,000 to the Jewish Board of Guardians and £500,000 to the Catholic Archdiocese of Dublin. The second million was divided into seventy-four parts and shared among family and friends. "We all got a bit off him," his brother said.

The £40,000 from the sale of the showjumper in Switzerland that the banker McAuliffe had raised with Haughey during the

1974 Dame Street meeting was lodged with Guinness Mahon (Zürich) under the name of Mrs Maureen Haughey. Some days after the 22 July meeting Haughey informed Fitzgerald that he didn't intend bringing the money back from Switzerland.

He continued to write cheques on his AIB accounts. Fitzgerald wrote a note to McAuliffe on 2 August:

At the time of writing, I am awaiting a return call from Mr Haughey and in the circumstances I will be telling him that the bank will expect him immediately to convert the D.M. into sterling for lodgement to his accounts which would appear to be deteriorating daily. I feel the time is coming when Mr Haughey's attitude towards us will have to be seriously considered and my present recommendation would be that he be asked immediately to regularise his accounts with the introduction of funds from any source available to him. Alternatively, that we would have no option but to withdraw facilities and ask him to take his accounts elsewhere.

This bit of hardball caused Haughey to lodge the Zürich money to AIB, but the situation continued to deteriorate, and the bank did not withdraw his chequebooks or refuse to honour his cheques. In a memo in October 1974, McAuliffe noted: "Haughey has abused our trust and we can no longer entertain hope that his accounts will be operated in a regular fashion. Accordingly, it is recommended that he be informed that debts will not be allowed exceed present figures and that we want clearance of the entire by the end of February, 1975, arranged for security to be completed forthwith."

It was a significant conclusion. The bank had decided that

Haughey's promises meant nothing and he could not be trusted not to write unauthorised cheques. Yet the bank took no firm steps to ensure that Haughey made no more withdrawals.

In November 1974 the assistant advance controller, a Mr O'Donnell, wrote to McAuliffe about Haughey.

> The directors discussed various measures which might be taken, but decided that dishonour of cheques was out of the question. Eventually it was decided that you should interview the customer along the lines that the debt (the overdraft) must be brought within the limit of £40,000 and that it might become necessary to take away his cheque book. The view was expressed that following the interview the bank's requirements should be advised to Mr Haughey in writing.

In January 1975 Haughey was appointed to the Fianna Fáil front bench as spokesman on health and social welfare, and so he could expect to be appointed to cabinet once the party was returned to office.

Also in January 1975, AIB initiated a series of more forceful attempts to have him deal with his financial situation. Following the lodgment of the Zürich money and the proceeds from the sale of Abbeville land to Cement Roadstone, his total debt stood at £129,000. He made an application to the bank for additional facilities and had meetings with McAuliffe in Dame Street. He admitted that his income was "negligible" compared with his outgoings, yet confirmed to the bankers that he was about to have a summer residence built on Innishvickillane. He was "extremely vague about source of finance" for this, an AIB memo noted. McAuliffe warned Haughey that his "audacious" application would exacerbate relations with the bank and could only provoke a refusal and a firm request for the return of his chequebook. Against McAuliffe's recommendation, Haughey insisted that his application be put to the regional board.

A memo dated 28 January 1975 recorded the board's decision to refuse the application: "Written demand to be made for provision of acceptable repayment proposals in respect of the indebtedness outstanding at present. In addition, debtor to be interviewed and requested to return any cheque books in his possession." Haughey was in trouble.

At a meeting in a bank head office building, Oldbrook House, in early February the new front bench spokesman was informed of the board's decision. "He was handed the secretary's letter which he carefully read," an AIB official noted. It demanded that Haughey hand over his chequebooks and make immediate arrangements for the very substantial reduction of his debt. Haughey was told "the haemorrhage" could not be allowed continue.

"Mr Haughey unequivocally accepted that he was at crisis point and would have to take immediate and resolute steps to satisfy the bank but he refused to hand up his cheque books." Traynor had been scheduled to attend the meeting but hadn't, because of the death of his father. Haughey asked for the weekend to consider his position and consult Traynor. He was granted what the memo-writer called "the required days of grace".

In early March Traynor presented himself at Oldbrook House for a meeting with McAuliffe and Sweeney, the central advance controller. He had a letter from Haughey granting the bank permission to discuss his affairs. He told the bankers he was going to conduct similar interviews with Northern Bank and with Pat O'Connor, Haughey's solicitor, following which he would draft a "composite picture" of Haughey's affairs which he would then discuss with Haughey on the following Saturday morning. The bank explained the "very serious and deteriorating situation" to Traynor, who "appreciated the gravity of the matter" and "promised he would have a very down-to-earth discussion" with Haughey.

On 19 March Haughey and Traynor returned to Oldbrook House and outlined their proposal. Traynor told the bankers he saw no possibility of Rath Stud or part of Abbeville being sold at that time, because of the economic situation and the impending wealth tax and inheritance tax legislation. Traynor suggested the borrowings be frozen at the current figures for six months, during which time Haughey would live on his income from politics of £7,000 per annum. However, a £2,000 per month advance for six months would be needed for Rath Stud.

Haughey was asked about his assets. He said he owned Abbeville and 250 acres at Kinsealy; 150 acres with a small house and stables at Rath Stud; a house in Co. Sligo; a house at Artane, Dublin; a site in Wexford; livestock; bloodstock; a share in a stallion; and a life policy.

He also gave details of his outgoings. He paid a stud manager and eight staff £18,000 per annum; paid domestic staff £5,000 per annum; and had other expenses of approximately £9,600 per annum. The bankers expressed scepticism that with such expenses Haughey would be able to survive on £12,000 together with his political income over the coming six months. Nevertheless, the bank went along with the proposal, agreeing to Haughey having fresh overdraft facilities for his stud farm but not for his personal expenses.

In September Haughey was back looking for more money. Michael Phelan, the new manager in Dame Street, was in favour of granting the request. "Despite the unattractiveness of the pro-position Mr Phelan recommends sanction bearing in mind the likelihood of Mr Haughey being a man of influence in the future and the fact that the additional amount will be repaid in March/April," the bank noted. It wasn't swayed by Phelan's view.

Regular meetings were taking place, with the bank pressing for its money and Haughey making promises. He told the bank he only owed it and the Northern Bank money, though the bank had information that he owed money to the Agricultural Credit Corporation and the Bank of Ireland, Raheny branch, the latter by way of his wife's bank account there. He continued to say he intended to sell the Rath Stud as well as lands at Kinsealy, promises he'd been making since 1971. He kept writing cheques, and the bank kept honouring them.

Haughey wasn't letting his difficulties get him down or cause him to lower his expectations. In 1976 he called to see Patrick Gallagher in his offices and walked away with an unsecured loan of £8,500. He told Gallagher he wanted the money to build a house for his daughter in Co. Wexford. The money was entered in the bank's books as two loans, one for £2,500 in Haughey's name, the other, for £6,000, in the name of Larchfield Securities, the company which had bought Innishvickillane and which was owned by the Haughey children. No interest was paid on the loans up to the time of the collapse of Merchant Banking in April 1982. As already noted, during the liquidation process Haughey and Larchfield were asked to repay the loans and did so. The total involved was £23,225.

By April 1976, a year after the deal brokered by Traynor, Haughey's debt with AIB was £246,871.There was a bank strike, and when it ended AIB discovered that Haughey had written cheques which increased his debt to the bank considerably. In

September 1976, when the debt had grown to £304,904, Phelan noted that during a meeting that month Haughey had said "the bank did not make use of his influential position and he indicated that he would be more than willing to assist the bank in directing new business, etc. He intends to devote a further ten years to politics." There is no further mention of this matter in the bank's documents.

An internal bank memo from this period noted that a final policy decision on the calling in of the debt or the returning of cheques "in this particular case" could only be made by the main board of the bank. The author felt sure "that the board will share [his] alarm at the unprecedented level of the debt, the huge drawings made in the past twelve months, and Mr Haughey's total disregard for previous board rulings and his own promises so firmly given."

On 14 September 1976 Haughey had lunch with the chairman of AIB, E. M. O'Driscoll, and a number of other senior executives. One bank memo was to record this as the culmination of the "very hard line" taken with Haughey at around this time, though what seems to have transpired was that Haughey put a proposal to the chairman involving the bank "rolling" the debt for seven years, after which time Haughey would sell Abbeville, and the chairman left "Mr Haughey in no doubt that [the] bank could not entertain such a suggestion." There is no evidence of any threat of harsh action.

Michael Kennedy, then regional manager for Dublin West, attended the meeting. He later said that, following general discussion, Haughey raised the topic of his indebtedness and suggested it "be allowed stand indefinitely without any specific arrangement in respect of repayment." In effect, the bank should write it off. O'Driscoll rejected the idea, and Haughey, Kennedy said, "was very disappointed." That was the end of the meeting.

In fact the culmination of the "very hard line" taken by the bank happened later that month.

On 30 September J. E. Casey, the senior lending manager with the bank, told James Denvir, an area general manager, that he should immediately demand the return of all Haughey's chequebooks. The showdown was to happen at a meeting in Oldbrook House the next day.

Haughey attended on his own and met Denvir, Phelan, the Dame Street manager, and a Mr Coyne, the assistant advances manager. Denvir demanded Haughey's chequebook, and Haughey blew his top. An AIB memo described the scene:

> At the outset Mr Denvir adopted the very hard line suggested by the banking department lending committee and having spelt out the bank's attitude to the major increase in the debt over the past year, he formally demanded Mr Haughey hand over his cheque books forthwith. At this point Mr Haughey became quite vicious and told Mr Denvir that "He would not give up his cheque book as he had to live" and "that we were dealing with an adult and no banker would talk to him [Mr Haughey] in this manner." Furthermore, he stated that if any drastic action were taken by the bank he could be a "very troublesome" adversary.

Following this outburst the meeting settled down, and once again the bankers found themselves discussing with Haughey all the ways he was going to get money and pay off his debts. It was the usual sort of thing: selling land, giving undertakings to pay the interest on his debts ("We gather he can make an arrangement with a colleague to provide this sum"). Meanwhile, of course, Haughey just needed a few small advances to get him by. By the end of the meeting the bankers who'd been detailed to take his chequebook off him were agreeing to advance Haughey more money.

The memo recorded:

A sum of £10,000 per annum to be advanced by the bank each year for living expenses for the next 2 years pending sale of 150 acres (at Abbeville) – no excesses whatsoever on such limit. He stated he has £10,000 from the Dáil, £6,000 from other income, and £26,000 in all should be sufficient.

Finally he stressed the importance of his position, prestige, etc, and on no account would he consider outright sale of Abbeyville now as it is in his constituency.

The memo then concluded with an extraordinary summary of the situation, given what had occurred: "Meeting concluded and he departed having been left in no doubt as to the seriousness of the situation and of the bank's firm intentions once and for all to freeze the debt and obtain payment in full in the short term."

Haughey's debt with the bank continued to grow. Since September 1976 interest which accrued was being put in a suspense account, meaning it was not being included in the bank's books as money which was likely to be paid. Haughey was not informed of the development.

The bank asked Haughey to try to get funds from the Agricultural Credit Corporation or Northern Bank, which he could use to pay off some of his debts to AIB. Haughey said he was loath to ask ACC, because there was an executive there with affiliations to Fine Gael. He said he didn't want to put pressure on

Northern Bank, as an executive with Haughey Boland was about to be appointed to a top job with the bank. AIB was stuck with him.

In December 1976 Haughey told the bank he'd sold Rath Stud for £350,000 to a Maurice Taylor from Northern Ireland. It was a good price, considering he'd told the bank he'd bought the land in the 1960s for £30,000. In March 1975 he'd estimated the value of the land at £200,000.

However, despite the excellent price received, the bank wouldn't be getting any money. Haughey had to pay £30,000 capital gains tax, and £264,000 to the Northern Bank Finance Corporation, which had first charge on the lands, and he needed £32,000 to buy nine acres he wanted added to his Kinsealy estate. That left only £24,000, and he needed that to pay "immediate sundry debts which have been outstanding for some time." AIB would have to wait.

> He now proposes next year to sell 30/40 acres of Abbeyville at £10,000 per acre and in this connection the County Council are already running a sewage scheme across portion of his lands and he has had consultations with them regarding expansion of the sewage scheme with a view to catering for a larger development within the area and he is confident that planning permission will be obtained.

On 20 December Haughey had sent a letter to Phelan, the manager in Dame Street, informing him of the Rath sale. The letter concluded:

> When I have completed the purchase of the nine acres here at Abbeville and discharged some other liabilities I

shall require accommodation of up to £350,000 from your good self for a further two years.

During that period I shall arrange to dispose of sufficient land here at Abbeville to discharge this liability and in the meantime interest will be paid as it falls due.

I would be very grateful if you could have the board agree to this proposal.

Thank you for the kind attention you have always given to my affairs.

An application form for the advance, dated the same day as the letter and describing Haughey as a farmer and TD, gave his income as £16,000. In the section of the form for the manager's comment someone typed: "Has been difficult to control over years." Haughey's debts to the bank were now at £338,000, so the request for total accommodation of £350,000 was not a significant increase. It was agreed in January 1977.

One positive aspect for AIB of the sale of Rath Stud was that the bank was now left with a first charge on Abbeville and the adjoining acres. AIB put a value of £600,000 to £700,000 on the Kinsealy property in December 1976, almost twice the value of Haughey's then debt of £341,358. It also had a letter of guarantee for £40,000 in relation to Innishvickillane.

Of course the securities were no good if the bank felt it couldn't move against Haughey because of who he was. By April 1977 Haughey had failed to make the first of the half-yearly interest payments agreed at the September 1976 showdown and had exceeded the agreed £350,000 limit. On 5 April he owed £401,929, with a further £49,438 in interest in the suspense account. At a meeting in Dame Street he was told he must not write any more cheques. Haughey gave his "firm undertaking" not to do so. Dame Street wrote to Oldbrook House:

> It was made clear to him that if he failed to honour his
> undertaking we would be forced to dishonour his cheques.
> It is our firm intention to keep him to this promise and
> your confirmation that it will be in order for us to take this
> course is requested.

The advances manager wrote back to Phelan:

> It must be clearly pointed out to Mr Haughey that the
> advance is to be brought back within these limits at the
> earliest possible date and the security matters finalised
> within the immediate future. On the basis that Mr
> Haughey has given a clear indication to you of the amount
> of cheques issued but not yet presented, we will agree to
> allow matters to run on for the present bearing in mind his
> firm promise that he will not draw on you further.
>   In this connection we are wondering has he given any
> indication that he would hand in his cheque books?
>   Should the occasion arise whereby further cheques,
> drawn on you without prior arrangement have to be
> deferred, no doubt you will contact the Area office.

It wasn't quite the backing Dame Street had sought.

Haughey continued to spend. Meanwhile on the political front
matters were improving. The June 1977 election saw Fianna Fáil
win just over 50 per cent of the first-preference votes and eighty-
four seats, a massive overall majority. A reporter who bumped
into Haughey on the day of the count asked him why he was

looking so pleased. "They're all mine," Haughey said, referring to all the new deputies.

Haughey got 11,041 first-preference votes, or 3,500 over the quota in Artane. Despite the fact that Haughey had been making controversial hardline statements concerning policy on Northern Ireland, Lynch brought him back into the cabinet just less than seven years after he'd sacked him for allegedly being part of a conspiracy to import arms. Haughey was appointed Minister for Health and Social Welfare, a significant brief.

Soon after his appointment to cabinet he decided he would have a house built on the island he'd bought off the coast of Co. Kerry some years earlier. Haughey bought the island in 1973 from two elderly brothers for £20,000. The construction by him of a holiday home on the island was to cost significantly more than that again, as all the materials used had to be taken out to the island by boat or by helicopter. However, and despite his troubles with AIB, money was no object.

Haughey told the Moriarty Tribunal that when deciding to build the house he didn't consider where the money would come from. "I don't think I thought of it in those terms," he said. "I just decided to go ahead with the building, leaving it up to Mr Traynor to fund the operation."

The construction of the house took place in 1977 and 1978. An account in Guinness & Mahon in Haughey's name and to which the money used to build the house was lodged had been opened in July 1976. Lodgments totalling £90,000 were made to this account in the period 1976 to 1977. Haughey told the Moriarty Tribunal he had not known of the account's existence at the time and that he did not know where the money came from.

During 1977 and 1978 there were debits totalling £15,000 to Dan Brick, the builder who worked on the Innishvickillane house, as well as payments totalling £20,000 to Collins Brothers, of Dublin. Other debits from the account related to the construction of the house and other matters, but it is estimated that the total spent on constructing the Kerry holiday home was £38,000.

Haughey's 1977 appointment to cabinet was bad news for AIB. Now if they were to confront Haughey they would be confronting not just a controversial and popular TD but a Government minister with obvious prospects of succeeding Lynch as Taoiseach. Haughey's busy schedule in his new department did nothing to curtail his spending. If anything, the spending got worse.

By October the debt was £456,000, and by June 1978 it had risen to £580,000. Subtracting the £135,678 which was in the suspense account, the figure was still £445,282. Another expression of concern winged its way from on high to Phelan in Dame Street.

It is totally unacceptable and a matter of concern to the bank that indebtedness to the extent quoted now outstands and the point has been reached when a full report to the board is necessary. We accept that due to the change in the political climate in the past year it has not been possible for you to tackle the situation as you or the bank would wish but, whatever about the forbearance shown up to this, it is imperative that Mr Haughey should now be interviewed with a view to obtaining his realistic proposals for dealing with his large and unwieldy debt.

Haughey had stopped calling to Dame Street to discuss his affairs, and Phelan was finding it difficult to see Haughey at all. Between late 1977 and late 1978, the size of Haughey's debt grew by £250,000 if interest is included, or by £150,000 if it is not. On occasion the minister deigned to fit visits from Phelan into his busy schedule. The bank manager would go to the office of the customer with the hopelessly overdrawn account and plead with him to do something about the situation. One such meeting occurred on 1 December 1978. Haughey's debt was by then more than £710,000.

> By appointment arranged at my request met CJH today at Dept of Social Welfare. Handed him a memorandum setting out the position on his various accounts, which memo high-lighted the heavy drawings on Abbeyville Stud account for various periods between Sept. 1975 and November 1978. Explained that I was under considerable pressure to make a report to my H.Q. on the situation and in particular the continuing heavy drawings on the Abbeyville stud account, despite the fact that as we were aware he had sold bloodstock to the value of approximately £40,000 at the recent Goff Sales. He admitted that he had been using the Abbeyville stud account for living expenses – this contradicted a previous statement he had made to me to the effect that the drawings from Abbeyville were connected only with the Stud and that he was operating his personal expenses on a cash basis. As to the proceeds of the sale of the bloodstock – £40,000 – he said he still had those funds, and intimated that he was intending to use them towards reduction of his indebtedness here.

By February 1979 Phelan and Haughey were having discussions about how much of a concession on interest accrued might be given by the bank if Haughey was prepared to try to address the debt. Phelan said the size of any such concession could be discussed only in the context of a concrete proposal from Haughey.

> I did state that the existing interest charge for the period from September 1976 up to September 1978 at £196,000 included a surcharge of approximately £40,000; that I would be confident of a favourable reaction to scrubbing that amount, but whether the bank would go any further or not would be difficult to say.

Haughey's proposal was that he might pay off £200,000. He talked, as usual, about the potential return from selling some of the Kinsealy land. Phelan noted: "He waffled a bit about a recent sale of a field across the road from Abbeyville at a very high price."

However, Haughey then raised an altogether different possible source for the debt repayment:

> Apart altogether from any monies from the sale of lands he told me that from a development in Baldoyle, which was now coming to fruition, there would be a sum of £200,000 coming to him. He expected this amount to be available in a month at the outside, and from the conversation it looks as if this is the reduction he intended to make in his debt here. The tax implications on this £200,000 was, according to him, a question that needed some consideration.

Haughey said he now had his bloodstock and farm operations working so that they provided approximately £30,000 per year, "which, he said, 'would allow him to live in the manner to which he had become accustomed'."

During his evidence to the Moriarty Tribunal Haughey was asked to explain the reference to a development in Baldoyle but said he had no idea what it could be. He was asked to think of anything which it might be referring to, but couldn't. "It puzzles me," he said.

In July 1979 Phelan wrote a letter to O'Donnell, the advances manager. Haughey's debt stood at £887,966 (£281,110 in the suspense account). Phelan outlined the latest version of his discussions with Haughey and the latest balance on the accounts.

> All in all, it is my considered opinion that this client does not believe the bank will force a confrontation with him because of his position. I feel that until his view in this regard is changed, no progress will be made. Despite various promises to the contrary drawings have continued on the account as is shown from the attached figures.

Phelan was in favour of resolute action. He wanted a letter he'd composed sent by registered post. "I fully appreciate that this action may have serious adverse repercussions for the bank," he wrote.

The letter he'd drafted for sending to Haughey read:

> I am instructed by my board to inform you of the bank's grave disappointment and concern that despite various discussions with you, over a considerable period, no acceptable proposals for dealing with your large indebtedness have emerged. I am further instructed to inform you that unless the bank is satisfied, within two months from this date, that realistic measures are being taken by you it

will be left with no option but to consider the steps open to it to resolve the situation …

If cheques are presented which if paid would have the effect of increasing the balance beyond the figure of £ - -, they will be returned unpaid, without reference to you. I enclose an up-to-date statement of your accounts.

O'Donnell's response was that the proposed letter should not be sent. Haughey's cheques were to continue to be honoured. Phelan was told to "go after the Gallagher deal," a reference to a deal Haughey was now talking about concerning the property developer Patrick Gallagher. An AIB memo of a meeting in Oldbrook House earlier in the year, on 23 February 1979, recorded how senior bankers discussed the Haughey debt and decided that Phelan should "propose to C.J.H. that he might consider a land deal under some guise with a member of the Gallagher family."

It was at about this time that Haughey seems to have begun to believe both that he could deal with his massive AIB debt and that he had to. He would soon be making his bid for the leadership of Fianna Fáil, and the debt was a threat to his success. He may also have felt that sources of funds would come on stream in the event of his being successful, and possibly even before that, given his strong chances of winning.

For a number of months Phelan had been unable to get to meet Haughey. Appointments were repeatedly made and cancelled; but then a meeting did occur, on 19 July at Leinster House. Phelan recorded how he "suggested that a cash offer of £767,000 might be acceptable. Gallagher deal idea to be considered with advisers." The next day Haughey offered £400,000 in full and final settlement before the year's end. Phelan said the offer would be rejected.

Phelan's memo also recorded: "The possibility of the bank being offered a £10 million Middle East deposit was mentioned [by Haughey] – no enthusiasm shown." The Middle East deposit was to come from Rafidain Bank, with an address at Leadenhall Street, London. Rafidain was a commercial bank wholly owned by the Republic of Iraq, fully under the control of the Central Bank of Iraq and, therefore, of Saddam Hussein. Haughey had visited Iraq as Minister for Health and Social Welfare to discuss the Aer Lingus subsidiary PARC taking over the running of a Baghdad hospital, and afterwards he began to take a particular interest in Irish dealings with Iraq. Rafidain was later involved with Irish beef exports to Iraq by Larry Goodman. Why exactly Haughey felt he could convince the Iraqi bank to place deposits with AIB is not known. The offer was not taken up.

In August 1979 AIB drew up yet another statement of the situation. Haughey was fifty-four years old. His gross debt to the bank was £913,279, of which £281,110 was interest placed in the suspense account. In the 26-month period June 1977 to August 1979 he'd made drawings on his overdrawn accounts totalling £179,000. A further £100,000 in interest was due to be added to the suspense account the following month. The interest rate was 26 per cent per annum.

The charge over the Kinsealy property was stamped to £350,000 by Haughey and his wife, Maureen. Phelan put a value of £1.3 million on the mansion and 248 acres. The charge over Larchfield Securities, the owner of Innishvickillane, was stamped to £40,000. Since the account had last been considered by the board in December 1976, "Mr Haughey's political career has changed dramatically rendering it extremely difficult for the manager at Dame Street to even interview the customer despite many appointments made and broken."

According to the note, it was in February 1979 that Haughey "at last" began to show an interest in trying to get the debt reduced.

> Vague suggestions have been put to Mr Haughey as to how he might redress present unacceptable situation. He appears to now reject the outright sale of land due to the publicity involved (he is paranoiac about this) but a possible arrangement with a member of the Gallagher family whereby land might be "parked" in a new vehicle, with Mr Haughey and a Gallagher as shareholders, and held under a declaration of trust (thereby avoiding publicity), was seen by Mr Haughey to have some merit but efforts to get him to go into detail on this with his advisors have so far failed.

The bank's law agent had advised that such an arrangement could be made.

> Mr Haughey fails to see the precarious position he is in and obviously feels that his political influence will outweigh any other consideration by the bank. As the point has now been reached where the account appears to be out of control, consideration must be given to the taking of a firm stand by the bank. If this is not done it seems inevitable that drawings will continue at the present rate of £12,000 per month approximately in spite of several assurances which he has given that "drawings would now be minimal."

There was an outbreak of nervousness among the Fianna Fáil backbenchers after the party suffered a serious electoral setback in the June 1979 local and European elections. Given the size of the Fianna Fáil majority following the 1977 general election, many of the party's TDs feared they would lose their seats if the June 1979 performance was repeated in a general election. Haughey, of course, was watching the situation with interest, though he has denied that he was in any way actively involved in trying to hurry Lynch's end. Whatever was the case, his debt to AIB was something which could ruin his chances if his political rivals got wind of it.

A real sense of crisis in relation to Haughey's finances developed in September, both on the part of the bank and of Haughey. Phelan went to Haughey's office on 6 September.

Mr Haughey appeared much more anxious than previously to get to grips with his affairs. Mr Haughey was in Gallagher company on 5th September and is aware that money and inclination is very much there to acquire land. Gave manager permission to discuss his entire situation with Des Traynor of Guinness Mahon.

Haughey told Phelan that Patrick Gallagher was "flush with cash" and wanted to buy land. The object of Phelan's meeting with Traynor was to draw up a scheme to sell part of Abbeville to Gallagher. "Mr Haughey is now positively prepared to acquiesce in a plan which will avoid publicity."

"Questioned as to why a lodgement is never made to the account he admitted that he 'snaffled' virtually all Stud income himself. He denied that he had any other bank account and dealt entirely in cash."

Phelan complained that Haughey continued to spend, despite his promises not to do so. Although Haughey had said in

July that spending henceforth would be minimal, he had in fact spent £31,776 during the following two months. "He seemed very surprised at the high figure of the drawings, and implied that Abbeyville had gone mad buying unnecessarily and that it obviously needed controlling."

The next day Haughey phoned Phelan and "stated categorically that he wants to handle this 'dangerous' situation once and for all." Notes in Phelan's diary show an increasing frequency of contacts from Haughey at this stage. Something said during a phone conversation in late September caused Phelan to note: "Borrowing abroad – G Colley" and on 3 October, "Iraqi money. List of outstanding cheques, Neill C [Niall Crowley] calling to CJH." On 10 November Haughey rang and said he'd sought out Patrick Gallagher on the previous Saturday. "Says O.K."

Meanwhile two by-elections held in November were won by Fine Gael. The fact that the constituencies concerned were in Co. Cork made Fianna Fáil backbenchers all the more nervous about going into the next general election with Lynch at the party's helm.

On 13 September Haughey telephoned and said he could reduce his debts by £500,000 but wanted to know what it would require to wipe the slate clean. On 18 September Traynor began discussions with the bank. The Gallagher scheme was raised. Traynor, as we have seen, was a senior adviser to the Gallaghers and had been on the board of some of the group's companies.

> The scheme mentioned did not seem a great surprise to him as obviously he had been thinking along the same lines, but whereas our scheme envisaged that all the money would be put up by P. G. he had at least two other people in mind who would also contribute.

There were two aspects he had to consider before involving solicitors. These two aspects were (1) Whether C.J. was absolutely serious in wanting to go ahead with this new scheme, and (2) he would have to look at the long term implications for the three people he had in mind who would be putting up the money, particularly in regard to their tax implications. He knew they had the cash available, but since he would be advising these people he could not just walk them into something for the sake of solving C.J.'s problem.

No names were given.

Traynor would discuss the matter with Haughey on Saturday, the bank memo noted. If Traynor did not make contact on Monday or Tuesday it was because the go-ahead had been given. It would take about three weeks for the scheme to be put in place.

Whatever happened that Saturday, Haughey's debt with the bank was not settled within three weeks. On 5 December 1979, when Jack Lynch announced his intention to resign as leader of Fianna Fáil, Haughey owed Allied Irish Banks in excess of £1 million. The bank knew it was in possession of information which would destroy Haughey's chances of replacing Lynch if it became publicly known. It also knew that hugely wealthy Irish businessmen were considering privately helping Haughey settle his debts. Nowhere in the AIB file is there any record of consideration being given to the ethical or political issues inherent in having the most powerful politician in the State beholden in this way to a number of senior business figures.

Two days after Lynch's announcement, Fianna Fáil voted on his successor. The contest was between Haughey and his old colleague George Colley. Haughey won by forty-four votes to thirty-eight. Four days later, on 11 December 1979, he was elected Taoiseach by eighty-two votes to sixty-two. Phelan wrote to him.

Dear Mr Haughey,

It gives me great pleasure to convey to you my warmest congratulations on your election to the high offices of leader of Fianna Fáil and Taoiseach and to offer you my sincere good wishes for success in both.

To say the task you have taken on is daunting is an understatement but I have every faith in your ability to succeed in restoring confidence in this great little nation.

With renewed congratulations and kind regards,

Michael Phelan.

Manager.

4

Banking Secrets

IN July 1997 I travelled to the Cayman Islands to report on the funeral of the banker John Furze. I flew from Dublin to London and from there to the Cayman Islands via the Bahamas. It takes ten hours from London, but because you are travelling westwards you arrive in the late afternoon if you take a morning flight. Most of the passengers on my flight got off in the Bahamas, and there were only forty or so of us left when the plane landed at the small, relaxed airport outside Georgetown, the administrative centre of the islands. It was hot. We walked down steps onto the tarmac and over to the low, modern airport building. The immigration official who checked my passport and asked me the purpose of my visit knew John Furze, whom it turned out was known on the island for his charitable work as a district governor for Rotary International: "Mr Furze was a very good man," she said, waving me on, seemingly approving of the fact that I had come so far to attend his funeral.

The Cayman Islands is a British dependent territory in the British West Indies. There are three main islands, and Grand Cayman, the largest, is only 100 square miles in size. The islands are low-lying and marshy. Columbus spotted them in 1503 but didn't bother stopping.

There are lovely beaches. The sea inside the reefs is calm, the water exceptionally clear. The islands have a reputation as the best scuba-diving location in the world. It was so hot and humid during my stay that to walk any distance was uncomfortable. I hired a motorbike. At night I'd sit on the verandahs of expensive shoreside restaurants and look at electric storms in the sky towards Cuba. Des Traynor, John Furze and their banker colleagues used to visit the same restaurants after the meetings they held on the island during the 1970s, 1980s, and early 1990s. I spoke to a waitress who remembered them.

Appropriately enough, the islands were used by pirates in earlier centuries. These days the Cayman economy is based on its secrecy laws, which make it a serious offence for anyone to divulge business information to an unauthorised party. Foreign authorities seeking information from Cayman bankers, accountants and lawyers must go to the Cayman courts seeking permission before any information can be handed over. The courts usually rule against disclosure. In 1997 the McCracken (Dunnes Payments) Tribunal failed in its attempt to have the Cayman courts order the Cayman bank Ansbacher Cayman Ltd to co-operate with its inquiry into payments to Charles Haughey. Furze opposed the application.

Cayman law provides for co-operation with foreign author-ities investigating acts which are illegal in the Cayman Islands, but as there is no income tax on the islands, failing to pay such taxes is not an offence. Foreign authorities investigating tax fraud get no co-operation. This is one of the reasons people and companies around the globe have lodged approximately $500 billion with Cayman banks and trust companies.

The islands have a population of approximately 35,000. Cayman Island citizens are the descendants of previous Cayman citizens, are mainly of mixed race, and jealously guard their right to citizenship. There are approximately 20,000 citizens. Foreigners wishing to establish a company in the Cayman Islands must have at least one Cayman director, and this creates lucrative employ- ment for the citizenry. Any public service jobs that exist on the islands are exclusively the preserve of citizens. Citizens of the islands are always assured of a relatively decent job, and many take regular breaks from employment, assured as they are of being able to find a reasonable job again whenever they feel the need for one.

The second category of persons on the Cayman Islands, about 7,000 in all, are the construction workers, domestic workers, cleaners, gardeners and service industry workers generally. In the main these people are from Jamaica. They can never become citizens, nor can their children, even if they are born on the islands.

The third category of persons are the bankers, insurance brokers, lawyers and accountants who run the islands' lucrative financial community. This group is mostly white, and its members come mainly from the United States and Europe. John Furze belonged to this third category. He lived in Governor's Harbour, an exclusive development not far from Georgetown. His large house, like the others in the development, backed onto a man-made inland waterway designed to allow the houses to have a berth for their boats at the end of their back gardens. Not far away, beyond some trees, was the Caribbean.

Furze was from England, though his sons were attending an American military college at the time of his death. His funeral took place at the Church of God evangelical Protestant church. After everyone else was seated a group of men marched in in formation and took their seats. They were former colleagues from Cayman Freemason Lodge Number 8153. There was a large wreath on the altar with the Freemason design of a compass inside an inverted compass. The pastor, Rev. Alson Ebanks, having listened to friends and family praise Furze for having lived life to the full, warned the gathering that faith and belief were required from those who wished for eternal happiness.

Back in Dublin in the 1960s the chairman of Guinness & Mahon bank was the late John Guinness. He later became well known when his wife, Jennifer, was kidnapped and held to ransom by Dublin criminals. Some years after the kidnapping he was to lose his life when, walking with his wife and others on Snowdon in Wales, he slipped and fell to his death.

Guinness was a descendant of Robert Rundell Guinness, who founded Guinness & Mahon bank in 1836 along with John Ross Mahon. The bank's name appeared in the prospectus for the first National Loan in 1923. It established a sub-office in London in 1873 which, by 1923, had become the bank's headquarters.

During the 1960s Traynor was introduced to Guinness and worked for his bank during difficult business dealings involving New Ireland Assurance and Cement Roadstone. He made a good impression. In 1969 he took up the offer from Guinness to leave Haughey Boland and join the board of Guinness & Mahon as an executive director.

At his first board meeting Traynor was struck by how many of the directors came from London, and how distinctly upper-class they were. A silver tea trolley was brought in at one stage, and people were asked if they wanted Indian or China. Traynor opted for China and then sat watching as everyone else selected Indian. He prospered in the bank, becoming *de facto* chief executive and developing a complex international financial structure which was at least in part a conspiracy to assist tax evasion. He created a secret bank within the bank, one to whose secrets only the select had any access.

Traynor joined the board on 11 December 1969. Very soon afterwards he and Guinness established a subsidiary of the Dublin bank in the Cayman Islands, which they called Guinness Mahon Cayman Trust. Around the same time Guinness was approached by John Collins, an employee of the Bank of Nova Scotia on the Cayman Islands, in relation to the funding of a land deal. Furze worked with Collins in the Bank of Nova Scotia and had already met Traynor. In an interview with Barry O'Keeffe of *The Irish Times* in the Cayman Islands in December 1996, Furze said he met Traynor in 1969, when Traynor was still with Haughey Boland, but he wouldn't say in what context.

Guinness Mahon Cayman Trust was given a B or restricted licence to trade in 1971. It prospered. As already noted, in 1972 most of the shares in Carlisle Trust were transferred to the Cayman Islands. In 1973 Furze and Collins suggested to Traynor that Guinness Mahon Cayman Trust be developed into a fully fledged operation. Everyone involved would make more money that way, they said. Traynor agreed. The company applied for and was granted an A or unrestricted banking licence for the Cayman Islands. It commenced operations as an authorised dealer on 1 January 1974.

Furze and Collins left Bank of Nova Scotia to become joint managing directors of Guinness Mahon Cayman Trust. Traynor was appointed chairman and was to remain in this position until his death. Furze told O'Keeffe that in the period 1973 to 1980, Traynor came to the Cayman Islands about once a year but that after 1980, because the business was growing, the company began to hold meetings every quarter. For many of these years Traynor would have travelled free, as he was a director of Aer Lingus. He served two terms on the airline's board, appointed by Haughey governments in both instances. Haughey, in his evidence to the Moriarty Tribunal, said he had never known of Traynor's business interests in the Cayman Islands, or of his frequent trips there. "I didn't know where the Grand Cayman was until all this tribunal business," he said.

Traynor, Furze and Collins also created subsidiaries of the Dublin bank in the Channel Islands. They established Guinness & Mahon Channel Islands and Guinness & Mahon Guernsey. The Guernsey company later changed its name to College Trustees.

Pádraig Collery, a computer expert and employee of Guinness & Mahon bank, was introduced to the workings of the offshore network by Traynor after he joined Guinness & Mahon bank as a senior official in 1974. Collery had previously worked for Lloyds Bank in London. His main area of responsibility with Guinness & Mahon was the management of the operations department, which was responsible for the maintenance of all the bank's customer accounts. He was also responsible for the bank's computer operations.

Traynor took Collery into his confidence. He had set up a system whereby wealthy Irish people he was in contact with and who were lodging money offshore could get access to their funds through Dublin if they wished. It was not always the case, but many of the people involved were hiding their money from the Revenue Commissioners. Also, exchange control regulations then in existence made it illegal to hold bank accounts abroad without the permission of the Central Bank. The controls do not seem to have been enforced. There were never any convictions for breaches of the controls. The regulations were lifted in 1992.

Because much of the money was being hidden from the Revenue and held abroad in contravention of the exchange control regulations, the very existence of the structure had to be kept secret. However, operating a commercial financial service which no-one knows about has its drawbacks, the principal one being that people cannot opt to avail of something they do not know exists. For this reason many if not most of the customers were people Traynor knew from his accountancy days or from his membership of the various private and state boards he belonged to. He seems to have had a practice of making approaches to people he got to know and offering to hold their money for them. The Cayman bank was not authorised to collect deposits in this jurisdiction.

As well as simply lodging money in offshore accounts, Traynor, Furze and Collins were also involved in managing offshore trusts for Irish customers. How much was involved in these trusts is not known and may never be known, but it may be hundreds of millions.

Furze made frequent trips to Dublin to discuss business and sometimes met senior figures in the financial services sector, whom he tried to interest in the discretionary trust service. While making his pitch he emphasised the secret nature of the whole system.

Furze would set himself up in a room in the Guinness & Mahon building in College Green and work on reconciling the records from both sides of the Atlantic. Sometimes in the evenings he and his wife would dine with Traynor and his wife, Collery and his wife, and Field-Corbett and his wife. They must all have felt very pleased with themselves.

Details of how the trusts operated are contained in an audit report of Guinness Mahon Cayman Trust drafted in 1987:

GMCT have a large proportion of customers having "managed company"'or "hold mail" status. In the former case GMCT provides directors or trustees for the client's company and has day to day control over the assets of the company in trust (although in normal circumstances the trustees act in accordance with the wishes of the undisclosed beneficial owner.) These clients have a number of key characteristics:

a. They are generally kept undisclosed except to the most senior manager of the company.

b. The principals do not sign any documentation.

c. The principals do not receive statements of account on a regular basis.

d. The principals only occasionally (maybe once every two or three years) visit the company to review their affairs.

e. Instructions are usually received by telex from solicitors or other trustees or by telephone from the principal. There is never any direct written instructions from the principal.

Much of the trust money was left in the Cayman Islands or in the Channel Islands. However, some of the funds invested with Traynor were kept in Dublin. This allowed people who had lodged money to get access to it if they so wished. Although the money was kept in Guinness & Mahon bank, an outsider such as someone from the Revenue Commissioners would not know from examining its books that the bank was holding these funds for Irish residents.

The accounts in the bank showed that its offshore subsidiaries and related companies had lodged funds with the Dublin parent. On the books in the offshore islands there were normal bank accounts with the names of the account-holders, and the balances, lodgments and withdrawals recorded for each account, just like any ordinary bank. However, with some of the accounts the money was really in Dublin, in a number of large accounts in the name of the offshore banks. Traynor and Collery kept secret "memorandum" accounts in Dublin which showed who owned what within these large pooled accounts, and who was making lodgments and withdrawals. In other words, a secret mirror image of the offshore accounts was kept in Dublin, but kept separate from the official books of the Dublin bank.

The structure is probably best explained with an example. If Joe Bloggs opened an account with £50,000 it would be placed in one of the large accounts held in Guinness & Mahon, Dublin, under the name, say, of Guinness Mahon Cayman Trust. On the Dublin books it would seem as if the Cayman bank had made a lodgment from the Cayman Islands of £50,000, adding this to its account which already held, let's say, £1 million. There would be no mention anywhere in the Dublin bank of Joe Bloggs. Traynor would communicate with Furze and instruct him to open an account in the Cayman Islands in the name of Joe Bloggs and record an opening balance of £50,000.

Meanwhile Traynor would open a new account in the secret memorandum accounts in Dublin, give it a code, say A/A30, and enter the opening balance. He would then make a new entry to the secret list he kept of who was represented by each code. He would write: Joe Bloggs – A/A30. He would also open a file in which he would keep all correspondence between himself and Mr Bloggs. Only Traynor, Collery and Traynor's secretary, Joan Williams, would know of or be allowed access to any of this Dublin material. Collery, a computer expert, kept the memorandum accounts in a "bureau system" he had established in the

Dublin bank's computer system. Only those who knew the password could get access to it.

Evidence illustrating how the system may have worked on the ground was given to the Moriarty Tribunal by David Doyle, son of the successful hotelier P. V. Doyle. Traynor was a close business associate of P. V. Doyle and, according to David Doyle, would lunch in one of the Doyle hotels in Ballsbridge most days of the week, invariably dining with other business people. Traynor's practice was to arrive early and wait at the door to the hotel for whomever he was to dine with that day. He also regularly attended the hotels for business meetings and board meetings.

Doyle said he was greatly concerned about his personal security in the early 1980s and decided he would open an account in Guinness & Mahon bank and move his funds there. Because the bank had only one branch in Dublin, he said, he believed this would guarantee a greater degree of privacy in relation to his financial affairs.

The account had no name but instead was identified by a number. Over time, he said, he became aware that the account moved to London and then to the Cayman Islands. He said he believed Traynor was the only person who knew about his account, and that he had never told his father about it.

To make deposits or withdrawals Doyle dealt with Traynor or Traynor's secretary, Joan Williams. Mostly these transactions occurred without appointment, with Doyle either calling into Traynor's office (which by then was in the Cement Roadstone offices in Fitzwilliam Square) or simply approaching Traynor when he was standing in a hotel lobby waiting for that day's luncheon companion.

During his evidence Jerry Healy, counsel for the Moriarty Tribunal, asked Doyle: "Do you mean you'd just go up to him and say, Mr Traynor, or Des, or however you addressed him, I want to give you some money for my account?"

Doyle: "Yes."

Lodgments would be in a draft or drafts, or even drafts and cash. One such deposit, which occurred in January 1987, involved a number of drafts made out to fictitious names and totalling £27,000, as well as cash totalling £2,000. Given that these transactions occurred in the lobby of the Burlington or Berkeley hotels, it must have been the case that Traynor would then sit down to lunch with the money in an envelope inside his jacket pocket or his briefcase. Perhaps the person he was meeting might also be making a deposit or a withdrawal. He was a walking bank.

Doyle said he could remember only one withdrawal during the lifetime of the account. Traynor gave him the money directly. His evidence was that he rang Traynor and told him what he wanted. Traynor said he would be in the hotel lobby at such and such a time a few days later and would see him there. When the two men met, Traynor handed over a draft for the amount requested.

Healy said Doyle's account of how he conducted his banking business was very unusual. "There is no bank in Ireland, England or anywhere else for that matter where the general manager or chief executive of the bank walks around and takes money from people at lunch parties or gives money to people at lunch parties or simply when he's passing through the doors of a hotel." Doyle said it hadn't seemed unusual at the time.

The commercial arrangement behind the Ansbacher deposits, as the secretive banking system was later dubbed, was that the offshore bank paid the Irish customers interest calculated at one-eighth of one per cent per annum less than the interest which it was receiving from the Dublin bank. It was not a heavy fee for the Irish customers to pay for the service they were getting. Many of them, while wanting to hide their money from the Revenue Commissioners, also needed to have access to it. With Traynor's system they could make lodgments and withdrawals simply by contacting him or his secretary. Withdrawals could be in draft form or in cash.

If customers feared that making a very large withdrawal might bring the money to the attention of the Revenue Commissioners, they could make a "back-to-back" loan. This involved their taking out a loan from Guinness & Mahon bank which was backed, or secured, by the money they had in their secret offshore account. The Revenue Commissioners, if they wanted to know where the funds came from, could be told the money was loaned from the College Green bank. The bank would have nothing on record showing that the loan was backed by the offshore deposits. The system had the added advantage that a company which, for example, took out such a loan for the purpose of its business could claim the interest it was paying to Guinness & Mahon as an expense and thereby lower its tax bill.

According to a submission made to the High Court in 1999 at the time of the appointment of the Ansbacher inspectors, £17 million had been borrowed by John Byrne's companies from Irish Intercontinental Bank in the 1990s, and the loans backed by money lodged in the Ansbacher deposits.

Traynor ensured that as few traces as possible of the secretive financial service he operated appeared in the records of Guinness & Mahon bank. As he was close to most of the businesses and business persons who were his customers, he could also endeavour to ensure that as little as possible appeared in their accounts or annual reports which might alert the Revenue Commissioners. On occasion he would contact companies and request them to change the wording of their annual reports and other documents in relation to the backing of loans. He once made such a request to the Doyle Hotel Group, which he advised and to which he issued loans from Guinness & Mahon. He was all the time watching to ensure that his secret financial service remained hidden.

While most of Traynor's clients were rich business figures with substantial assets, they were not the only sort of customers he canvassed. Back in the 1960s Denis Foley was a rate-collector in Tralee, Co. Kerry. In 1965 construction work was under way on the Mount Brandon Hotel in Tralee, and Foley was asked if he would help find bands to play in the hotel's ballroom. He agreed. As well as finding bands he also became involved in publicising the hotel's dances. He got on well with his employers and was in time given the job of booking bands for the Central Ballroom, in the Central Hotel in nearby Ballybunion. The top bands in the country at the time came to play in both venues. So well did Foley get on that he became the owner of a one-quarter interest in the Central Hotel.

The ballroom business was largely a cash business. Foley got one-third of his annual pay, or £480, from the Tralee hotel "on the books" and the rest of it, £1,000, under the table. The un-declared money was used by him to buy bank drafts, which he kept in a dresser in his home in Tralee. Occasionally, worried that the drafts might become out of date, he would bring them to the bank and exchange them for new ones. In fact this was unnecessary, as drafts, unlike cheques, remain negotiable no matter how old they are.

John Byrne was one of the owners of the Mount Brandon and Central hotels. Traynor was his accountant for the Mount Brandon venture, and it may have been during a visit to Tralee for the opening of the Mount Brandon – attended by Lemass – that Traynor introduced himself to Foley: "Hello. I'm Des Traynor. Haughey Boland." The two men got to know each other, though Foley later said he never discussed his off-the-books payments with Traynor. It seems that someone, however, mentioned Foley's income to the Dublin accountant.

Traynor would visit Tralee once or twice a year to work on the hotel's accounts or those of other Kerry clients of Haughey Boland. During these visits over the years he and Foley would meet and discuss how business was going, and in particular the booking of bands for the ballroom.

Later, when Traynor had moved on to Guinness & Mahon bank, his visits became less frequent. However, he was still doing business with the Mount Brandon Hotel. The hotel was run by a company called Prince's Investments. Byrne and the Clifford brothers, Thomas and William, were the directors. In 1975 it took out a loan for £116,000 sterling from Guinness & Mahon. The loan was secretly backed by money in the Ansbacher deposits. Byrne said later that this was done without his knowledge and without permission from him for any funds belonging to him to be used in such a way. Byrne and the Cliffords, along with Foley, were the directors of the company, Central Tourist Holdings, which owned the Central Hotel. It took out a loan from Guinness & Mahon to pay for the hotel's refurbishment. Again it was backed by funds in the Ansbacher deposits.

According to Foley, he and Traynor had a chance encounter in the mid-1970s in the foyer of the Mount Brandon. Traynor invited Foley to join him for tea. Out of the blue he said to Foley: "What's your financial position? Because I'm now in a very good position to get a good rate through Guinness & Mahon for any money that you might wish to invest."

Foley took a number of years to consider the matter but in 1979 decided to take Traynor up on his offer. He had accumulated drafts worth £50,000 and still kept them in his dresser. More than half of this money was from his work in the dance-halls. The rest, about £20,000, was money he'd collected for an unsuccessful campaign to be elected as a Fianna Fáil candidate in the 1977 general election, money he had raised but hadn't spent and hadn't returned. Of the total, about £14,000 came from members of his family.

Having decided to take Traynor up on his offer, the aspiring Fianna Fáil TD brought the bank drafts he'd collected over the previous ten years up to Dublin, to the offices of Guinness & Mahon in College Green. He was shown up to an office, and Traynor came to see him. Foley handed him the drafts. He was given two deposit slips, but he signed nothing. He presumed his investment would be well hidden from the Revenue Commissioners. His money, he was told, was being placed with Klic Investments. It went into the Ansbacher deposits.

During a routine examination of Guinness & Mahon bank in 1976 a Central Bank officer, Adrian Byrne, learned of the backed loans being issued to Irish residents and suspected they were part of an improper tax service. In 1978 Byrne and a colleague further formed the view that the bank was not being particularly well run, and was not particularly profitable. The Central Bank had no authority to inform the Revenue Commissioners of what it had discovered, and Traynor made sure to remind it of this fact. The Central Bank did have the power to request the resignation of banking directors whom it considered were not fit persons to hold such office. Consideration was given to making such a request in relation to Guinness &

Mahon but, Byrne was to later tell the Moriarty Tribunal, it was decided not to take such a step, as it could lead to the collapse of the bank, the precise event the Central Bank was primarily charged to prevent.

Instead of moving against Guinness & Mahon the Central Bank decided to seek an assurance from the merchant bank that it would wind down its involvement in giving loans to Irish residents backed by offshore deposits. Traynor gave a commitment to do so, and the Central Bank accepted it. He then proceeded to bury his secret financial service even deeper than it was already buried.

By 1979 Traynor was running a growing business looking after people's funds by way of a network of subsidiaries in the Channel Islands and the Cayman Islands. In the very last month of the decade when his long-time friend was elected to the most powerful office in the land, Traynor rounded up enough money to settle his debt with AIB. The identity of one of the main contributors is known, but who the others were remains unclear. Haughey was later to claim he knew only one of the sources of the money. He speculated that Traynor might have obtained the funds from customers whose money he managed. He was aware, Haughey said, that Traynor had substantial funds at his disposal.

5

Horse Dealers
and Hoteliers

HAUGHEY was elected leader of Fianna Fáil on 7 December 1979, and on 11 December he was elected Taoiseach. As he was being elected in the Dáil and family and supporters were watching from the public gallery, Des Traynor was opening an account in his own name in Guinness & Mahon bank. Over the coming weeks money was lodged to this account which was later used to settle the new Taoiseach's massive debt with AIB. On the first day he held the office of Taoiseach, Haughey was collecting money.

Traynor had become centrally involved in settling Haughey's debt with AIB in September 1979. According to the bank's file on Haughey, Traynor had at first mentioned the possibility of land at Kinsealy being sold to Patrick Gallagher or his group. Later the proposed scheme changed and the money was to come from Gallagher and two other unnamed individuals. In December Traynor told the bank that the scheme would not now be going ahead, as the parties involved were concerned about their names being raised in the Dáil.

With Haughey elected Taoiseach, Traynor stopped mentioning schemes for the sale of land and instead cut to the chase: how much would AIB be willing to settle for. He met Niall Crowley, the then chairman of the bank. Pat O'Keeffe, then deputy chief executive, soon became involved. Traynor had offered £600,000 as a full and final settlement of the debt, which by this stage was £1.143 million. The offer was rejected. Further negotiations saw the bank gaining another £150,000. The two sides agreed on £750,000 as a full and final settlement. The money was eventually transferred to AIB by way of a Guinness & Mahon draft.

Traynor was collecting money at the same time that he was negotiating with AIB. The opening lodgment to the Guinness & Mahon account that he opened on 11 December was for £150,000. Who the money came from has never been established. It came to Guinness & Mahon bank from the Rotunda Branch of the Bank of Ireland, where the money trail runs cold.

Five days later £350,000 was lodged. On 18 January 1980 a further £50,000 was lodged, and on 26 January a further £150,000. On 14 February the final lodgment, of £80,662.55, was made. The total came to £780,662.22. When AIB was paid off Haughey had £30,662 left over for himself.

The largest lodgment to the account, £350,000 on 16 December, has been linked to Patrick Gallagher. On the day Haughey was elected Taoiseach, a Friday, Gallagher was among those invited to an evening drinks party in Kinsealy. On the Sunday Gallagher and his brother, Paul, were drinking in a pub close to Patrick Gallagher's home when a telephone message came through from his wife saying that he was wanted by Haughey. He and his brother finished their pints and were driven to Abbeville. Once in the house Paul waited in the drawing-room and Patrick was shown to the library.

Haughey said that now he was Taoiseach he wanted to tidy up his financial affairs. "What's the bottom line?" Gallagher asked. Haughey said £750,000. "You're well in a position to carry a certain amount of that yourself," Gallagher said. The men agreed, and the bottom line was reduced to £600,000. Gallagher went out and discussed it with his brother, then came back and said he'd contribute half.

Because the money would be coming from company accounts, Gallagher needed something tangible in return, and he suggested a proposal to buy Kinsealy land. Haughey said he would have Traynor work something out. An agreement was subsequently worked out, but the money was handed over before the deal was made. A cheque for £300,000 made out to Guinness & Mahon bank was handed to Traynor some time shortly after the conversation with Haughey. It seems a further £50,000 was added from another source before the total was lodged to the account opened by Traynor to receive funds for the settlement of Haughey's debt.

Traynor finalised aspects of the matter with Gallagher. The two men drafted a document which outlined an agreement whereby the Gallagher Group would purchase thirty-five acres of Abbeville land at £35,000 per acre, a high price, given that the land was zoned agricultural. If the deal had gone ahead the total involved would have been £1.225 million. The deposit involved was £300,000 or an unusually high 25 per cent of the value of the deal. Under terms outlined in a document dated 27 January 1980 and signed by Gallagher and Charles and Maureen Haughey, the deal would not go ahead if the group could not find a stud farm agreeable to the Haugheys, the price of which would be deducted from the price being paid for the Kinsealy land. The sixty-acre stud farm was to compensate them for the loss of Kinsealy lands near a stud farm being developed by Eimear Haughey. It would have to be within twenty miles of the General Post Office in O'Connell Street, Dublin. No solicitors were involved in the drafting of the £1.225 million agreement.

No mechanism was included for dealing with any disputes which might have arisen, there was no subsequent correspondence between the two sides in relation to the deal, and no effort was made by the Gallagher Group to progress it. If the deal was not completed by 1986 then it fell, and the deposit was to be kept by the Haugheys. Gallagher later said he had no need for the usual formalities as he had complete trust in Haughey.

In the event the Gallagher Group collapsed in 1982. The land agreement document was discovered among the group's papers by the receiver, Laurence Crowley, and he kept it in his personal custody because of its obvious sensitivity. He was later to say he considered going to court to have the money paid back, as he doubted the bona fides of the deal worked out between Gallagher and the Haugheys. This would have necessitated the appointment of a liquidator, who would then pursue the Haugheys. However, Crowley was warned that given the unorthodox way Gallagher often conducted business, it would be difficult to prove the agreement was bogus.

The returned funds would have been distributed among the group's creditors; and the Revenue Commissioners, as the preferential creditors, were briefed about the matter. They gave consideration to taking a court action. Such an action, of course, would have created huge if not fatal political difficulties for Haughey. Crowley shared the legal advice he had with the Revenue. The then Revenue chairman, Séamus Páircéir, decided in May 1984 not to pursue the matter. In a letter to Crowley recording his decision he said he had not let Haughey's "status" influence his decision, which was an "administrative" one. He agreed with the legal advice received by Crowley, that the case would be difficult. The chances of success "would not seem to me to be great." The Revenue Commissioners subsequently levied capital gains tax on the deal, as if it had been a normal commercial one, and £80,000 was paid.

The documents in the AIB file on Haughey show it believed that Gallagher and two others were going to help him sort out his £1-million-plus debt. Looking at the lodgments to the Guinness & Mahon account, it seems one contribution of £300,000 was made (Gallagher), two contributions of £150,000 each, as well as two of £50,000 each and one of £80,662. Whatever the source of the lodgments, Haughey was able to collect enough money to settle his debts within just over two months. What his plans were for dealing with his finances in the future is not known. His evidence to the Moriarty Tribunal was that he always presumed Traynor would be able to "keep the show on the road."

Traynor, it seems, had been doing just that from about the time Haughey was selected for a cabinet position by Lynch in 1977. As already noted, Haughey was able to have a holiday home built on his Kerry island during 1977 and 1978. During 1979 there were a number of significant lodgments to his account in Guinness & Mahon, the origins of which remain a mystery. This, of course, was when AIB was still trying to get him to deal with his overdraft. The lodgments were: 2 February, £15,000; 20 February, £18,750; 23 February, £20,000; 7 March, £3,575; 12 March, £2,425; 21 September, £34,998; 26 October, £10,000. The total is £104,748. Haughey's salary as a TD in 1979 was £9,590. He did not lodge his salary cheque to this or any bank account.

These were significant lodgments but were not big enough to deal with his massive debt to AIB. In his evidence to the Moriarty

Tribunal more than thirty years later Haughey contested the view when it was put to him that money to deal with his AIB debt began to flow in the moment he became Taoiseach.

> Well, I think that's putting an entirely false coincidental aspect. The point was, as I was becoming Taoiseach, I decided that it was, for two reasons it was necessary to settle the AIB situation: one was, as I say, for the public perception of it; and the second was for the pressure being exercised by AIB. And, therefore, I asked Des Traynor to enter into discussions with AIB to resolve the matter so that I could go ahead – go into the office of Taoiseach with a clear sheet from that point of view, as it were.

As he took over as Taoiseach for the first time he seems to have been determined to sort out both his own and the State's finances. His first public action as Taoiseach was to address the nation on television. The broadcast went out on 9 January 1980 and was an extraordinary one, given his personal circumstances and his general attitude towards his personal finances. "I wish to talk to you this evening about the state of the nation's affairs ... The picture I have to paint is not, unfortunately, a very cheerful one ... As a community we are living way beyond our means."

According to Terry Keane, Haughey soon grew disillusioned with the office of Taoiseach. Despite having realised his dream, he did not, she said, feel he had the kind of power he had dreamed of achieving. Being Taoiseach of the Irish Republic was not at all like being his hero, Napoleon. "I have no real power," Keane says he told her; the effort to get to the top was not worth it. According to others he wanted very much to be Taoiseach but did not have plans for what he would do when he became Taoiseach.

The campaign for his election to leadership of the party had been contentious, and he had won only qualified support. There were many within the party and outside it who were concerned about the whiff of sulphur which surrounded Haughey and who felt he should not be trusted with such high office. His old UCD debating partner Garret FitzGerald, now leader of Fine Gael, made a controversial reference to Haughey's "flawed pedigree". Haughey's mother was in the public gallery at the time the comment was made. George Colley and Des O'Malley were both unhappy with Haughey's elevation to the leadership. Colley, who had suspicions about the source of Haughey's wealth, pledged only qualified support for the new leader.

A tussle soon ensued within the party organisation over the operation of its fund-raising activities. The chief source of corporate support for the party came by way of the Fianna Fáil General Election Fund-Raising Committee, which was part of the party organisation but not under the control of the party leader. The committee, which was chaired by Ken O'Reilly-Hyland, operated from room 547 of the Burlington Hotel, Dublin, one of the Doyle Group hotels. Des Hanafin, the secretary of the committee, was instrumental in the abolition of Taca in 1969. Hanafin was distrustful of Haughey and questioned his motives for wanting to get information from the committee about the sources of corporate support. A long and bitter battle was set in train.

Although he was elected in the hope that he would achieve a better result than Lynch in the next general election, Haughey never came close to an overall majority such as that achieved by his predecessor. His first general election as party leader took place on 11 June 1981. Support for Fianna Fáil, at 45 per cent, constituted a 5 per cent drop on Lynch's 1977 achievement.

FitzGerald formed an unstable coalition Government, which lasted less than a year.

After the February 1982 general election, when Fianna Fáil again failed to achieve an overall majority, O'Malley publicly challenged Haughey. The challenge failed, and Haughey was elected Taoiseach. O'Malley's failure helped Haughey consolidate his hold over the party and, in a more powerful position than he had been hitherto, Haughey told Hanafin he was fired. Hanafin, however, told Haughey that he had no authority to sack him, as the fund-raising committee was not under the party leader's control.

Haughey managed to have himself re-elected Taoiseach, having made an £80 million deal with the independent deputy Tony Gregory. He proceeded with his campaign to get control of the fund-raising committee. All the committee's members apart from Hanafin were invited to Kinsealy. Seated in the bar he'd had constructed inside the house, Haughey asked each member to sign a document instructing Hanafin to hand over the fund-raising accounts to the Fianna Fáil headquarters. Only one member refused, Gerry Creedon of Gypsum Industries. Hanafin refused to comply until the fund-raising accounts were audited, but by the middle of 1982 Haughey was in complete control of his party's fund-raising activities. Paul Kavanagh, a successful Dublin businessman who admired Haughey, became the party's chief fund-raiser and remained in that position for Haughey's period at the helm of the party. Kavanagh declined an offer of payment for the work.

As far as his personal financial affairs were concerned, Haughey had no intention of taking to heart the advice he'd broadcast to the State soon after coming to power. Although there were dealings with Guinness & Mahon bank prior to 1979, principally in relation to Innishvickillane, it was after his settlement with AIB that Haughey's relationship with the merchant bank really took off. Traynor was brought to the bank in order that he might bring the affairs of his friends and business colleagues with him, but Haughey may not have been the type of customer the merchant bankers had in mind. Not only was he really a retail rather than a merchant bank customer, he couldn't afford his lavish way of life and had a strange idea about what banks were for.

In December 1980 Haughey got a loan of £150,000 from Northern Bank Finance Corporation, the bank with which he had dealings during the 1970s. Between the taking out of the loan and its repayment, in January 1983, £52,000 was paid to the bank by way of interest. The interest payments came from Haughey's principal Guinness & Mahon account, as did the final settlement. Where the money originated from is not known, though some may have come from a bank loan taken out in the Cayman Islands.

The Government Haughey formed in 1982, subsequently dubbed the GUBU Government, fell in late November. In December 1982, as it became clear to Haughey that he was not going to form the new Government, he had to face up to the fact that he might not be getting any more large donations for a while, appeals for political support being less effective when they came from the leader of the opposition. He applied to the Central Bank for exchange control permission to borrow the sterling equivalent of £400,000 from Guinness Mahon Cayman Trust. Traynor handled the application, and the purpose of the loan was stated to be for the conversion, development and extension of the Abbeville Stud, though Haughey was later to say the money was really needed for his recurring expenses. The loan was to be repaid by 31 January 1985, and the security was said to be guarantees from Mr and Mrs Haughey and the depositing of the deeds to the stud with Mars Nominees, a subsidiary of Guinness & Mahon bank. The Central Bank approved the application the day after the request was received, and a letter was sent to Traynor so informing him. It was a sensitive matter, and the file was kept apart from the Central Bank's normal filing system. Traynor was given the names of officials within the bank with whom he should deal should any problems arise. In the event it seems from the Central Bank files that the loan was not settled until some time in 1987, when Haughey had been returned to power.

How or whether the loan was paid off is not clear. Haughey told the Moriarty Tribunal in September 2000 that he could not remember applying for the £400,000 sterling loan. "I'm not sure I do [remember it] but now I see this letter here in front of me, I accept it is my letter and I made the application." The letter would have been drafted by Traynor and given to him to sign, he said. He did not recall ever wondering how it would be repaid. "It was an operation carried out by Des Traynor and I presumed it would be attended to by him."

The tribunal produced a letter dated 2 January 1985 which was from John Furze to Haughey and had been sent to him at his Kinsealy address. The letter had subsequently been given to the Central Bank. It began: "We wish to refer to our recent telephone discussion in connection with the extension of the present facility ..." Furze said Guinness Mahon Cayman Trust was willing to extend the facility. Haughey rejected the suggestion that the content of the letter meant he had spoken to Furze.

"No. I would never have had a telephone conversation with Mr Furze. I am quite clear in my mind that the only time I ever spoke to Mr Furze, I met him quite *en passant*, at Des Traynor's funeral. That was the only conversation I ever had with Mr Furze."

After the collapse of his Government in November 1982 Haughey entered what was to be a long and for him frustrating period as leader of the opposition. He and Traynor managed to keep the show on the road, but while enough money was gathered to maintain Haughey in the life-style he'd chosen, there was no surplus, and the accounts which were maintained for him in Guinness & Mahon were often seriously overdrawn. It wasn't a drought but it was a dry period.

During the period Haughey was to have four accounts in Guinness & Mahon bank, all of which he was to say later were opened without his knowledge. According to his evidence to the Moriarty Tribunal, he spent the 1980s working as leader of the opposition while living in a mansion, believing he had no personal bank account.

The information available concerning these bank accounts is patchy. The same is true concerning the origin of the money lodged to the accounts. The total credited to Haughey's principal Guinness & Mahon account between January 1979 and June 1987 was £1,245,530. At least some of the money from the Cayman loan may form part of this.

In May 1983 a second resident current account with Guinness & Mahon was opened. It was closed in January 1984. During the seven months of its existence, £211,344 was lodged to the account. In November 1981 a loan account in the name of Charles Haughey and Harry Boland was opened. Before the account was closed, in September 1984, a total of £229,756 was lodged to it. Another loan account was open from September 1981 to October 1981, and the total lodged was £74,996.

The total lodged to the four accounts was £1,761,627. Some of this money was credited to both accounts, and some came from loans secured from other banks. Nevertheless the total is enormous compared with Haughey's known income from politics or farming.

Tracing the origin of all the money has not been possible, because much of it travelled through accounts controlled by Traynor before being lodged to Haughey's name. Some of these accounts were in the name of Amiens Securities Ltd. The microfiche files for that company in the Guinness & Mahon archive are incomplete. Someone removed them, most probably Traynor.

Sandra Kells, finance director with Guinness & Mahon, told the Moriarty Tribunal that since 1979 Guinness & Mahon had operated a system whereby statements from accounts were prepared each month and copies kept in large lever-arch files. Every three years the statements were sent from the operations department, controlled by Pádraig Collery, outside the bank for microfiching. From 1983 a new computer system automatically generated monthly statements onto tape, which was then sent outside the bank for microfiching. Paper files were also kept for as long as the customer's banking relationship existed and for a period of twenty years thereafter. If the files were missing it was because someone purposely took them out of the system.

The comprehensive nature of the filing system may have contributed to Haughey's attitude towards microfiches as expressed during his evidence to the Moriarty Tribunal. "I have no great faith in those microfiche things. They are a whole new thing in my world. I never heard of them before and I don't know what validity they have. They are a kind of, some kind of banking mumbo-jumbo."

Some of the Amiens records are available. In May 1983 £120,000 was transferred from an Amiens account to the Haughey accounts in three transactions. They occurred on the following dates: 5 May 1983, £10,000; 9 May 1983, £80,000; 19 May 1983, £30,000.

Three lodgments to the Amiens account amounting to £120,000 occurred between 3 May and 2 June 1983. The source of these lodgments was a loan account in the name of the hotelier P. V. Doyle. Doyle was the founder of the Doyle Hotel Group, which has already been mentioned on a number of occasions. Rich, hard-working, religious and private, Pascal Vincent Doyle was known for his involvement in charities and was a member of the Dublin Catholic Diocesan Finance Committee. He was friendly with Haughey and with Traynor, who was a long-term associate, friend, and trusted adviser. Like most who were so close to Traynor, he came to have dealings with the Ansbacher deposits.

When his company bought the Clifton Ford Hotel in London in 1983 it used a £1 million sterling loan from Guinness Mahon of London, with the money apparently backed by a similar amount lodged with Guinness Mahon Cayman Trust. The guarantee for the loan was supplied from Dublin, by Guinness & Mahon, where the Ansbacher deposits were held. The Doyle Group was to tell the Moriarty Tribunal in 1998 that the back-to-back arrangement had been made by Traynor without the group being informed, and that it was Traynor who organised that the money be deposited with the Cayman bank.

Born in 1925, Doyle was one of seven children born to a farmer and builder in Dundrum, Co. Dublin. He was educated at Westland Row Christian Brothers' school, the same school attended by Traynor, but dropped out early, having failed in Irish. At the age of twenty-two he entered the construction business and soon afterwards moved into the hotel industry, building new hotels in Dublin. He built the Montrose, the Skylon, the Tara

Tower, the Green Isle, the Burlington, the Berkeley Court, and finally the Westbury, just off Grafton Street. In 1982 the hotelier Colm Rice reflected on Doyle's achievement: Doyle "recognised that there was a new affluent Irishman emerging – the kind of customer who on average would dine out once a week, ordering, say, prawn cocktail, a steak (well done), fruit salad and coffee. PV went after him and they have continued to do business in a remarkably expanding way. His insight was remarkable."

Doyle gave his own view of the reason for his success in 1984 by criticising his competitors. "Dublin hotels were still catering for the ascendancy class." By the end of his career, with the construction of the Berkeley Court and the Westbury, he was supplying the class with which he had risen with the Doyle equivalent of the former "ascendancy class" hotels.

He was appointed chairman of Bord Fáilte by Peter Barry of Fine Gael in 1973 and survived a number of changes of Government. As well as being a founder-member of the finance committee of the Dublin Catholic Archdiocese he was a member of the board of the Meath Hospital, the Employment of the Blind board and the Central Council of the Federated Dublin Voluntary Hospitals. He was chairman of the National Kidney Research and Treatment Project.

Doyle was widely respected for his work rate and for his endeavours not just for his own business but for Irish tourism generally. He owned hotels in London and New York and was also involved in building houses and apartments in Dublin. He was a teetotaller but smoked. He liked dancing.

The loan account in Guinness & Mahon was opened for Doyle by Traynor in May 1983 just days before the first draw-down. A colleague of Doyle's, George Carville, told the Moriarty Tribunal he had a vague recollection of Doyle telling him he had guaranteed a loan to Haughey, and that Haughey had under-taken to pay it back. Haughey told the Moriarty Tribunal that in 1983 Traynor told him Doyle was providing financial assistance. He said he did not know why Traynor chose on this occasion to reveal the identity of a financial benefactor, something which Haughey said Traynor had a policy of not doing.

Doyle took out a second loan for Haughey's benefit in 1985, this time for £50,000. The money was drawn down in five tranches of £10,000. The final draw-down was in April 1986.

It may be that all the interest which accrued on these accounts was met by Doyle. Doyle died before Haughey ever paid back the money, if it was ever intended that he should do so.

Another identified source for some of the money Haughey spent during his years as leader of the opposition was a man rich enough to buy the Doyle Group with a personal cheque. On 19 February 1985, £50,000 was lodged to an Amiens account in Guinness & Mahon. The cheque for this lodgment was from the O'Connell Bridge branch of the Bank of Ireland, from an account belonging to Dr John O'Connell. O'Connell had in turn been given a cheque by an extremely wealthy Arab bloodstock breeder, Mahmoud Fustok, who'd asked him to pass it on to Haughey.

O'Connell is a colourful character. He was a Labour Party TD from 1965 to 1981, an independent TD from 1981 to 1985, during which time he was Ceann Comhairle, and a Fianna Fáil TD from February 1985 to 1987, in which year he lost his seat but was appointed to the Seanad by Haughey. He was re-elected to the Dáil as a Fianna Fáil TD in 1989 and from 1989 to 1992 served as a backbencher during Haughey's last governments. He was appointed Minister for Health by Haughey's successor, Albert Reynolds, in 1992 and served in that position to February 1993, when he resigned. During his period he opened up the sale of condoms, the sale of which had, until then, been confined to pharmacies.

O'Connell joined Fianna Fáil around the same time he conveyed Fustok's £50,000 to Haughey. Fustok is a Saudi Arabian billionaire bloodstock breeder, diplomat and relative of the Saudi Crown Prince. He is the eldest of nine children born to a wealthy Saudi oil family prominent in horse-racing in Egypt and Lebanon. He studied petroleum engineering in the University of Oklahoma, during which time he regularly visited the race tracks in New York and Chicago. After university he developed his passion for horses, buying a 500-acre stud farm in Kentucky and another in France. He is so rich that he and some associates once tried to make a killing by cornering the world's silver market through buying up a significant proportion of it. The Hunt brothers from the United States, whose fortune was once estimated at $6 billion, were involved. They spent hundreds of millions of dollars on the scheme, lost $1.5 billion, and had to pay a fine of $130 million. Fustok and a company based in the Bahamas owned by two sheiks, were involved in the conspiracy. Fustok transported tons of silver bullion in armour-plated trucks from New York warehouses to Kennedy Airport, New York, for transport to Switzerland. The removal of so much silver from the market caused prices to rise; but when the scheme was discovered the price collapsed.

According to O'Connell, he first met Fustok at Goff's bloodstock sales in Co. Kildare, and the two men became friends. Sources in the bloodstock industry say O'Connell used to act as Fustok's agent here, buying and selling horses for him and overseeing his affairs. It was at Goff's that O'Connell introduced Fustok to Eimear Mulhearn, Haughey's daughter, who in turn invited Fustok home to meet her father in Kinsealy.

O'Connell said he used to see Fustok regularly in Ireland and less often in London. Fustok was very interested in his own well-being and would question O'Connell, a doctor, about medical matters.

According to O'Connell, it was he who suggested to Haughey that Crown Prince Abdullah of Saudi Arabia be invited on a State visit. During the visit in June 1988 the crown prince gave jewelled gold daggers to members of the cabinet, including Haughey. Maureen Haughey was given a diamond necklace. Haughey subsequently told the Dáil that reports that the necklace was worth £250,000 were "exaggerated".

O'Connell told the Moriarty Tribunal that in or around February 1985 he had dinner in London with Fustok, during which Fustok asked him to pass on a payment of £50,000 to Haughey, money he said he owed the then opposition leader. O'Connell said he did as requested, not knowing anything of the circumstances behind the debt.

O'Connell lodged the Fustok cheque to his account in the Bank of Ireland. The cheque was lodged on 22 February. O'Connell's cheque for Haughey was dated some days earlier, 18 February. O'Connell said he contacted Haughey to tell him about meeting Fustok, and Haughey asked him to make the cheque out to cash. O'Connell did so and delivered it to Haughey in Dublin.

Fustok informed the tribunal, by fax, that the money was owed to Haughey for a horse but that as he had so many racehorses and as his records did not go back as far as 1985 he could not provide details of the horse in question. As he was resident in the United States the tribunal could not force him to give evidence. The tribunal wrote to him a number of times but, the tribunal disclosed in early 2000, he eventually stopped replying.

In his evidence Haughey said he had been interested in trying to convince Fustok to establish some of his extensive bloodstock business in Ireland but failed to convince him to do so. Fustok subsequently bought one of his yearlings. Haughey said: "I feel that his offering to purchase the yearling from us was by way of recompense for not acceding to my request. I think it may have been a sort of gesture on his part." He never had any further dealings with Fustok.

Haughey was asked why a normal commercial transaction involving Abbeville Stud was dealt with in such a way, not identifying the payer or the payee. He replied: "First of all it would give me flexibility and secondly because I was anxious at all times to keep my own financial affairs as confidential as possible."

No documents recording the sale have been produced by any of the parties involved. Eimear Mulhearn told the Moriarty Tribunal she had no records relating to the sale. She said she ran the stud farm but her father negotiated the sale to Fustok. She had never received any money from it and never knew the price paid. Nor did she witness the horse being selected by anyone on Fustok's behalf or being removed from the stud farm.

The cheque from O'Connell was dated 18 February and lodged to Guinness & Mahon bank on 19 February, to an Amiens account. During his evidence to the tribunal Haughey resisted the suggestion that he must have passed the cheque to Traynor. He suggested he might have given it to Haughey Boland. He said he could not remember cheques or cash ever passing between himself and Traynor.

Haughey and Fustok obviously got on well. Keane, in her *Sunday Times* memoirs, said that once Haughey became Taoiseach she saw less of him. There were some Sunday morning meetings, she wrote, in Government Buildings. Also sometimes when he was abroad on Government business he would arrange that they would meet in Paris. They would stay in friends' houses, she said, often in "the magnificent château in Chantilly owned by Mahmud Fustok, the fabulously rich Saudi businessman." She wrote that she never met Fustok but did see the gold and jewel-encrusted dagger his brother-in-law, the Saudi crown prince, gave Haughey during a State visit here. She was not shown the diamond necklace given to Maureen Haughey during that same visit.

O'Connell played a pivotal role in securing an Irish passport for Kamal Fustok, a close relative of Mahmud Fustok, in the early 1980s. At the same time he was also involved in securing passports for others associated with Fustok's horse-trainer in the United States. All are understood to be Lebanese nationals. These passports were processed before the introduction of the controversial passports-for-sale scheme in 1987. Kamal Fustok's passport application was granted on 3 June 1981, just before Haughey's minority Government left office. Some of the passports were granted by the then Minister for Justice, Seán Doherty, against the advice of Department of Justice officials.

The Cayman Islands loan, the Northern Bank and the ACC loans, the Doyle loan and the payment from Fustok are the sources of some of the money lodged to the four accounts Haughey had with Guinness & Mahon during the 1980s. Many other lodgments remain unexplained. It is worth listing the details concerning each of the four accounts, given that some of the unexplained lodgments were for what were considerable sums in those days. It gives an impression of what was happening in relation to the personal finances of one of the most powerful political figures in the State during the decade.

During Haughey's first year as Taoiseach there were two lodgments to his principal Guinness & Mahon account. The first, for £40,000, was on 10 September 1980. This may have been in part the proceeds of a loan, for £50,000, Haughey took out with the Agricultural Credit Corporation in September 1980. The second, for £150,000 on 31 December 1980, was the proceeds of the loan he took out with Northern Bank Finance Corporation.

In 1981 there were lodgments on 4 August and 12 August, for £33,726 and £13,726, respectively. No records exist in Guinness & Mahon which identify the source of these lodgments.

On 4 March 1982 there was a lodgment of £67,135; on 22 June 1982 a lodgment of £1,000; on 9 September 1982 a lodgment of £100,000; and on 13 September 1982 there was a lodgment of £75,000. The total for 1982 was £243,135, a good haul. The £75,000 lodgment was most probably the proceeds of another loan from ACC. The sources of the other lodgments are not known.

On 4 January 1983 there was a lodgment of £200,000, and six days later a further £100,000 was lodged. On 4 May a further £20,000 was lodged and on 19 May a further £30,000. The total for 1983 therefore was £350,000. Haughey's exchange control permission application to the Central Bank was granted in December 1982. A note in the Guinness & Mahon files shows Pádraig Collery informing Traynor in January 1983 that he had debited the Guinness Mahon Cayman Trust sundry sub-company account with the sterling equivalent of £200,000, and credited this sum to the GMCT "S" account. This money was then moved from the S account "as per advice." The S account being referred to is most likely Haughey's Ansbacher account, which may have been opened at around this time, and the lodgment would have been to Haughey's principal Guinness & Mahon account.

It seems the lodgment to the Haughey account in Guinness & Mahon from his Ansbacher account was immediately used to pay off the loan taken out with Northern Bank Finance Corporation. A payment of £154,433 was made on 4 January 1983. Haughey, in his evidence to the tribunal in September 2000, suggested it was possible the Cayman loan could also have been used to repay unspecified borrowings which he said Traynor could have made in 1980 to help settle Haughey's debt with AIB. There is no evidence of any such borrowings in 1980 from any bank or individual.

The lodgment of £100,000 to Haughey's Guinness & Mahon account on 10 January 1983 has been linked to a cheque for £100,000 drawn on an unidentified AIB account.

The lodgments made to the account in 1984 were small beer. On 20 January £500 and £2,547 were separately lodged, on 8 March £1,008, on 11 December £911, a total of only £4,866. The £2,547 was a transfer from another of Haughey's accounts with the bank.

On 2 January 1985 there was a lodgment of £326 and on 9 April 1985 a lodgment of £20,000. The next lodgment to the account was not until 29 May 1987.

Haughey's second current account, as we have already seen, was opened in May 1983. On 9 May two lodgments were made, one of £30,000 and one of £80,000. Four days later £10,000 was lodged, and on 14 September 1983 £80,000 was lodged. The first lodgment, of £30,000, was an in-out transaction, meaning the funds passed though the account on the same day. The second lodgment, of £80,000, came from an Amiens account. The £10,000 lodgment came from the account held in the name of Haughey and Harry Boland. The £80,000 lodged in September is thought to have come from the ACC, from another loan Haughey got from that bank around that time.

The third account in Guinness & Mahon was in the name of Haughey and Harry Boland. Boland did not know an account had been opened in his and Haughey's name in November 1981. On 18 January 1982 £53,897 was lodged to the account. On 5 May 1983 £10,000 was lodged, and on 20 January 1984 £50,000 was lodged. On 11 September 1984 £115,859 was lodged.

It is not known where the first lodgment, of £53,897, came from. The £10,000 came from an Amiens account, and the £50,000 came from an account in Traynor's own name. The £115,859 came from Haughey's principal current account.

On 2 September 1981 a loan account was opened in Haughey's name, the fourth of Haughey's 1980s Guinness & Mahon accounts. On 1 October £74,996 was lodged, a sum which was advanced by ACC to Haughey that same month. This was the only lodgment made to the account and cleared the loan.

As well as the loans Haughey received from Guinness & Mahon over the years, his current accounts were often substantially overdrawn. In April 1985 the bank's credit committee, at Traynor's urging, agreed to let Haughey maintain an overdraft of up to £200,000, without any security being supplied.

In fact no major drawings were made from his principal account after June 1983, apart from the £115,859 transfer in September 1984 to the account in Haughey's and Boland's names, and a debit of £20,000 sent to Haughey Boland to fund the bill-paying service and funded by a lodgment of the same amount the previous month.

Similarly there was only one small debit from Haughey's second current account after September 1983. As we have already seen, the account was opened in May 1983, and closed in January 1984.

In general, apart from the £20,000 sent to Haughey Boland in April 1985 and funded by a lodgment of the same amount the previous month, there were no major drawings from the Haughey accounts in Guinness & Mahon from January 1984 up to when his last account was closed in June 1987. It would seem Haughey used the bank to the greatest extent he could, but had to back off around January 1984.

Thereafter the large monthly cheques needed to feed the bill-paying service being provided by Haughey Boland were coming from somewhere else. Some of this money came from the loans taken out by P. V. Doyle. Another £100,000 came from the Irish Permanent Building Society and was, according to Dr Edmund Farrell, managing director of the society, intended for Fianna Fáil.

Edmund Farrell was managing director of the Irish Permanent Building Society from 1975 to 1993, having inherited the job from his father, Edmund Farrell Snr, who had taken over as secretary of the Irish Temperance Permanent Benefit Building Society a decade before Edmund Jnr was born. Edmund Jnr, having studied medicine, joined the society in 1972 at the age of twenty-five. Three years later, after the death of his father, he took over the running of the organisation. It was reputedly Edmund Snr's dying wish that his son succeed him. Despite his young age and his lack of experience, Edmund Jnr did well, increasing the society's assets and opening new branches. When he parted company with the society in 1993 it was the largest in the State.

As noted earlier, in 1979 Farrell oversaw the purchase from the property developer Patrick Gallagher of a new Irish Permanent head office in St Stephen's Green, for £7.5 million. The purchase created some controversy at the time, as Gallagher had bought the building just one month earlier for £6.5 million, from a company belonging to John Byrne.

Edmund Jnr lived a privileged existence. His interests were said to be jogging, swimming, fishing, fine wines and haute cuisine. He was interested in boxing and closely followed the career of Barry McGuigan. The year he took over as managing director of the Irish Permanent he bought a large house, Grasmere, in Westminster Road in Foxrock, Co. Dublin, an address popular with denizens of the top levels of the Irish financial sector. According to reports from the time of his parting with the society, the house, on a sizable site, was bought for £250,000 and some time afterwards sold to the society for £275,000. It was then extended and substantially refurbished, at a cost of £450,000, before being sold back to Farrell for £275,000.

Transactions concerning the Foxrock house led to Farrell's dramatic suspension by the Irish Permanent in March 1993. A statement was issued on the evening of 10 March: "The board of directors of the Irish Permanent Building Society has announced that it has suspended the society's chairman, Dr Edmund Farrell, from executive office pending further investigation of past transactions regarding the residential property occupied by Dr Farrell."

The suspension was followed by the inevitable court hearing. The society sued Farrell for being in breach of his duties from April 1986 to June 1992, for an "unauthorised" increase in his salary in 1986 and an "unauthorised" payment of £100,000. Farrell counter-sued for unfair dismissal. The case was settled in 1997 in a deal which left Farrell and his wife, Zora, with Grasmere and a pension fund worth £800,000 but which also involved a £150,000 payment to Irish Permanent. The bank also got ownership of a condominium in Boston reported to be worth £100,000 and to have been bought with the society's money.

Each side had to pay its own legal costs of more than

£300,000. Before the case was settled it was said in court that Farrell had used devices to extract large sums of money from the society, though Farrell's counsel said his client vehemently denied any wrongdoing. Farrell's solicitor said afterwards that all the transactions mentioned in the proceedings had been known of by the society's board at the time. In 1998 Farrell sold his Foxrock home for £2 million.

An associate of Haughey's in the 1980s formed the impression at the time that Farrell was very much in awe of Haughey, and that this was the reason for Farrell's largesse with the funds of the society he managed. This view essentially matches the evidence given by Farrell to the Moriarty Tribunal.

According to Farrell, he first met Haughey at a Fianna Fáil fundraising lunch in the early to mid-1980s. Soon afterwards Haughey was a guest at Farrell's Blackrock home. Haughey and Farrell began to meet for lunch about once a year, though at one period this grew to about three times a year. Farrell dined with Haughey twice in the Taoiseach's office.

He had other social and business meetings with Haughey. He would meet the party leader along with other executives of the building societies to discuss matters of interest to the sector. Haughey was a guest of the society's at the first Barry McGuigan world title fight, and Farrell was a guest of the State during a dinner held in Dublin Castle for Queen Beatrix of the Netherlands, who was on an official visit. Contact between the two men all but ceased following Farrell's bust-up with the society in 1993.

In 1986 Farrell authorised two payments totalling £100,000 from the society. He told the Moriarty Tribunal the money was intended for Fianna Fáil and not for Haughey. It was paid in two amounts of £50,000 each. The cheques were made out to Fianna

Fáil but did not go into the account operated by party head-quarters in Mount Street. Headquarters had no record of receiving £100,000 from the Irish Permanent. In fact the cheques found their way to Haughey's offices in Leinster House. They were endorsed on the back by Haughey and lodged to an account called the party leader's account, of which more will be heard later in this book. The account was one controlled by Haughey from his offices in Leinster House. Farrell said he knew nothing of any party leader's account and would not have sent a donation to the party anywhere other than to party headquarters.

The first cheque, for £50,000, was dated 19 March 1986 and was signed by Farrell and J. G. Treacey, a director of the Irish Permanent. The second cheque, again for £50,000 and made out to Fianna Fáil, was signed by the same two men. On the cheque stubs the payments were each described as a "sub" to Fianna Fáil. Neither Farrell nor Treacey could remember how the payments came to be made.

During the period April to October 1986 five withdrawals were made from the party leader's account which coincided with lodgments to the Amiens account in Guinness & Mahon then being used to fund Haughey's bill-paying service. The total involved was £75,000. The sixth lodgment, for £25,000, was by way of a cheque made out to cash and signed by Haughey and Bertie Ahern.

A number of payments during this period were lodged to the party leader's account and the money then transferred from that account to the Amiens account by way of cheques signed by Haughey and Ahern. For most of the payments which came his way by this method during Haughey's time as leader of the opposition, the original source of the funding is not known. In 1984 £46,000 may have passed through the leader's account for his benefit. In

1986, £34,000 over and above the Irish Permanent payments may have passed his way. In 1987 the amount was £34,460.

In January 1987 six cheques signed by Ben Dunne and amounting in total to £32,000 were lodged to an Amiens account in Guinness & Mahon. These cheques were later to be dubbed the "bearer cheques".

Ben Dunne's father had a practice whereby he occasionally made out cheques, for not inconsiderable amounts, to "bearer" and then distributed them among his top executives. The cheques were drawn on a particular account and the chequebooks for this account kept in an old leather briefcase in his office. Ben Dunne junior continued the practice when he took over the running of the family companies. As with his father, these bearer cheques were used by him as something akin to legal tender. Sometimes he'd keep some of them for himself.

Dunne said in evidence to the Moriarty Tribunal that he would have one of his aides fill out some of these cheques and he would then sign them. He might distribute a few of them there and then and keep others in his pocket to give to people later, or to keep for himself.

Six of these bearer cheques, written out in January 1987 by his financial adviser, Noel Fox, and totalling approximately £30,000, were lodged in two tranches to an Amiens account in Guinness & Mahon. The amount involved was greater than any individual Dunnes executive, other than himself, would get under the bearer cheque system, Dunne said. Even Fox wouldn't receive that amount.

"There is a possibility that if I didn't give them to Mr Haughey I would have given them to Mr Fox to give to Mr Haughey," Dunne told the Moriarty Tribunal. However, he had no memory of this. Fox said he knew nothing about how the cheques could have got to Haughey or to Traynor.

Dunne said he had no dealings with Traynor in early 1987 and his name had never come up in discussions with Fox. Likewise, there had been no mention of Traynor during a meeting between him and Haughey arranged by Fox in 1986. How these cheques came to be lodged to Guinness & Mahon bank has not been explained.

When Haughey's long period as leader of the opposition came to an end in February 1987 he had an overdraft of more than a quarter of a million pounds with Guinness & Mahon bank. He may also have had a debt at the bank's Cayman Islands subsidiary equal to half a million pounds. He was struggling.

6

Helping Ciarán

DURING the 1980s, as Haughey bided his time before his return to power, there was time to give attention to the affairs of his son Ciarán. Ciarán, the third born of his four children, had been apprenticed as a plumber after leaving school, but by the mid-1980s he had befriended a former American helicopter pilot named John Barnicle and was showing a strong interest in training as a helicopter pilot. The idea was hatched that the two men could form a small charter helicopter company which, if all went well, would provide a living for both of them. The only Irish competitor company then in existence was Irish Helicopters, a subsidiary of Aer Lingus. The two men decided they would call their company Celtic Helicopters.

Neither man had any capital, but Ciarán's father decided he would do what he could to support his son's venture. Des Traynor soon became heavily involved. Between them Haughey and Traynor organised £160,000 in capital, half of it coming by way of a loan from Guinness & Mahon and the rest from mutual friends and acquaintances. The exact breakdown of how much

each invested is not clear, nor is it clear that all the money given
went to the Helicopters. Ciarán Haughey and John Barnicle, for
their part, each contributed £60. Ciarán Haughey later told the
Moriarty Tribunal he knew his dad was helping with setting up his
company but had not known whom he was asking for support.
The directors of the new company included Paul Carty, the
Haughey Boland accountant. He and the accountancy firm were
to continue to have a say in the running of the company's affairs
over the years.

Celtic Helicopters opened an account with Guinness &
Mahon bank in March 1985 and was granted an overdraft facility
of £80,000. There were also two lodgments to the account, one
for £5,000 and one for £75,000. The £5,000 came from Dr John
O'Connell, then a Fianna Fáil TD. The second lodgment was
based on a transfer from an Amiens Securities account opened
by Traynor on 17 January 1985 and closed on 17 April 1985.

The Amiens account received lodgments totalling £85,000
during the three days 26 to 28 March. The first lodgment, for
£10,000 on 26 March, was the proceeds of a cheque made out to
Dr Michael Dargan. The second, for £15,000 and on the same date,
was the result of a transfer of £12,420 sterling from a Guinness
Mahon Cayman Trust account. The third, for £10,000 on 27
March, was the result of another transfer of £8,200 sterling from
the Guinness Mahon Cayman Trust account. The fourth, on the
same date and for £25,000, was the result of a transfer of £20,712
sterling from the Guinness Mahon Cayman Trust account. On 28
March £10,000 was lodged, this being a transfer from the Guinness
& Mahon account of Purcell Exports Ltd, the company associated
with Séamus Purcell. The donations identified by the Moriarty
Tribunal came to just over £37,000, leaving some £43,000 that it
couldn't account for. The donors or investors identified were Dr

John O'Connell, £5,000; Joseph Malone, £15,000; Séamus Purcell, £12,000; and Cruse Moss, £4,987.

Haughey senior and Traynor showed little regard for the niceties of political correctness or corporate ethics while raising capital for Celtic Helicopters. At the time, Traynor was on the board of Aer Lingus, the parent company of the only Irish competitor to the planned venture. He had been appointed to the board by Haughey and was chairman of a board sub-committee which monitored the affairs of the state enterprise's commercial subsidiaries, including Irish Helicopters. Within their own circle Traynor and Haughey made no attempt to hide the fact that Traynor was acting as adviser, fund-raiser and banker to a company which was setting up in competition with an enterprise he had detailed information on as a result of his being on a State board. Not only did they not try to hide the fact but Haughey even asked another member of the Aer Lingus board if he would act as chairman of the new company, and make an investment.

One of the points often made in relation to business people giving money to Haughey is that there is no clear evidence of his ever having done anything in return. Terry Keane, in her memoirs, says the idea involves a misunderstanding of Haughey's nature. He would simply expect people to give him money, and when they did he would think no more of it. Others say that what you would get in return was inclusion. Many people admired Haughey hugely and were anxious to secure or maintain his friendship. Also, Haughey was shameless about asking people for money. The story of Celtic Helicopters illustrates this.

Joseph Malone is a successful Irish businessman who in the course of his career worked mostly in the tourism sector. Like many of the people who feature in this book, he was a member the 1960s Fianna Fáil fund-raising organisation Taca. Malone started his career working in car hire in the 1950s, set up his own company and sold it to a British firm in 1964. In 1967 he took up a position in New York as chief executive, North America, for the Irish Tourist Board, and in 1976 was appointed director-general. He was appointed to the board of Bord Fáilte in November 1982, just before Haughey's Government was replaced by FitzGerald's Fine Gael – Labour coalition. The hotelier P. V. Doyle was on the board at the time.

In 1982 Malone joined the Smurfit Group and a year later took up a position with an American company, General Automotive Corporation (GAC), in Ann Arbor, Michigan. In 1988 he took up the position of president of three hotels in Boston. He retired in 1992.

Malone twice served as a director of Aer Lingus. His first term ended in 1985, the year Celtic Helicopters was established. He was re-appointed by the Haughey Government in August 1991 and served to December 1993. Appointment to the board of Aer Lingus was a prestigious appointment, one of the most attractive in the state sector, and brought with it an entitlement to free international air travel.

Some time around 1985 in the course of a conversation between the two men, Haughey asked Malone if he would take up the position of chairman of a company his son Ciarán was establishing called Celtic Helicopters. Malone was embarrassed because of his membership of the Aer Lingus board. There was no way he could serve on the board of the new company, so he turned down Haughey's request.

Some time later a further discussion took place between Malone and the then leader of the opposition. Malone was out in

Abbeville. "Ciarán happened to come in," he told the Moriarty Tribunal, "and Mr Haughey said to Ciarán, tell Joe and his friend all about Celtic Helicopters, your new investment, or your new company. Then, it was a kind of off the cuff remark, the suggestion was made perhaps you would like to invest in it." Malone discussed the matter with his "friend" when they were driving back from Abbeville. He felt the great man had been offended by his earlier refusal to become chairman, and, having explored the matter with his friend, he decided to make the investment. He later contacted Haughey and told him so. Malone bought shares worth £15,000 and asked that they be put in the name of his son, Joe Jnr, who was a friend of Ciarán's. It later emerged that the friend he was with in Kinsealy, and with whom he'd discussed the matter afterwards, was P. V. Doyle. Malone thought Doyle might himself be an investor, and internal G&M documents suggested this might be the case, but Haughey was "as confident as I can be" that Doyle was not an investor. The hotelier's estate did not include any reference to a shareholding.

Michael Dargan was a long-time associate of Traynor's from the board of Cement Roadstone, where he served as chairman up to 1987, when Traynor replaced him. The two men also served together on the board of Aer Lingus. Dargan was chief executive of Aer Lingus from 1969 to 1974 and was on the Aer Lingus board up to 1986. He was chairman of the state-sponsored company at the time Celtic Helicopters was set up as a rival to Irish Helicopters. He was on a number of other boards, including Fitzwilton, the holding company associated with Tony O'Reilly.

Dargan was involved in bloodstock breeding, had his own substantial stud farm, and had dealings with stud companies with which John Magnier was associated. Magnier was a bloodstock breeder who had risen to the very top of the business and, with a little help from the tax-free status given the industry by Haughey in the 1960s, had become one of the wealthiest men in Ireland. Haughey once appointed him to the Seanad.

In March 1985 an accountant at Coolmore Castlehyde and Associated Stud Farms, one of Magnier's companies, sent a cheque for £10,000 to Dargan, the payment being the dividend due for a stallion called Thatching. After Dargan received the money it ended up in the Amiens account in Guinness & Mahon bank and formed part of a larger sum of money which was ultimately paid to Celtic Helicopters. Dargan was later to say this happened without his knowledge, that he never made a contribution to Celtic Helicopters or to Charles Haughey, and that he was never asked to. It was Traynor who had diverted the cheque, he said.

Dargan was in business with his son, who was in the United States at the time of the Thatching transaction. Dargan said he used Guinness & Mahon bank for transferring money to his son. He knew Traynor very well. It was because of his personal relationship with Traynor, Dargan said, that he brought some of his personal financial affairs to Guinness & Mahon. Traynor opened an account for Dargan with Guinness Mahon Cayman Trust.

Around the same time as the £10,000 went to Celtic Helicopters, five other cheques to Dargan were lodged to the Amiens account in Guinness & Mahon. Dargan was a director of the Bank of Ireland from the mid-1970s to the late 1980s. Dealing with Traynor or his secretary, Williams, he sent money to or through the Cayman account without seeking the necessary exchange control approval. At one point during his evidence to the Moriarty Tribunal, Dargan said he didn't know what exchange control regulations were. He said he would have been sending money abroad "every month" but that all the money involved would have been untaxable earnings from his bloodstock activities. During his evidence he mentioned that he had lived in a house in north Co. Dublin so large that it had eleven rooms in the basement. He kept all his files in this basement, but when moving to a smaller house he had discarded many of them.

Dargan denied ever authorising a payment to Celtic Helicopters. He also said he would have noticed if the £10,000 had gone missing and never did. There is a possible explanation for this scenario. It emerged during the Moriarty Tribunal that Traynor would sometimes switch amounts he was handling which were in different currencies. If someone wanted, for instance, to retrieve £10,000 in Irish pounds from a sterling account and someone else wanted to lodge a similar amount of Irish money to an offshore account, Traynor would give the Irish money to the person wanting to make the withdrawal, and then record the transactions in the memorandum accounts as if a separate lodgment and withdrawal had actually been make. This saved him from exchanging the currencies and having to worry about exchange control regulations. So Traynor may have given Dargan's £10,000 to Celtic Helicopters and at the same time given an equivalent amount of money to Dargan's son, that money coming from the offshore account of someone who had agreed to invest in Celtic Helicopters.

Cruse W. Moss was chairman of GAC, the company Malone worked for in Michigan. GAC and the bus-building company Bombardier had a major contract with CIE in the early 1980s. A joint-venture manufacturing operation based in Shannon built approximately 850 buses for CIE. GAC ultimately took over the entire operation, which closed in the late 1980s. Malone suggested to Moss that he invest in Celtic Helicopters, and Moss invested £5,987. Haughey told the tribunal that he had met Moss a number of times. GAC eventually collapsed. In 1990 Moss sold back his Celtic Helicopters share to the company for £7,802.

John O'Connell invested £5,000 in Celtic Helicopters just a month after he joined Fianna Fáil. The payment was made after he was summoned to Haughey's offices in Leinster House. Haughey told him about his son's new company "and asked me to make a contribution or if I had any friends who would make a contribution." Haughey said he was asking "a few friends" for contributions of £5,000 each. O'Connell wrote out a cheque. "I had joined the party in January of 1985 and this was March and I presumed that a lot of members of the party had been asked to contribute."

Séamus Purcell operated a major livestock exporting business in Co. Tipperary which used Waterford port. He admired Haughey and was thankful for support Haughey had given in the past to the beef sector. He told the Moriarty Tribunal that in 1985 he received a call from Haughey asking that he meet him for lunch in the Berkeley Court Hotel. No reason was given for the request, and Purcell did not ask. The two men met and had a general discussion on the meat industry while dining. When they were leaving the hotel Haughey mentioned that his son Ciarán was starting a new company and "needed a bit of capital." Haughey asked for £12,000. Purcell agreed. Haughey told him Traynor would be in touch.

When Traynor subsequently contacted him he asked if Purcell wanted shares in return for the payment. Purcell said he did not. No amounts were discussed. The money was subsequently transferred between accounts. Bank records show that £10,000 was transferred, not £12,000.

Michael Smurfit, the millionaire businessman and head of the Smurfit Group, told the Moriarty Tribunal that around the time of the establishment of Celtic Helicopters he was asked by Haughey if he would make a contribution to the new company. "We declined to get involved in the company but decided to give it some business after it was formed." He said his company still did business with Celtic Helicopters.

From its early days, Ben Dunne and the Dunnes Stores Group used the services of Celtic Helicopters. Dunne used the company to such an extent that he later asked Ciarán Haughey to look for a helicopter which would be suitable for carrying him and his friends when they were going on golfing trips. He was to have a number of financial dealings with Ciarán Haughey and Celtic Helicopters.

Part Two

1987–1992

7

Back in Business

I N early 1986 Garret FitzGerald made what was generally accepted to have been a disastrous reshuffle of his Fine Gael – Labour coalition Government. Haughey quickly moved a motion of no confidence in the Government. Des O'Malley, who had never been happy with Haughey as leader of Fianna Fáil, had formed a new party, the Progressive Democrats, and it was riding high in the public opinion polls, only a few points short of replacing Fine Gael as the second most popular party in the State. Mary Harney had left Fianna Fáil with O'Malley. Pearse Wyse and Bobby Molloy had also left and joined the new political grouping. FitzGerald survived the no confidence vote, but from then on it was downhill for him and his Government. Haughey was looking for a kill.

The stance Haughey took in this period against the Anglo-Irish Agreement, going so far as to try to wreck it, and the duplicitous role he and his party played during the divorce referendum, when the party's stated position of neutrality on the issue was belied by its activities on the ground, did nothing for his reputation. Haughey issued a personal statement during the divorce campaign in which he expressed his "unshakeable belief" in the importance of the family as the basic unity of society. Divorce, he said, had an appeal for some individuals, the attraction of "superficial freedom".

In January 1987 Dick Spring and his Labour Party colleagues refused to support cutbacks in health and social welfare and resigned from the Government. FitzGerald called a general election. Haughey's moment had come, but once again he was to be denied his dream of an overall majority.

Polling was on 18 February 1987. That day Haughey's old friend John Byrne wrote a cheque for £50,000. The cheque, drawn on the account of a company called Skellig Investments, was made out to Guinness & Mahon bank, and Byrne told the Moriarty Tribunal he couldn't remember why he had written it. Because of who the payee was, he said, he must have given the cheque to Traynor. It was not intended as a payment to Haughey, he said.

The cheque was lodged in an Amiens Securities account in Guinness & Mahon, and where it went afterwards is not known, the records having been removed from the Guinness & Mahon archiving system, most probably on Traynor's instructions. The likelihood is, however, that the money was used by Haughey. The £50,000 would not have been enough to keep him going for more than a month and a half, such was his expenditure.

The existence of O'Malley's Progressive Democrats was the crucial political factor after the 1987 general election. Fianna Fáil won eighty-one seats, three short of what was needed. Haughey would not be able to wield power unless he satisfied the desires of at least one of the opposition parties. It was the kind of limitation on Haughey's powers that FitzGerald had hoped for. It emerged that if he was going to maintain a minority Government, Haughey would have to adopt a policy of financial rectitude. Alan Dukes, who replaced FitzGerald at the helm of Fine Gael, said his party would not oppose the Government as long as it seriously addressed the dire economic situation. This strategy was to be dubbed the Tallaght strategy, because of where it was announced.

Given Haughey's impatience and dictatorial tendencies, it was a frustrating position for him to find himself in. However, it was later to be generally acknowledged that the decisiveness with which Haughey then set about turning around the public finances and setting in train a number of positive, confidence-building and growth-building initiatives, was a critical and positive turn-around in the State's history.

Whereas he had famously overseen a publicity campaign against FitzGerald's Government centred around the phrase "Health cuts hurt the old, the sick and the handicapped," in government he adopted a policy of fiscal rectitude and drastic cutbacks in public services. Fine Gael and the Progressive Democrats abstained on the vote on the first Fianna Fáil budget. Haughey's Government championed social partnership, the establishment of the Irish Financial Services Centre, a cultural initiative in Temple Bar, Dublin, and the renovation of Government Buildings in Merrion Square. On the North Haughey worked for the Anglo-Irish Agreement which he had opposed so strongly in opposition. His ratings in the public opinion polls increased as he set about pursuing the sort of harsh, decisive policies he had shied away from before because of concerns about the public's response.

As well as dealing decisively with the State's finances, Haughey launched a programme to put his own financial situation on a better footing. Eleven cash lodgments totalling £106,8000 were made around the time of the 1987 general election to the

Amiens account to which the Dunne bearer cheques were lodged. The eleven lodgments were all for round-figure sums. The origin of much of this money is not known.

The Amiens account to which the cheques were lodged was the one through which the various loans taken out by P. V. Doyle and used by Haughey were discharged. On 22 February 1988 there was a lodgment to the account of £195,00 and on 24 February of £47,700. These lodgments brought the balance to £302,950. The account was then used to settle the loans taken out by Doyle for Haughey. This occurred after Doyle had died but before Traynor informed Doyle's family and the executors of his estate that the debts were still outstanding. The money came from an account in the Bank of Ireland, but from which particular account it is not known. The tribunal examined the Amiens account to see if the money eventually given to Traynor by the Doyles was later debited from the Amiens account and transferred to the Bank of Ireland, but found no such record.

The tribunal did note that debits were made from the account which appeared to match credits to the Haughey Boland No. 3 account, the one used for the bill-paying service operated for Haughey.

Doyle died in February 1988, after a short illness, and his death was covered extensively in the media. The 65-year old businessman was the subject of tributes from across the political spectrum as well as from figures in commerce, tourism, and the Catholic Church. Haughey issued a statement:

He was a man of great charity and humanity. His contribution to Irish life over a wide area was of great value and
importance. He was generous with his time and his advice

Charles and Maureen Haughey with their neighbour, Mrs Pat O'Connor, at a reception in 1960.

Seán Lemass (Taoiseach), Jack Lynch (Minister for Finance) and Charles Haughey (Minister for Agriculture) leaving for London in 1965 to negotiate the Anglo-Irish Free-Trade Area Agreement.

Haughey with his solicitor, Pat O'Connor, at the time of the Arms Trial.

At the helm.

Maureen Haughey and Mrs Pat
O'Connor, ready for the hunt.

Terry Keane.

Taoiseach at last: Charles Haughey on the day of his election as Fianna Fáil Party leader.

With Albert Reynolds in the background.

At the ard-fheis.

After the heave.

En famille.

At Arbour Hill with Brian Lenihan.

Opening the International Financial Services Centre in 1988. Mark
Kavanagh is to the right of Haughey.

to all who sought it and he had a special interest in young people. He was one of the world's great hoteliers and will be especially remembered for his services to the Irish tourist industry.

Soon after Doyle's death Traynor asked for a meeting with Doyle's son, David, and another executive of the Doyle Group. At the meeting in the Berkeley Court Hotel in March 1988, Traynor said Doyle owed Guinness & Mahon money he had taken out in loans to facilitate Haughey. Haughey had made some of the interest payments but then had stopped doing so, Traynor explained. The position, Traynor said, was that there wasn't "a hope in hell" of the loans being repaid by Haughey.

As we have seen, this was not entirely true: the debt had already been settled by way of a transfer from an unidentified account in the Bank of Ireland. When money was later received from the Doyle estate, to pay off a debt which had already been settled, it was lodged to the Amiens account in Guinness & Mahon. It is not necessarily that Traynor cheated the Doyle family out of any money. A representative of the Doyle Group said it believed that whatever Traynor did was done for good reasons. Haughey also denied that Traynor had acted in any way dishonourably in relation to the Doyle family or the Doyle Group when he failed to explain that the debt had already been repaid.

Haughey said he'd never known that the financial help he was receiving from Doyle was a loan. "I wasn't certain, but I certainly wouldn't have thought that it was by way of loan, probably by way of donation or maybe by way of personal loan to Mr Traynor for donation." Traynor had not mentioned the matter to him after his original comment that Doyle was helping out, he said.

It appears that at least one of the interest payments made to the loan accounts during their existence was made by Doyle rather than Haughey. This payment was for £9,966. Other payments were made in cash, and their source cannot be identified. The total interest paid on the first loan account was approximately £112,000.

The Moriarty Tribunal identified a number of cheques from Doyle which were lodged to the Amiens account, including one for £3,500 for which the associated cheque stub contains the note "to cash loan H." It may be that Doyle paid all the interest payments made on the first loan account during its five-year existence. The total involved in the two loan accounts, including interest, was £301,138, and it may be that Doyle and his estate paid out most of this amount as a result of his agreement to facilitate Haughey.

It was a considerable amount even for a man of Doyle's wealth. His estate when he died was valued at £4,723,022. It may be that the loan account was not the first time Doyle provided financial assistance to Haughey.

8

Tralee Again

DURING its sittings the Moriarty Tribunal spent a considerable amount of time trying to get to the bottom of a number of transactions involving John Byrne's hotels in Co. Kerry. Traynor, of course, was deceased. Byrne had not known what Traynor had been up to until it was brought to his attention by the tribunal, so all that could be established was the money trail. What lay behind the transactions is not clear, nor is it clear who benefited. At issue was £260,000 lodged to Guinness & Mahon bank in July 1987, and a further £42,000 lodged in October. The money was lodged to the Amiens account to which the Dunne bearer cheques were lodged. What happened to it subsequently is not known.

As we have seen, not only was the Fianna Fáil TD Denis Foley personally involved with the Ansbacher deposits, but so too was Central Tourist Holdings, the company which owned the Ballybunnion hotel and in which Foley held a 25 per cent stake. The other directors of the company, besides Foley, were Byrne and the Clifford brothers, Thomas and William.

The directors had borrowed money from Guinness & Mahon

bank and refurbished the Central Hotel for use mainly as a dance hall and bar. The business did not prosper, and when in 1986 the company sold the hotel there were insufficient funds to discharge creditors. A settlement was agreed between Haughey Boland, on behalf of the company, and the Revenue Commissioners and Guinness & Mahon bank. The directors each made payments of approximately £7,000 to fund the settlement.

Traynor was involved in having a cheque for £42,000 drawn on the company's Guinness & Mahon account in October 1987 as part of the exercise of settling with the bank. However, the cheque ended up in an Amiens account in Guinness & Mahon, rather than with the bank itself.

What had happened was that the loan Central Tourist Holdings had from the bank was backed by funds in the Ansbacher deposits and had been paid off a year earlier, in September 1985. At the time the total amount owed to Guinness & Mahon bank was £135,000 and the entire debt was cleared by way of a transfer from the Ansbacher deposits. John Byrne said he did not know at the time that the debt had been paid off, or that it had been backed by money in the Ansbacher deposits.

When Haughey Boland was completing the accounts for 1985 for Central Tourist Holdings it wrote to Guinness & Mahon seeking information on any loans then outstanding. False documents were produced within the bank and issued to the auditors, purporting to show the loan as still in existence. The auditors reported that the company had a loan, the interest on which was deductible against tax. The documents would also have been used by the company in its negotiations with the Revenue Commissioners in relation to its closing settlement. The main motive for pretending the loan was still in existence, however, may have been to hide the fact that the loan had been repaid, lest the Revenue begin to question where the money had come from and thereby discover the Ansbacher deposits.

When the money from the sale of the Ballybunnion hotel was forwarded to Guinness & Mahon, ostensibly to repay the company's loan, it went into the Amiens account rather than to the bank. The Revenue Commissioners would not have known this.

The Brandon Hotel, in Prince's Street, Tralee, was run by a company called Princes Investments. Byrne and the two Clifford brothers were the directors. It took out a loan for £116,000 sterling from Guinness & Mahon in 1975 and the loan was secretly backed by money in the Ansbacher deposits. In December 1984 the balance in the loan account was £172,138 sterling. On 4 September 1985, the loan was cleared with £186,986 sterling from the Ansbacher deposits. This is the same date on which the Central Tourist Holdings loan was cleared in a similar way.

Again bogus documents were produced within the bank for Haughey Boland, purporting to show the loan as still in existence, and forwarded to Haughey Boland. This happened for two years in a row.

On 23 July 1987, £260,000 was sent to Guinness & Mahon bank from Tralee, ostensibly to repay the loan. However, the money took a circuitous route on its way to Dublin. A cheque drawn on the Princes Investments account in Co. Kerry was used to buy what is called a banker's payment in Dublin, and that document was then lodged to the Amiens account in Guinness & Mahon. Banker's payments are usually used for payments from one bank to another. A huge trawl through the records of all its branches for the period around July 1987 was undertaken by AIB for the Moriarty Tribunal before the source of this banker's payment was identified. The circuitous route taken seems to have been aimed at hiding the trail between the Amiens account and the hotel's account in Castle Street, Tralee.

Where the money went next is not known. Byrne, when he gave evidence about this matter, was of little assistance to the tribunal. As in the instance of the Central Tourist Holdings transactions, he said that all these matters concerning the repayment of the loan had occurred without his knowledge and without his giving any consent to Traynor to conduct any such transactions. It was all "very mysterious," he said at one stage, but "if it happened it happened." Despite its inquiries into the matter, no evidence was produced by the tribunal to show who received the £260,000 sent from Tralee.

Haughey expressed bafflement when the subject was raised during the evidence he gave in private to the Moriarty Tribunal. During these sessions he would be given notice the day before of what was to be raised the following day. When questioned about the £260,000 he said, "I saw these references to Princes Investments, and I just can't understand why they are there. I mean, they are nothing to do with me whatsoever."

Asked if he knew if Byrne was ever approached by Traynor in relation to his (Haughey's) finances, Haughey said:

No. I don't know that, but I don't think he ever was and I think Mr Byrne has said from time to time publicly and definitely that he never subscribed personally to my finances, never subscribed to my personal finances at any stage. But, I mean, I don't understand why these … I never heard of Princes Investments in my life and I know nothing about these transactions … I just, when I saw them here in these documents as matters you were going to raise, I was baffled. Because I don't know or see how you can suggest that these had anything to do with me.

9

A New Disciple

I N May 1987, on Ben Dunne's instructions, the manager of
Dunnes Stores (Bangor), Matt Price, wrote out a cheque for
£285,000 sterling. The payee was a company called Tripleplan, and the cheque was sent by Price to Dublin, to Noel Fox.
No-one had ever heard of Tripleplan, and Dunnes Stores had
never had any dealings with the company. Tripleplan was in fact
a British-registered company, a legal entity with no assets, and
soon after the cheque was written out the company was
dissolved. Its directors were John Furze and John Collins, the two
Cayman Island bankers involved in running the Ansbacher
deposits. Secretarial services for the company were supplied by
Sam Field-Corbett's Dublin-based Management Investment
Services Ltd. The Tripleplan cheque made its way to Guinness &
Mahon bank, where it was used to settle the debt Haughey had
with that bank as his long period in opposition came to an end.

Ben Dunne is a strange man. In 1987 he was at the head of one
of the wealthiest business families in Ireland. His upbringing, and
by all accounts those of his siblings, was far from conventional.

His father, Ben senior, had opened a shop in Cork in 1934 and proceeded to build a retail empire over the following two decades. He opened the State's first supermarket, at Cornelscourt, and reportedly used on occasion sit outside in his car with his wife watching the customers entering and leaving. *Dunnes Stores better value beats them all* was the company's famous catchcry. He ran his shops personally up to 1963.

In April 1963 an unlimited company, Dunnes Holding Company Ltd, was formed, and the entire business transferred to that company. The following year a trust, the Dunnes Settlement Trust, was established to hold the ordinary shares in Dunnes Holding Company. The trust was a discretionary trust, the purpose of which was to provide for Dunne's children and grandchildren. The trust was to have a life term of twenty-one years, to 16 March 1985.

There were five children: Ben, Frank, Margaret (Heffernan), Elizabeth (McMahon), and Therese. When Ben senior died in April 1983 the management of the Dunnes company was assumed by the children. Ben became joint managing director along with his brother, Frank. The sisters were also on the board and active in the affairs of the company. During the next ten years the Dunnes operation expanded considerably, with a number of new outlets being opened in new shopping centres around the State. Ben Dunne was in charge of this aspect of the Dunnes operation, as well as the grocery side of the business. Margaret Heffernan was in charge of personnel and women's underwear; Elizabeth McMahon of women's wear, and Therese Dunne of children's wear.

Ben Dunne Jnr left school at the age of sixteen to begin working in his father's business. When he and his siblings took control after their father's death, Ben became the main force within the group. He took sole and complete control of the financial side of the business. During the ten-year period 1983 to 1993 turnover rose from about £300 million per annum to about £850 million per annum. He was in charge of a growing, thriving, highly successful business.

He devised a method of getting influence and control over companies which supplied goods and services to Dunnes Stores, a system which created a number of companies which were in effect subsidiaries of Dunnes. The Fine Gael minister Michael Lowry ran one such company.

Lowry had started his working life as an apprentice with Butler Refrigeration in Thurles, Co. Tipperary, in 1971. He worked his way up to sales manager, a position which brought him into contact with Dunnes Stores, a company with which Butler Refrigeration conducted business installing and maintaining refrigeration units. In 1987 Lowry was elected a Fine Gael TD for Tipperary North. His contact with Dunne and the donations for the party he secured from Dunne were to play a critical role in his rapid rise in the parliamentary party.

Lowry left Butler Refrigeration soon after being elected TD and started doing consultancy work for Dunnes Stores. A company he established, Garuda Ltd, trading as Streamline Enterprises, started to conduct work for Dunnes after Ben Dunne told Lowry he was no longer going to use Butler Refrigeration and offered Lowry the work. An arrangement was arrived at between Dunne and Lowry whereby Streamline would work for Dunnes Stores and be paid in such a way that it would make modest annual profits. The auditors to the company would be Oliver Freaney & Co., auditors to Dunnes Stores. Dunnes Stores' chief accountant, Michael Irwin, on secondment from Oliver Freaney, would have full access to the books of Lowry's company.

A second part of the arrangement was that Dunne would give Lowry personal bonuses based, essentially, on how pleased Dunne was with the work Lowry was doing for him. Lowry was later to tell the McCracken Tribunal that Dunne said: "The bottom line is, if you are good for Dunnes Stores and if you achieve the savings that I think are possible, I will certainly make it worth your while and your company will be successful and you will be a wealthy man."

Lowry received a number of large payments from Dunnes Stores, amounting to hundreds of thousands of pounds, which were given to him in such a way as to facilitate tax evasion. Much of the money was lodged to offshore accounts, and it meant that Dunne, whatever about his motives, soon had information with which he could destroy one of the senior figures in the second largest political party in the State.

In his report after the McCracken Tribunal Mr Justice Brian McCracken came down hard on Lowry.

> By evading tax in the way in which he did, Mr Michael Lowry made himself vulnerable to all kinds of pressures from Dunnes Stores, had they chosen to apply those pressures. The threat to disclose the payments and the offshore accounts could have been used by Dunnes Stores to obtain favours, as indeed could a threat to cut off this source of income to Mr Lowry.
>
> It is an appalling situation that a Government minister and chairman of a parliamentary party can be seen to be consistently benefiting from the black economy from shortly after the time he was first elected to Dáil Éireann. If such a person can behave in this way without serious sanctions being imposed, it becomes very difficult to condemn others who similarly flout the law.

In the general election following publication of the McCracken Report, Lowry, standing as an independent, topped the poll in Tipperary North. At the time of writing he has not been charged with any offence.

Dunnes Stores conducted a lot of business in the Far East, obtaining goods which were imported for sale in the Republic. As far back as the 1970s Ben Dunne, having discussed the matter with his father, set about establishing a number of companies in Hong Kong which he controlled in a similar way to Lowry's Garuda Ltd. He went into business with a Hong Kong national called Tse Kam Ming or Laurence Tse. Under the arrangement Tse was to own a company, Wytrex, which would purchase goods for the Dunnes Group and transport them to Ireland. Dunne would then organise payment for Tse but would pay approximately 5 per cent above what was required. This surplus would then accumulate within the Hong Kong company. Once every year or so Dunne, during a trip to the Far East, would collect the surplus in banker's drafts made out to fictitious names, and bring them home. He would collect up to £200,000 at a time. At other times the surplus would be transferred to a Swiss trust, called Equifex, and at other times to a company in the Isle of Man called Tutbury Ltd. All of this provided Dunne with a method for getting his hands on money which properly belonged to the trust.

The Dunnes trust, as already noted, was established in March 1964 and was to exist for twenty-one years. When that period of time came to an end the trust applied to have its life extended for a further twenty-one years. The Revenue Commissioners, however, fought the application. Huge amounts of money were at stake. If the Revenue Commissioners were successful, the value of the trust would have been deemed to be distributed among the Dunne beneficiaries, who would then have become liable for a huge capital gains tax bill. A £30 million assessment was raised by the Revenue Commissioners some time in 1986 or 1987, that is, just around or before the time of Haughey's return to power. As the capital gains tax rate was then 40 per cent, the assessment meant the Revenue Commissioners put a value on the trust of £75 million. The family appealed the assessment, and it was dismissed following a three-day hearing in camera before the Appeals Commissioners in 1988. On foot of legal advice from senior counsel, the Revenue Commissioners decided not to pursue the matter further.

In 1981 Ben Dunne was kidnapped by the IRA. The full details of what happened have never been disclosed, but it is generally believed to have been a hugely terrifying time for the multi-millionaire businessman. It seems Dunne was kept in the boot of a car and suffered great cruelty at the hands of his abductors. Haughey was Taoiseach at the time. The Gardaí were adamant that no ransom would be paid and tried to prevent any such payment being made from the group's turnover. The telephones of more than forty potential intermediaries were tapped by the Gardaí.

Dunne was released. The kidnapping received enormous media coverage, and hundreds of people turned up in the Pro-Cathedral in Dublin for a service to give thanks for his safe return. The psychological torture he had undergone affected him hugely and may have contributed to his subsequent development of a cocaine habit and the events which, a decade later, were to lead to his removal from the helm of the family company.

Dunne gave evidence to both the McCracken and Moriarty Tribunals. In the witness box he would crouch forward as if listening intently to the questions being put to him by the barristers. He addressed the men as "sir." He sometimes seemed to have difficulty expressing himself. During the course of the Moriarty Tribunal new payments to Haughey would be discovered, such as the Tripleplan cheque for £285,000 sterling, and he would not be able to remember anything about them. He would often say he had vague, unsure recollections. "I have a vague memory, somewhere in the back of my head," he would say, touching the back of his head with one of his huge hands and frowning as if concentrating on trying to find it.

Some time in 1986, Ben Dunne asked Noel Fox to organise an introduction for him to Haughey, then leader of the opposition. Fox was a partner with the accountants Oliver Freaney & Co., a trustee of the Dunnes Settlement Trust, a financial adviser to Ben Dunne, and a neighbour and associate of Haughey. Margaret Heffernan was to say subsequently that Haughey and Dunne became "very close" and that she was uneasy about the relationship. The relationship was to last almost exactly as long as both were in their respective positions of power.

As we have already seen, six cheques written by Fox, signed by Dunne and made out to bearer were lodged to Guinness & Mahon bank in January 1987. The Tripleplan cheque which wiped out Haughey's overdraft with the merchant bank was written in May 1987, and as it was made out to an obscure company run by Furze and Collins, Traynor must have been involved.

Some time in 1987 Fox received a phone call from Traynor. The two men, both accountants, knew each other though not very well. Fox knew Haughey well and presumably knew that Traynor had a role in managing Haughey's financial affairs. This telephone call has been given as the genesis of the series of payments Dunne was to make to Haughey over the following five years. Fox told the McCracken Tribunal that the approach occurred in November, and others, as we shall see, subsequently said they received similar approaches around the same time.

However, Fox later retracted his evidence to the McCracken Tribunal. He agreed with counsel for the Moriarty Tribunal that the Tripleplan cheque showed that the approach from Traynor must have come earlier in 1987. The Tripleplan cheque was dated 20 May 1987; Haughey was returned to power in February. If the Tripleplan cheque followed an approach from Traynor, then that approach occurred between February and May, almost immediately in the wake of Haughey's return to power. Everyone who has given evidence on the matter has said Haughey was Taoiseach at the time of the approach. As Fox said to the Moriarty Tribunal, referring to the Tripleplan cheque, "In the course of the McCracken Tribunal I could not remember exactly when I was approached, but I must draw the inference that it was much earlier than that cheque." He further said: "I now believe that he must have made the approach prior to May 1987."

Whatever about the timing, there is no confusion about the purpose of the approach. Traynor told Fox that Haughey had a "business problem" and that he, Traynor, was approaching about half a dozen people asking them to contribute £150,000 each towards settling the matter. What the problem was was not explained, but the total, £900,000, roughly equated to the debt Haughey may have had with Guinness & Mahon bank and its Cayman Islands subsidiary. Fox agreed to make an approach to Dunne.

At the time Fox and Dunne would meet every morning at 8 o'clock in the Dunnes Stores head office in Stephen's Street, Dublin. The two men were close. As already noted, Fox was a member of the Dunnes Stores trust and a partner with Oliver Freaney, auditors to the Dunnes Group. When in the years following the Tripleplan payment the auditors were trying to work out how to treat the matter in the Dunnes accounts, Fox referred them to Dunne.

On the morning after the 1987 telephone call from Traynor, Fox told Dunne of Traynor's approach. Dunne said he would take some time to consider the matter. During a subsequent con-versation, in which Fox emphasised the need for confidentiality in relation to the matter, Dunne said: "I think Haughey is making a huge mistake trying to get six or seven people together ... Christ picked twelve apostles, and one of them crucified him."

Dunne then said he would pay the whole amount but would not be able to do so immediately. He wanted to obtain the money from abroad and it would not be ready until later. He was planning to use money from the "slush fund" in the Far East to make the payments to Haughey, and the delay was because he had to let the money accumulate before the required amount would be available.

In May the Tripleplan cheque was written. Some time in late November Traynor got back on to Fox and said Haughey urgently needed the sterling equivalent of £205,000. Traynor told Fox where the money should be sent. He gave him some account details in London. John Furze, Traynor said, was the banker looking after the transaction. Fox had never heard of Furze.

Dunne agreed to make the payment even though he couldn't get the money from his Far Eastern operation. He told Fox to get on to Matt Price in Bangor again and get a sterling cheque for the required amount. Price got on to Dunne and verified the request from Fox before drawing a cheque on a Dunnes account with Ulster Bank for £182,630 sterling. He sent the cheque to Fox, and Fox passed it on to Traynor.

The cheque was sent to Guinness Mahon & Co. in London on 8 December 1987, where it was lodged to the Dublin bank's account with that bank. It was then transferred into the Ansbacher deposits in Dublin. Earlier that month Traynor had organised a £100,000 overdraft with Guinness & Mahon for Amiens Securities and used it to pay off a debt Haughey had with the Agricultural Credit Corporation. On 15 December the Amiens account was credited with the Irish equivalent of the Bangor cheque, this being £204,055. Some of this was used to settle the overdraft. On 22 December 1987, £59,000 was withdrawn in two cash withdrawals. The merchant bank would have had to put in a special order for this amount of cash. No receipt was given to whoever collected the money. It was most probably taken by Traynor or his driver for delivery to Haughey.

The remainder of the Dunne payment was transferred from the Amiens account to the Haughey Boland account used to fund Haughey's bill-paying service. Within a month the entire amount had been spent. Haughey dealt quickly with the money, but once again the unfortunate auditors for Dunnes Stores were to spend years trying to make sense of the payment.

During the following year, 1988, Dunne sought the only favour from Haughey the McCracken Tribunal discovered when it examined the matter almost ten years later. Haughey called the then chairman of the Revenue Commissioners, Philip Curran, to his office and asked him to meet Dunne. Curran agreed. The contact happened in the same year as the Dunnes' three-day appeal against the £30 million tax bill, heard before the Appeal Commissioners.

Curran was asked at the tribunal whether he had gone to Haughey's office or Haughey had gone to his. He paused, smiling at the idea of Haughey coming to his office. In Haughey's office, Curran said. The Taoiseach told him "business was booming and Ben and the family were making an awful lot of money and that there was some problem they had about, I think it was the family trust and the question of capital acquisitions tax."

This was indeed the issue Dunne wanted to discuss. Noel Fox attended the meeting with Dunne. They met Curran in his office in Dublin Castle. Dunne was not precise in outlining what his difficulty was, and Curran asked him to go away and draft a submission, which he would then consider. Dunne never took up the offer.

It seems Dunne was not the only source of funds for Haughey around this time. The lawyers working for the Moriarty Tribunal failed to discover who funded Haughey's bill-paying service during the entire year of 1988. The funds, according to the tribunal, did not come from the usual sources. In the story of Haughey's finances from 1979 to 1996, the year 1988 is a greater mystery than all the others. Although some funds were identified as having come in that year, these were not used to fund the bill-paying service that year, with the service being run with other donations of which nothing whatsoever is known. So the Dunne payment which is about to be described was allowed sit in the Ansbacher deposits until it was later needed. Also in 1988 there were two lodgments to an Amiens account which have remained a mystery: one for £195,000 on 22 February, and another for £49,700 two days later. Both were inter-bank transfers. When Haughey was asked about the transfers he said he knew nothing about them.

By the time Traynor next approached Fox looking for money for Haughey, funds had accumulated in Dunne's Far East operation. This time, July 1988, Traynor wanted £471,000 sterling. He said the money should be paid into an account with Barclays Bank, Knightsbridge, London, to the account of John Furze. The details were passed to Dunne, and he arranged for the money to be sent from Equifex, Switzerland, through a firm of Swiss solicitors, to the Furze account. From London the money was transferred to Guinness Mahon & Co., London, and from there to the Ansbacher deposits in Dublin. This time the payment would not come to the attention of the Dunnes auditors.

Dunne's dealings with Haughey were meanwhile extending to Haughey's family. As already noted, Dunne and his company used Celtic Helicopters from soon after the company was established. On 21 October 1988 Dunne gave Ciarán Haughey a cheque for £100,000. The cheque was drawn on an account in the Bank of Ireland, Marino, used by Dunne for making personal payments and was made out to cash. Ciarán Haughey was later to tell the McCracken Tribunal that the payment was for consultancy services. Dunne, he said, had asked him to look at different types of helicopters to see which one would be best suited to his needs. Ciarán Haughey was in the United States doing a course with Bell Helicopters and travelled to look at a helicopter he thought might suit the supermarket tycoon. Dunne, he said, paid him £100,000 for doing this.

The tribunal did not believe Haughey. Instead it opted to believe Dunne's story. He said Ciarán Haughey personally piloted the helicopter which he used and did a lot of piloting for him, putting in long hours. The payment, according to Dunne, was a bonus payment to Haughey junior.

It was late spring 1989 when Traynor next contacted Fox seeking money for Haughey. This time he was looking for £150,000 sterling, and again Fox passed the request on to Dunne. The instructions about where to send the money were different, but the money again came from Equifex and, in June 1989, was lodged to the Ansbacher deposits.

Haughey, as we have seen, was at this time the head of a minority Government implementing policies of financial rectitude. On 27 April 1989, he returned from a trip to Japan designed to encourage more investment in Ireland. While he was away a private member's motion supported by the opposition parties had called for £400,000 to be allocated towards alleviating the suffering of haemophiliacs who had contracted AIDS through the use of infected blood products. Haughey's Government was offering £250,000, not much more than Dunne had that same month been asked to give Haughey personally. Haughey, upon his return from Japan, suffered the humiliation of his Government being defeated in a Dáil vote. It was an embarrassing but not a fatal political development, but Haughey threw a fit, during which he threatened to call a general election.

On 25 May Haughey, riding high in the opinion polls and frustrated with being beholden to the opposition, called a general election. He launched himself into the election campaign, hoping for his long-sought dream of an overall majority. As we shall see later, huge amounts of money began to swirl around the party, as Paul Kavanagh and his fund-raising team set about the job of raising money for the campaign. Haughey began to grab some of this money for himself.

Politically Haughey's problem was that the public were suspicious of his motives. The State's financial difficulties were being sorted out – although by way of cutting back on public services rather than collecting taxes from the people who had undeclared money in the Ansbacher deposits or the Irish banking system generally. The need for an election was not clear. Haughey's popularity fell as the election campaign progressed; and when the votes were counted his party had lost four seats. Just when everything had been going well for him, Haughey had made one of the worst mistakes of his political career.

He still managed to get back into power. In July he agreed to enter coalition with his arch-rivals, the Progressive Democrats. It was a traumatic moment for Fianna Fáil, but for Haughey it meant he was still the Taoiseach. Without the deal his political career might have ended with his finances still in a less than healthy state. He had been given a reprieve, but time was running out.

In February 1990 Traynor again contacted Fox, this time looking for £200,000 sterling. Dunne arranged for the money to come from Tutbury, in the Isle of Man. Again the money was lodged to the Ansbacher deposits. This payment meant that the total which had been given to Haughey by Dunne since 1987 now exceeded £1 million sterling, an amount significantly greater than the amount agreed when contact had been made in 1987. However, it seems neither Dunne nor Fox were paying particular attention to this. Dunne was later to say that he would have noticed how much money he was giving Haughey if it had been paid over in one or two lump sums, but because it was a continuing matter and because so much money was under his control, he failed to notice.

In November another £200,000 sterling winged its way from Dunne's Far Eastern stash to Haughey's account in the Ansbacher deposits. This time the money went by way of the Bank of

America in London. This payment wasn't discovered until after the Moriarty Tribunal, when Gerry Ryan was appointed by the Tánaiste, Mary Harney, to investigate the companies involved in running the Ansbacher operation. Ryan reported the payment to the Moriarty Tribunal, and Dunne later told the tribunal that while he must have authorised the payment, he had no memory of doing so. He couldn't remember who would have supplied details of where to send the money but assumed they would have come by way of Fox. Fox, for his part, insisted he had nothing to do with the payment. Even though he had been Traynor's contact point for all the other transfers to the Ansbacher deposits, he insisted he'd had no involvement in the November 1990 payment. There the matter rested.

In June 1991 Dunne was contacted by John Barnicle, of Celtic Helicopters, and Ciarán Haughey and asked if he would help them acquire land near Dublin Airport. He later told the Moriarty Tribunal:

> Mr Barnicle asked me to consider lending him the money
> for this proposed acquisition. I contacted my solicitor, Mr
> Noel Smyth, and Mr Smyth arranged through a company
> called Abbervanta Ltd for the loan in question to proceed.
> A facility of £185,000 was granted based on a lien over a
> deposit of £110,000 put up by myself in a legal charge on
> the property. And I undertook to guarantee the payment
> personally and to redeem the loan if requested.

Three years later the property was sold again, the loan was fully repaid, and Dunne got his money back.

In November 1991 Dunne gave Charles Haughey a further

£210,000 sterling. By this stage Haughey's coalition Government was under pressure. In May 1991 a "World in Action" television programme concerning the Goodman group of companies had led to the establishment of a tribunal to inquire into the beef industry. In the autumn of 1991 a controversy erupted over substantial profits made by directors of Greencore, formerly Irish Sugar, at the expense of the State. The chairman of Greencore, Bernie Cahill, was chairman of Feltrim PLC, an exploration company which was headed by Conor Haughey and which, it later emerged, had been floated on the stock exchange to provide Haughey with a job. Cahill had agreed to become its chairman following a request from Charles Haughey. The Cork businessman had no involvement in the Greencore dealings.

The financier Dermot Desmond was at the heart of another huge scandal which erupted around this time concerning dealings in the former Johnston, Mooney and O'Brien site in Ballsbridge. The site was bought by a company linked to Desmond, UPH, for £4 million and later, following a number of transactions, sold for £9.4 million to Telecom Éireann. Michael Smurfit was chairman of Telecom Éireann and had a beneficial interest in UPH. John Glackin, an inspector appointed under the Companies Acts to investigate the matter, reported that when Telecom Éireann was buying the site, Smurfit was not aware that Desmond, who was acting as an intermediary for the vendors, still had a beneficial interest in the deal. At the time, the site had been sold on by UPH but it was still owned by companies which Glackin said were linked to Desmond. Desmond publicly contested the findings of the report.

The political establishment was in crisis, and it was thought by many that Haughey was in some way linked to all these scandals. Four backbenchers issued a statement saying it was time for him to go. Haughey showed no intention of resigning as party leader, and members of his party from this point on were to grow increasingly uncomfortable with him.

With all this scandal circulating and pressure mounting on Haughey to resign, it was no wonder that in November 1991, when Dunne called to Kinsealy, he found the Taoiseach to be somewhat depressed. Dunne had been playing golf in Baltray, north of Dublin, and had called Haughey on the telephone and arranged to drop in for a cup of tea. Dunne had three bank drafts in his pocket for £70,000 sterling each. The drafts were made out to fictitious names and were "profits" from the scheme involving the excess payments being made to the Far East by the Dunnes Group. The money came from Tutbury Ltd, in this instance, and the drafts were intended for Dunne himself and two others.

Because he felt sorry for Haughey, Dunne, acting on impulse as he was about to leave, put his hands in his pockets, took out the drafts and handed them over. "Look, that's something for yourself," he said. Haughey took the drafts. "Thank you, big fella," he said. The drafts were conveyed to Traynor and lodged to the Ansbacher deposits.

The drafts were the last payment from Dunne disclosed to the McCracken Tribunal, but in fact there was one more. This was the so-called grocery cheques payment and it occurred nine months after Haughey had been forced to resign as Taoiseach and leader of Fianna Fáil.

Three cheques totalling £180,00 were written on the Dunnes grocery account in November 1992. The cheques, made out to cash, were drawn up under Dunne's instructions, and he then added the dates and his signature. The cheques were for

£49,620, £50,962, and £79,418. The three figures total £180,000 exactly. The cheques were dated 20, 23 and 27 November. The first two were cashed on 25 November and the third on 1 December. Dunne and his solicitor, Noel Smyth, were in the Far East on business on the dates on which the cheques were apparently written. There is no evidence or any indication that Fox was involved in these transactions.

Traynor organised that the cheques be lodged to the account of John Byrne's company, Carlisle Trust. Traynor was, of course, a director of this company, but Dunne has said he never gave any money or cheques directly to Traynor, nor did he instruct anyone to give the cheques to Traynor. Dunne said he had a vague recollection of giving the cheques to John Barnicle, for the benefit of that company after Barnicle had told him the company was in financial difficulty. However, Dunne said, this was only a very vague recollection. Barnicle, for his part, denied ever asking Dunne for money for his company or ever having received the cheques.

Subsequent to the lodgment to the Carlisle account two cheques were drawn. One, for £100,000, was made out to Celtic Helicopters and another, for £80,000, was made out to cash. This latter cheque was lodged to an account of Kentford Securities, a company Traynor controlled and used in an identical way to Amiens Securities.

A month before the money was paid out Dunne and his wife and his solicitor, Noel Smyth, and his wife had had dinner with Charles and Maureen Haughey in Abbeville. Dunne said there was no mention on this occasion of the three drafts he'd given Haughey a year earlier, or of Ciarán's helicopter company being in need of a cash injection from a benevolent millionaire. Some months later Dunne was to have a panic attack in Florida, and his siblings would decide he was no longer a suitable person to have running the family business.

Altogether, during the period 1987 to 1992 Haughey, as far as we know, got £1.8 million from Dunne and not the £1 million Dunne had originally agreed to pay over. It was a lot of money and made Dunne by far the most generous benefactor to Haughey during this period. Other sums were coming from other sources.

10

Money for the Boss

IN 1997 the question was raised in the Dáil of the possible misuse by Haughey of the Fianna Fáil party leader's allowance account. The then Taoiseach, Bertie Ahern, told the Dáil the account had not been misused. The account, he explained, was one funded by the Exchequer and used to finance personnel, press and other normal supports for a party leader. "I am satisfied, having spoken to the person who administered the account, that it was used for bona fide party purposes, that the cheques were prepared by that person and countersigned by another senior party member."

"There was no surplus and no misappropriation," Ahern said. "The account as far as her excellent recollection goes was normally short, not the other way around. I have spoken to her at some length."

It was a bizarre statement. The person who administered the account was Eileen Foy, a long-time private secretary of Charles Haughey who had previously worked for Jack Lynch. The "senior party member" who Ahern told the Dáil countersigned the cheques was, in fact, himself. Ahern chose not to inform the Dáil of this. Two years later, when he appeared before the Moriarty Tribunal, Ahern said he sometimes "for administrative convenience" signed blank cheques so that Foy would not have to chase him down whenever she needed a cheque. In fact, it emerged that he sometimes signed whole books of blank cheques.

There was another aspect of Ahern's comments in the Dáil which sat uneasily alongside the evidence subsequently heard by the tribunal. Ahern told the Dáil the account, as far as Foy's "excellent recollection goes," was normally short. He presumably knew Foy well, having worked with her for years in Leinster House. During her evidence to the tribunal Foy had great difficulty remembering even the most basic of facts. Although she was in charge of administering it, she couldn't remember the names of any of the donors to a fund raised in 1989 for a life-saving operation for Brian Lenihan. This was despite the trauma and emotion surrounding the operation, and the secrecy which surrounded the fund-raising. She couldn't remember large round-sum withdrawals from the party leader's account, some by way of cheques made out to cash. When Foy was asked about the conversation she'd had with Ahern prior to his 1997 Dáil statement, and whether she'd said anything to him which might have caused him to refer to her excellent recollection, her answer was that she couldn't remember.

If, when he said there was no surplus and no misappropriation, Ahern meant that the amount given by the Exchequer to Fianna Fáil was used by the party in legitimate ways, leaving nothing to be misappropriated, then he was correct. However, over the years there was money lodged to the account over and above what the party received from the Exchequer. Between 1984 and 1992, the period examined by the Moriarty Tribunal, the surplus was more than £500,000. The source of much of this money has not been identified. Where the source has been traced, the donors have said the money was intended for either Fianna Fáil or to pay for the medical treatment of Brian Lenihan.

What in fact happened with most of the surplus is that it was passed through the Fianna Fáil party leader's account before being used by Haughey to support his expensive life-style. The Fianna Fáil party leader's account was an important element in Haughey's personal finances for at least eight years. Ahern was the counter-signatory for the account for this period and never noticed what was happening.

All qualifying political parties in the Dáil receive a leader's allowance, with the amount varying according to the size of the party's representation in the Dáil and whether it is in Government or in opposition. Government parties get less than parties in opposition, all else being equal, the rationale being that Government parties have access to the resources of the civil service.

The Fianna Fáil party leader's account was in AIB, Baggot Street, about ten minutes' walk from Government Buildings. During the period 1984 to 1992 there were three signatories: Haughey, Ahern, and Ray McSharry. The total amount paid by the Exchequer to Fianna Fáil and lodged to the account during the period was £1.05 million. The total amount lodged was £1.5 million.

The size of the annual excesses lodged to the account during Haughey's period in opposition has already been noted. The excess in 1984 was £46,000. The following year the amount lodged was roughly equivalent to the party leader's allowance. In 1986 the excess lodged was £134,000. This included the £100,000 received from the Irish Permanent.

In 1987 the excess lodged was £34,460; in 1988 there was no excess of any significance. In 1989, the year Brian Lenihan was sent to the United States for a liver transplant, an excess of £220,302 was lodged to the account. Much of this was money the donors later said was given to help save Lenihan's life. In 1990 the excess lodged to the account was just £6,000, while in 1991 the excess was £100,417. The account was dormant from June 1992 until it was closed in January 1993.

Foy gave evidence to the tribunal indicating that she administered the account in a competent and methodical way, as one would expect of a personal secretary to the Taoiseach and leader of Fianna Fáil. She said she would receive invoices for payment, prepare associated cheques, have them signed by one of the co-signatories, and then bring them to Haughey for his signature. McSharry seems not to have been involved to any extent, so it was Ahern who would sign the prepared cheques, which would then be brought in to Haughey. She said that sometimes Haughey would tell her to write out cheques and leave the payee blank.

Foy would despatch the completed cheques to their appropriate destinations. When she got statements on the account from AIB, Baggot Street, she would conduct a reconciliation exercise. All withdrawals were by way of cheques, and she used a ledger to record the date of each cheque, the payee, the sum, and the purpose for which the cheque was drawn. Apart from the fact that no external audit of the account was conducted, it was normal competent administration. Apart from Foy, only Haughey ever knew the balance in the account.

Lodgments and withdrawals that were significant in the amount of money passing through the account were being made by Haughey. Cheques for cash for as much as £25,000 were written. When asked about it by the Moriarty Tribunal, Foy could not remember the reasons she had been given for these withdrawals. "I was obviously given a very logical explanation at the time," she said when asked about a 1989 cheque for £25,000 made out to cash, signed by Ahern and Haughey, and lodged to G&M bank.

The 1989 cheque was dated 16 June 1989, the day after the general election of that year. It was the discovery of the cheque in the G&M archives that led the Moriarty Tribunal to the Fianna Fáil party leader's account. Haughey, in his evidence to the tribunal, said he had no memory of the cheque. He had no recollection of giving such a cheque to Traynor and said he hadn't lodged it himself. "I never made a lodgment to a bank for the last thirty years," he said. "I am getting tired of this matter ... I don't know why, after twenty or thirty or whatever number of years it is, that this one cheque has been taken out, looked at, examined, theories evolved about it. I told you that I don't remember the cheque."

Haughey used to cash his monthly pay cheque. Foy would bring it to AIB, Baggot Street, cash it, and bring the money back to her boss. He used the money for what he later described as "out-of-pocket expenses". There were also a lot of cash withdrawals from the account, many of them for very significant sums. At one stage the bank expressed its concern to Foy about her carrying so much cash. For security reasons she would sometimes travel to the bank with Haughey's driver, a plain-clothes garda.

At one stage Haughey used the account to bail out a Fianna Fáil TD whose financial difficulties were a threat to the Government. The cattle business run by the Sligo-Leitrim TD John Ellis had collapsed. Farmers who'd sold him cattle found themselves holding useless cheques. Ellis was facing being declared a bankrupt as a result of proceedings being taken by National Irish Bank (NIB), Swinford mart, and Manorhamilton mart. The amounts involved were £263,450, £13,600, and £12,400, respectively. If the pursuit of these amounts led to Ellis being declared a bankrupt, then, under the terms of the Electoral Act (1923), he would be disqualified from holding his seat. Such a development was a threat to the Government.

In late 1989 Ellis told his friend Albert Reynolds, the Minister for Finance, about the summons he had just received from NIB. Around late November Ellis met representatives of the bank and told them he had no money to pay his debts. "I understand that around the same time Albert Reynolds was informing the bank of my dire circumstances and, in effect, pleaded for leniency for me," Ellis said in a statement in 1999 to the media. Reynolds initially denied this, but later said it could have happened. Whatever was the case, NIB agreed to accept £20,000 as a full and final settlement of the £243,450 debt owed by Ellis. It was a much better settlement than Haughey had managed to negotiate with AIB ten years earlier.

The TD's problems were far from over. Haughey was being kept informed of the proceedings being taken against his TD for Sligo-Leitrim. His coalition Government was being supported by the independent TDs Tom Fox and Neil Blaney, but its voting position was unstable. The loss of Ellis would add to that instability. Ellis was called to the Taoiseach's office.

Haughey said his bankruptcy and the subsequent loss of his Dáil seat could cause the collapse of the Government and must be avoided. The next day Ellis was again called back to Haughey's office. Haughey had something for him: a bundle of banknotes amounting to £12,000. Ellis passed the money on to his solicitor, who in turn used it to settle matters with Swinford mart. The money had come from the party leader's account.

In March 1990, when his dealings with Manorhamilton mart were coming to a head, Ellis received another call from the Taoiseach's office. Again a bundle of cash was waiting for him, this time £13,600, and again the money came from the party leader's account. In both instances, presumably, the money was withdrawn from AIB, Baggot Street, by Foy, using a cheque signed by Ahern and Haughey, before being brought back to Government Buildings.

Foy told the tribunal that after cabinet meetings senior ministers would sometimes adjourn to Le Coq Hardi for lunch, and the bill would later be sent to her for payment out of the party leader's allowance account. The Coq Hardi was a famously expensive restaurant in Pembroke Street in Ballsbridge. It was often used by Haughey, sometimes with Terry Keane. It had private rooms. Foy was not particularly surprised that £15,000 was paid out of the party leader's account for Coq Hardi meals in the period April to December 1991. Cheques from this period made out to the restaurant by her and signed by Ahern and Haughey were produced by the Moriarty Tribunal. Foy said she believed most of the cheques would have been blank when Ahern signed them.

In February 1991 a cheque for £8,332 was written on the account and used to buy a draft in French francs made out to the expensive Parisian shirtmakers Charvet. In September of that same year a cheque for £7,500 was used for a similar purpose. Charvet are a very exclusive shirtmakers who keep busts of regular customers and can charge hundreds of pounds for a single shirt. Haughey was known to the staff in the shop, and it seems he may have frequented it for decades. He once visited the shop with his then press officer, Frank Dunlop, when visiting Paris as Taoiseach.

Bertie and Charlie.

With Dermot
Desmond.

Ben Dunne and Noel Smyth.

At home with the family.

John Byrne.

Des Traynor.

Joan Williams.

Haughey on screen while giving evidence at the Moriarty Tribunal.

Leaving the court hearing on criminal charges arising from his evidence to the McCracken Tribunal.

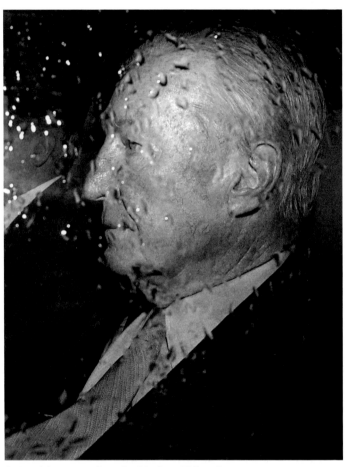

Being driven away from the Moriarty Tribunal.

Other withdrawals examined by the Moriarty Tribunal showed large sums being withdrawn and lodged to Amiens Securities accounts in Guinness & Mahon. Looking at the withdrawals over the years, it is obvious that Haughey and Traynor knew when surplus money had been lodged, and how much was available for Haughey's personal benefit.

When first contacted by the Moriarty Tribunal and told she would be called to give evidence, Foy said, she decided to look for her old records to see if they would help her answer the questions the tribunal wanted to put to her. She said she believed Haughey had brought the records with him to Kinsealy in 1992, when he lost the leadership of Fianna Fáil, so she went out to Abbeville to ask him for help. Her inquiry concerning the records was met with silence.

She also went looking for help from a friend and former colleague, Catherine Butler. Butler was another of Haughey's private secretaries and seems to have operated as a competent and forceful personal assistant. Foy told Butler the tribunal wanted her (Foy) to answer certain questions and that she was having difficulty remembering dates. She wanted Butler's help. The two women met in a pub to discuss the matter. Butler said in evidence that she asked Foy if she still had the files on the account, to which Foy replied that she'd destroyed them. Butler said she'd asked Foy about the files because she could remember helping carry a number of plastic bags to Foy's car in 1992, after Haughey had been ousted. These bags, Butler said, were filled with files concerning the party leader's account. Foy said this aspect of Butler's evidence was "rubbish".

During the meeting Foy asked Butler if she could make use of the diaries she knew Butler had kept since she'd begun working for Haughey in 1981. Butler agreed but subsequently changed her mind, deciding that Foy should depend on her own memory. She had not at this stage herself been contacted by the tribunal and decided she should destroy her "intimate personal" diaries. This she did, not wanting to get dragged into the tribunal and not wanting her diaries to fall into the hands of others. Her diaries, she said, contained "the utmost personal political secrets of Charles Haughey."

Butler was eventually contacted. When she informed her employer, Seán Mulryan, head of the property development group Ballymore Properties, he sacked her. In an account to the High Court in July 1999 Butler said that when she informed Mulryan that she was being called to give evidence, he replied:

> Well, we might as well have this conversation now – I have a business to run and I have to protect my business and my reputation and if you're going to be called before Moriarty, it'll have huge implications for me – never mind reading about you in the newspapers, which was very complimentary by the way – I cannot employ you or have you associated with my company – well, not publicly anyway – so I want you to become a self-employed consultant.

Butler said she pointed out that no suggestion of impropriety was being made against her, and that Mulryan responded: "I know you have done a great job for me and have helped me with certain named projects and a named individual and all that, but the fact of the matter is that you are guilty by association." When she asked what he meant by that, she said he replied: "Guilty by association with Haughey."

A High Court order restraining her dismissal from her £60,000 per annum job was secured and later lifted after certain undertakings were given by Mulryan. Some time later Butler settled with Ballymore in a deal which reportedly involved Butler receiving £1 million.

Ray McSharry's involvement with the party leader's account was always minuscule and came to a complete end when he was appointed a European Commissioner in 1989. Ahern, his schedule becoming more crowded as the 1980s progressed, adopted a policy of sitting down with Foy every so often in her office outside Haughey's and signing a number of blank cheques. He did this, he told the Moriarty Tribunal, for "administrative convenience" – so that Foy could get on with her job without having to be chasing after him. This practice became more prevalent as Fianna Fáil passed from opposition to government in 1987, and as Ahern's position increased in importance in the years after 1987. He became so elusive that the secretaries in Haughey's office dubbed him the Scarlet Pimpernel.

The signing of blank cheques by Ahern created an opening for Haughey. Haughey had always passed some payments through the account, but he now moved his use of the account to a much higher gear. Such was Ahern's lack of involvement in monitoring the account in the later stages that he never knew that money being raised for Lenihan – possibly in excess of £200,000 – had passed through the account.

Foy, who had difficulty remembering details, gave the impression at the Moriarty Tribunal that Ahern would regularly sign large numbers of blank cheques, even before 1989, when the pressures of his position began to make it extremely difficult to reach him. While Foy was troubled and hesitant in her evidence,

Butler was assured to the point of aggression. Her view was that prior to 1987, when Fianna Fáil was in opposition, Ahern was easy for Foy to find, as he occupied the chief whip's office next door to the party leader's office. During this period, she said, it was only on rare occasions that he was asked to sign blank cheques. In the period from 1987 to 1990, when Ahern was a Government minister, it became more difficult to reach him, and the practice of signing blank cheques grew. In January 1990 the Republic took on the presidency of the EU, and it became all but impossible to get an appointment with Ahern. The practice of signing blank cheques grew even more frequent, and this continued to be the practice right up to Haughey's resignation in February 1992.

Butler said she had once witnessed Ahern sign a complete book of blank cheques. This occurred around February 1991, she said. "It was a new chequebook. I sat at a round table next to Bertie Ahern and beside Eileen Foy as he did it. He signed the whole chequebook."

Butler, of course, unlike Foy, had no direct involvement in running the account, but she did work alongside Foy and, according to herself, had an excellent memory. (Foy's counsel put it to her that her memory was too good, bizarrely so.) Haughey, during his evidence, said Butler was "super-competent," though he made the remark while stating that evidence she had given concerning the frequency of his contacts with Des Traynor was mistaken.

Ahern was a signatory of the Fianna Fáil party leader's account throughout the whole of Haughey's tenure as party leader, having been invited by Haughey to assume the role. He became a signatory when he became chief whip, but remained a signatory after he left that position. He told the tribunal he had no involvement in the day-to-day running of the account. One or two days a month Foy would bring cheques to him to sign, he said.

> She would assemble the invoices, do a list of the companies and the creditors to be paid, normally bring that typed list, not all the invoices but bring the typed list, to me. She would go through what companies there were, they were fairly straightforward, usually PAYE, social welfare, salary cheques, the company that would supply the newspapers, advertising companies, maybe hotels if the party had taken out rooms, you know she would go through those and I would sign them.

He said that in the main the same payees came up every month and that Foy tended to give him more information than he needed about each cheque. About 1,600 cheques went through the account between 1984 and 1992, and he would have signed most of them, he said.

For administrative convenience a system developed where he would sign the cheques brought to him by Foy and then sign a few more which were blank. At particular times, for example during the run-up to an election, he might sign more blank cheques than usual. He suggested that this might explain his signature being on a cheque dated 16 June 1989, which was the day of the count of the general election of that year. The cheque was made out to cash and was for £25,000. It was co-signed by Haughey and lodged to an Amiens account with Guinness & Mahon.

Ahern said he had no memory of ever signing cheques made out to cash for figures such as £5,000, £7,500, or £10,000, all these being cheques which the tribunal discovered made out to cash and signed by Ahern and Haughey. Copies of cheques made out to cash and which were lodged to the Amiens account, signed by Ahern and Haughey and retrieved by the tribunal, were: £25,000 on 16 June 1989; £5,000 on 4 April 1991; £10,000 on 11 September 1991; and £7,500 on 18 September 1991. Ahern said he presumed he'd signed all the cheques when they were blank. Withdrawals by cheque which coincided with lodgments to the Haughey Boland account were: £10,000 on 24 April 1986 and £25,000 on 29 October 1986. These were most probably cheques signed by Ahern and Haughey.

Some of the details remain unclear, but what can be stated is that the opportunity existed for Haughey to lodge money to the account and to withdraw money from the account without his actions being queried. Because of the nature of the account he could lodge cheques which were made out to Fianna Fáil. This is precisely what happened.

Butler gave the impression that she had a lot she could say about Haughey. Haughey liked to compartmentalise his life, to keep his political associates in the dark about his financial dealings and vice versa, but for thirteen crucial years Butler was in a position to monitor his affairs, political, financial, and personal. An obviously intelligent woman, she was a close observer of Haughey during the years when he was at his most powerful.

She said she was a regular visitor to the Haughey home at the weekends, where Haughey would be conducting business of a political and personal nature. She kept his diary and arranged appointments. She remembered people visiting Haughey in Kinsealy for meetings in the library. Traynor, she said, would meet Haughey about once a week, most often at the weekends. This had been occurring since the early 1980s, when she'd started to work for Haughey, she said.

She copied out Haughey's personal telephone book in Kinsealy for use in her office, so she could set up calls for her boss whenever asked to do so. She could remember lining up calls with Noel Fox, Ben Dunne, Noel Smyth, Traynor's secretary Joan Williams, Jonathan Guinness, John Byrne, and Larry Goodman. She said there was "regular" contact between Haughey and Goodman.

Another person she said she could remember telephoning was Pádraig Collery, the former Guinness & Mahon banker. Collery told the McCracken Tribunal that his contacts with Haughey began in 1994, following Traynor's death, yet Butler's employment by Haughey ended in 1992. This mystery was never resolved.

Butler said she remembered lining up calls to Edmund Farrell, the managing director of the Irish Permanent Building Society, who'd authorised two payments totalling £100,000 in 1986. Further payments were authorised by Farrell during 1989, as we shall see in the next chapter. In August 1991 another cheque from the society was made out to Fianna Fáil, this time for £40,000. It failed to get to the party. The cheque somehow got to the Department of the Taoiseach instead, where it was endorsed by Haughey and lodged to the party leader's account. This cheque was recorded in the society's books as having been issued for the local election campaign of that year.

Farrell also gave some personal political donations, though of a much lower order. In the period 1987 to 1992 there was a direct debit sending £100 per annum from his personal funds to the party.

The total payments from the society which were authorised by Farrell and ended up with Haughey in the period 1986 to 1991 were £170,000. This puts the society among the larger of Haughey's donors. Farrell said he never intended any of the contributions from the society to go to Haughey personally, rather than supporting his political activities. He did authorise a contribution from the society towards a retirement present for Haughey in 1992, after he had been asked by members of Haughey's staff if he would support such an idea. He contributed £2,000, which went towards the purchase of a painting.

11

Brian Lenihan

BRIAN Lenihan was a popular man, both with the general public and among those who knew him well. A sophisticated and well-read man who combined these merits with a widely respected political nose, he devoted his life to politics and the Fianna Fáil party. His intellect and his passionate political beliefs were better known to those who were close to him than they were to the general public, or even the party faithful, as Lenihan had a seemingly irrepressible inclination to hide his intellect. He had many friends and admirers who thought he did himself a disservice in the image he so often chose to portray to the public.

Like so many of his generation, Lenihan had a formidable capacity for boozing and was once famously contacted by telephone by a civil servant who'd guessed his minister had stopped in a particular pub in Kilcock while on his way from Athlone to Dublin.

One of Lenihan's strongest political traits was his loyalty to party and to party leader. He felt that loyalty was an essential element in the operation of a healthy democracy and perhaps placed an undue emphasis on this quality. He, Haughey and Donogh O'Malley, who died young, were a Fianna Fáil triple act from the 1960s who strode through Dublin on their way from minister's desk to hotel dining-room to late-night bar, acolytes of Seán Lemass intent on modernising their party and the State it so frequently governed. They were interested more in the creation of a modern economy and European-style democracy than in the fight with the old enemy. It must have been exciting to be young and one of a small band intent on transforming a moribund State into an exemplar of western European democracy.

Lenihan remained close to Haughey as Haughey moved from his modest house in Raheny to his Georgian home in Grangemore and from there to his mansion and estate in Kinsealy, all without any obvious source of funding. Newspaper articles appeared detailing Haughey's lavish life-style and repeating the rumours which were abroad about how this life-style was funded. Lenihan, placed as he was so close to Haughey and at the very top of Fianna Fáil, was more privy than most to information and impressions which would have supported the rumours which were abroad. Yet he remained loyal, right up to the time when Haughey, finding himself in a corner during the 1990 presidential campaign, saved his own skin by sacking Lenihan from the Government.

Lenihan was said to have been of the view that his old friend was corrupted by greed as the years passed but perhaps believed that, all matters taken into account, it was better to have a figure such as Haughey as leader than to bring about the damage which would result to the party if he was confronted. Or then again, perhaps he felt that, all in all, the type of behaviour engaged in by Haughey was not such a serious matter and was more than compensated for by Haughey's ability. We do not know. He served his political career alongside Haughey and never spoke publicly on the matter of his friend's unexplained wealth.

Born in Dundalk in November 1930 but brought up in Athlone, Lenihan grew up in comfortable surroundings in a home with an emphasis on education, public service, and political engagement. His father, Paddy Lenihan, joined the IRA when he was a student in University College, Galway, and fought on the pro-Treaty side during the Civil War. Paddy Lenihan worked as a teacher in Belfast and later worked for the Revenue Commissioners in Dundalk, during which time he met Lemass and the two men became friendly. When Fianna Fáil entered government in 1932 Lemass asked Paddy Lenihan to leave the public service and build up a company called General Textiles (Gentex), then flourishing under Lemass's policy of protection for Irish industry. Paddy Lenihan acceded to the request.

Brian Lenihan studied in St Mary's College, Athlone, University College, Dublin, and King's Inns. While training as a barrister he took a great interest in politics and was never truly interested in any other career. His father was on the Fianna Fáil national executive, and Brian Lenihan was a candidate for Longford-Westmeath in the 1954 general election. He was unsuccessful but afterwards threw himself into the reorganisation of Fianna Fáil then being driven by Lemass, with whom Lenihan was particularly friendly. Haughey too was involved in this programme, and the two men became friends and colleagues.

Following his defeat in 1954 Lenihan moved to Co. Roscommon to work on securing a seat for himself there. The woeful state of the economy was a cause of much suffering, through material deprivation and the emotional hardship created by emigration. At local train stations throughout the county teenagers would bid adieu to their parents before setting off on their journeys to England or the United States. Because of the practice of late marriages, the fathers bidding farewell to their children could be as old as seventy, their chances of seeing their children again slim.

Lenihan wanted to put an end to this misery through the resuscitation of the economy, the creation of jobs, and the provision of education to those who might still have to leave. He was made a senator in 1957. Two years later Lemass succeeded de Valera as party president. In 1961 Lenihan was at last elected to the Dáil. Lemass appointed him parliamentary secretary in the Department of Fisheries.

In 1964 Lenihan was appointed Minister for Justice, and during his time in that position be introduced a bill to undo the robust censorship of films and books then in place. O'Malley introduced free second-level education, a move which began the Republic's move back towards having educational standards equal to the western European norm. In March 1968, following O'Malley's early death, Lenihan replaced him as Minister for Education.

Lemass retired in 1966 and was replaced by Jack Lynch. After the 1968 general election Lenihan was appointed Minister for Transport and Power and Haughey Minister for Finance. When the arms crisis erupted Lenihan remained supportive of Lynch, in line with his views on party loyalty, but kept on friendly terms with Haughey. His continued links with someone about whom so many questions existed lowered his standing in the eyes of those who believed Haughey unworthy of high office.

Lenihan lost his Dáil seat in 1973, was appointed to the Seanad, and set about establishing himself in a new constituency, Dublin West. He was also during this period a member of the European Parliament. (Up to 1979 members were selected by the Government rather than directly elected.) When Fianna Fáil won a landslide victory in the 1977 general election Lenihan was returned to the Dáil. He was to remain there until his death in November 1995.

When, following Lynch's retirement in 1979, Colley and Haughey contested the leadership, Lenihan voted for his old comrade, though only after giving lengthy consideration to the matter. When Haughey drew up his cabinet he granted Lenihan his long-held political dream: he made him Minister for Foreign Affairs. The two men worked hard on creating a new relationship with Britain, though the push was to fail, colliding as it did with the hunger strike in the Maze prison, the Falklands war, and the overselling of a summit meeting between Haughey and Margaret Thatcher.

In 1987, when Haughey was returned to power, Lenihan, who had remained loyal to Haughey during Dessie O'Malley's attempt to remove him, was appointed Tánaiste and Minister for Foreign Affairs. This Government, as we have seen, was aided by Fine Gael's adoption of its so-called Tallaght strategy. Haughey is credited with having allowed his cabinet colleagues the freedom to get on with their various tasks. Lenihan was in his element.

But within two years disaster struck. By 1987 he had already developed problems with his liver (unrelated to his drinking), and by 1989 he was seriously ill. Despite attendance at the Mater Private Hospital in Dublin, the illness progressed. He lost weight, and his appearance began to shock those he came into contact with. Lenihan seemed doomed.

According to Catherine Butler, it was she who broke the news to Haughey that his old friend's medical problem was critical. She told the Moriarty Tribunal she was out in Kinsealy at the weekend, as was common practice, and was in the library when she told Haughey what she had learned from medical experts who had examined Lenihan: he would die within weeks from liver failure if he did not undergo an expensive transplant operation in the Mayo Clinic in the United States. Haughey, she said, wept at the news. When he had gathered himself he declared that whatever it cost he would make sure his old friend got the vital operation.

The following week Haughey had a meeting in Government Buildings with his chief party fund-raiser, Paul Kavanagh. Haughey asked Kavanagh to organise a discreet appeal for funds to send Lenihan to the United States. Something between £150,000 and £200,000 was needed, Haughey said, amounts significantly in excess of what was eventually required. The money was needed within weeks, because of Lenihan's condition, Kavanagh was told. He went away and drew up a list of likely contributors. He noted down the names of sixteen people. The names were: Ben Dunne; Dan McInerney; Larry Goodman; S. F. Rafique; Michael Behan; Fred Danze Agua; Leo Cafolla; Séamus Tully; Tadhg Gallagher; Edmund Farrell; Oliver Barry; Gus Kearney; John Horgan; J. P. McManus; Oliver Murphy; and John Magnier. Cafolla was a close friend of Lenihan's; all the others on the list, according to Kavanagh, were party supporters.

When Kavanagh brought the list back to Haughey, Haughey drew a line through Dunne's name. "I never asked for a reason," Kavanagh told the Moriarty Tribunal. "His style was, and I had worked with him for ten years, I knew when he did something like that, that was it. You didn't ask why."

The question arises why Dunne's name was on the list in the first place, and why Haughey crossed it out. At the time Dunne was in the middle of his extraordinary period of largesse towards Haughey, but Haughey's version of events is that he did not know this. Dunne was handing over tens of thousands of pounds to Fine Gael but was not giving money to Fianna Fáil other than a few small payments to a small number of TDs and one constituency organisation. When asked about it later, Haughey could not recall drawing the line through Dunne's name or think of why he might have done so.

Despite Dunne being ruled out of the fund-raising drive, the money for Lenihan's vital liver operation was soon collected. The fund-raising took place during the months of May and June, the same time as a major fund-raising drive was under way for the general election called by Haughey after his minority Government suffered a defeat in the Dáil vote on compensation for haemophiliacs.

If the condition of the State's finances was such that there was no room for generosity towards the haemophiliacs, there was nevertheless plenty of money abroad. More than £1.7 million was brought in for Fianna Fáil during Kavanagh's election fund-raising campaign. Kavanagh had a system whereby he tried to collect the money centrally, but many contributors wanted to make their payment directly to senior members of the party, so that politicians to whom they might want to have access would know of their donations. Some of this money, tens of thousands of pounds and perhaps more, was kept for their own campaigns by the individual politicians rather than passed on to Kavanagh for use by the party headquarters.

Some people so admired Haughey, Kavanagh said, that they gave him money to do with as he pleased. When he was asked at the Moriarty Tribunal to name people who had made such payments, he withdrew the comment.

The money which did get to the party was noted in a receipts book kept at party headquarters in Mount Street and lodged to the appropriate bank account. Money coming in for Lenihan was kept separately. Kavanagh was working with another Fianna Fáil supporter, the meat factory owner Peter Hanley. Kavanagh contacted some of the people on his list, and Hanley contacted others. The money for Lenihan was to be sent to Haughey's office in Government Buildings, where it was looked after by Eileen Foy. She put the money into the party leader's account. This was so the money raised for Lenihan would not become confused with the money raised for the party.

Haughey took an active role in soliciting funds for both the party and the Lenihan fund. He sought assistance for Lenihan from the VHI. In early May the chief executive of the VHI, Tom Ryan, got a call from Haughey's office asking him to go there. He went, and met Haughey. "He referred to Brian Lenihan's illness and proposed treatment in the USA," Ryan told the tribunal. "He outlined the likely total cost and likely hospitalisation bill, and asked would the VHI pay the hospital account." Ryan gave Haughey an outline of the board's attitude to such applications.

Applications for significant ex gratia payments had to be sanctioned by the VHI board, and the matter was listed for consideration on 18 May. Before the meeting Ryan briefed the chairman, Des Cashell, about the matter. The board approved the application, as was the case with most applications which reached it, as they were considered to have the approval of the management. The amount eventually paid by the VHI was £57,000. Noel Fox was a member of the board.

Haughey was also looking for assistance from other sources. In the run-up to the general election Edmund Farrell attended a speech by Haughey in the Berkeley Court Hotel in Ballsbridge. Haughey gave an address on the International Financial Services Centre, then being built in the Dublin docks area. Haughey, in his evidence to the Moriarty Tribunal, said the address represented a turning-point in the financial history of our country … It was a major announcement, of considerable significance and we went ahead when we returned to government and established a financial services centre much against the comments and cynical remarks of the body politic in general at the time. Anyway, that's the financial services centre today which has, as I say, changed the whole political history, financial history mainly, of this country.

Afterwards, as the two men were preparing to leave the hotel, Haughey made an approach that Farrell later told the Moriarty Tribunal he found "inappropriate and surprising". Haughey, in his evidence, said he found the idea of such an approach "totally out of kilter," could not recall the approach, but accepted Farrell's evidence.

Farrell said Haughey approached him and said campaign funds were low. Farrell responded by referring to a letter seeking donations to Fianna Fáil which had already been received by the society. Haughey then said he was referring to his own rather than the party's funds. Farrell said later he was surprised that Haughey's personal election machine was not capable of generating the required funds, and that he had "no idea" why Haughey had chosen to approach him on that occasion and in such a public way.

After the encounter Farrell responded both to the approach from Haughey and to the letter from Fianna Fáil. He wrote out two society cheques, one to Haughey for £10,000 and one to Fianna Fáil for £65,000. Both cheques were countersigned by another director of the Irish Permanent, J. Enda Hogan.

He later said he chose to give Haughey £10,000 because he believed anything less would not be appropriate.

He was a man of integrity, he was the prime minister of the country, we were a large establishment and if any contribution was to be made, it would be difficult or embarrassing, for example, to send down £500 . . . I thought £10,000 would be an appropriate amount.

Meanwhile, on the morning of 7 June 1989, Haughey telephoned Farrell and asked him to come to his office in the Department of the Taoiseach. The chief executive of the building society, without knowing the purpose of the requested meeting, left his St Stephen's Green offices and travelled the short distance to Haughey's office in Merrion Street. When the two men sat down to talk Haughey explained that expensive medical treatment was needed for Brian Lenihan, that the Lenihan family was unable to raise the necessary funds, and that a discreet fund-raising effort was under way. Farrell immediately said the society would be prepared to make a contribution and asked whom a cheque should be made out to. "To myself," said Haughey.

Back in his office, Farrell wrote out a cheque for £20,000 to "C. J. Haughey (B. Lenihan)". He had it delivered to the Department of the Taoiseach along with a note which read: "On behalf of the members of the society, we are pleased to enclose a cheque for £20,000 to help meet the expenses of Mr Lenihan's operation." He enclosed the cheque for £10,000 for Haughey's personal political fund at the same time.

On the same day on which Farrell sent the two cheques to Haughey's office in the Department of the Taoiseach he also wrote cheques for £65,000 for Fianna Fáil and £25,000 for Fine Gael. Five days later he wrote out a society cheque for £10,000 for the Labour Party.

When the two cheques totalling £30,000 arrived at Haughey's

office he endorsed them on the back. The two cheques then found their way to the Bank of Ireland branch in Dublin Airport, where they were lodged to the account of Celtic Helicopters. A withdrawal of £30,000 was then made from the account by way of a cheque made out to cash and dated 13 June, and that cheque returned to the Department of the Taoiseach. From there it was brought to the AIB branch in Baggot Street, presumably by Foy. That happened on 20 June. The cheque was exchanged for cash.

When details of the treatment of the £20,000 Irish Permanent cheque intended for the Lenihan fund were first aired by the Moriarty Tribunal, Haughey broke the silence he had maintained up to that point in relation to the tribunal's revelations. He issued a statement to a number of media outlets, sending it himself from a fax machine in Kinsealy. It read:

> It was Charles Haughey as leader of Fianna Fáil who initiated and spearheaded the humanitarian project of raising a fund which would enable Brian Lenihan's wife and family to take him to the Mayo Clinic in the United States for a life-saving liver transplant operation.
>
> With the help of a group of loyal friends and supporters this was achieved and the operation was successful in saving Brian's life. The funds raised were properly applied. A full statement on the utilisation of the fund subscribed will be made later when we have access to the records.

Haughey subsequently issued a second statement in which he said the Irish Permanent contribution was "inadvertently" lodged to the Celtic Helicopters account but that when the mistake was noticed the matter was rectified and the money moved to the party leader's account. He said an examination of that account's records would support this.

However, the Celtic Helicopters cheque for £30,000 made out to cash and co-signed by Ciarán Haughey was not lodged to the party leader's account. There were two separate lodgments to the account on 20 June, one being for £7,288.63 and the other for £36,000. As a cheque for £25,000 from Larry Goodman was lodged to the account on that day, the Celtic Helicopters cheque could not have formed part of the £36,000 lodgment. A bank official questioned about the matter said no other lodgment of £30,000 was made at or around this time, and that it was "more probable than not" that the Celtic Helicopters cheque was exchanged for cash over the counter.

Despite this evidence, Haughey insisted when he came to give evidence about the matter that the £30,000 cheque had been lodged to the party leader's account. He repeated his view that the cheque was lodged despite counsel for the tribunal saying that he was not correct. "Why are you saying these things?" Haughey said. "Are you just trying to humiliate me?"

The approach to Goodman for a donation had been made by his fellow meat plant operator, Peter Hanley. Goodman's business empire at the time had a turnover equivalent to a few per cent of the Republic's gross domestic product. He told the Moriarty Tribunal he personally wrote out a cheque for £25,000 following the request from Hanley for a contribution towards the Lenihan fund of between £10,000 and £20,000. The cheque was made out to "Fianna Fáil (party leadership fund)". Goodman said he had never heard of the party leader's fund before.

The cheque was written on 13 June 1989 and put in the post. It was not banked until a week later.

Not all the donors to the Lenihan fund have been identified but they are known to include the following:

Éamon de Valera, chairman of the Irish Press Group, founded by his father and namesake, issued an Irish Press cheque for £10,000 following a request for a donation from Dan McGing, a partner in Coopers & Lybrand and member of the boards of ACC Bank and the Irish Press Group. The cheque was sent to Coopers & Lybrand, auditors to the Irish Press. Where it went thereafter is not clear. De Valera was later invited to a luncheon held in a Ballsbridge hotel to thank donors to the Lenihan fund. De Valera was one of the few donors to come forward to the Moriarty Tribunal and informed it he had authorised a donation. He couldn't remember who else was at the thank-you luncheon held after the transplant operation.

Séamus Tully, a successful businessman involved in the Donegal fishing industry, gave £20,000. He told the tribunal he made the donation after he was contacted by Kavanagh and told "the boss" was setting up a fund for Lenihan. Kavanagh, he said, told him he was contacting seven to ten people to ask them for £20,000 each. Tully later met Lenihan in the Dáil bar when he was in Leinster House as part of a delegation of fishermen, and Lenihan thanked him for his support.

The bloodstock breeder John Magnier gave £20,000. He made the donation after Kavanagh called to see him in his stud farm in Coolmore, Co. Tipperary, and the two men had lunch together. Magnier gave the money in two drafts for £10,000 each, one made out to Jim Murphy and the other made out to Jim Casey, both being fictitious names. He wanted the donation to remain anonymous, he told the Moriarty Tribunal. He sought the opportunity to state during his evidence that "Mr Charles Haughey never approached me directly or made any personal request for funds for himself, the Fianna Fáil party or the Brian Lenihan fund." Nor, he added, had any indirect approaches ever been made by Haughey. He had been approached by Fianna Fáil for donations.

Nicholas Fitzpatrick, a director of the aircraft parts company Atron, gave £10,000. His name was not on Kavanagh's list. Fitzpatrick is a brother of Ivor Fitzpatrick, whose firm of solicitors was used by Haughey during his dealings with the McCracken and Moriarty Tribunals and with the criminal charges which arose from the McCracken Tribunal. A further £5,000 was donated by Oliver Murphy.

Where the rest of the money lodged to the party leader's account that year came from is not clear. Not all the people on Kavanagh's list actually gave money, and not all the money lodged that year was for the Lenihan fund. The total paid from the party leader's account towards the cost of Lenihan's treatment around the time of that treatment was less than £80,000. Total lodgments other than the exchequer payment were £220,000.

The tribunal identified roughly £160,000 which it could link to identified donors. Although all this donated money did not go into the party leader's account, the amount which did was larger than the amount identified as coming out of the account for Lenihan. When this point was put to Haughey by counsel for the Moriarty Tribunal, Haughey responded: "You are wrong, you are wrong, and I think you are trying to make a false accusation, and I reject it."

He also, at another point, said:

My efforts on behalf of Brian Lenihan at that time were the most compassionate thing I have ever done in my life. And I think it's absolutely preposterous that this whole genuine charitable effort on my part at that time should now, twenty years or so later, be sought to be turned against me in the most cruel fashion, that I would deliberately divert to my own purposes money which was subscribed by well-meaning people for the good and salvation of my friend Brian Lenihan.

Eighteen months after the successful transplant Haughey instigated a further bit of fund-raising. In January 1991 there was still a bill for £12,914 outstanding from Lenihan's trip to the United States. The bill was for travelling expenses incurred by Lenihan which had been picked up by the Department of Defence. It was paid in February 1991, with a transfer from the party leader's account. On the same day which the withdrawal occurred a lodgment of £25,000 was made. The lodgment was the proceeds of a personal cheque from Philip Monahan and his wife.

The Moriarty Tribunal had all but completed its investigation into the Lenihan fund when it was contacted by AIB and told it had discovered another document linked to the party leader's account, this being the cheque from the Monahans. Up to this point no-one had come forward to tell the tribunal about the payment.

A number of people were involved. Paul Kavanagh said in evidence he had forgotten that in 1991 Haughey had called him in and told him £50,000 more was needed urgently for the Lenihan fund. He said it was only when the 1991 cheque was brought to his attention, along with some of the surrounding circumstances, that he remembered.

Kavanagh said that at the time of the request from Haughey he was preparing to leave the State for a number of years. He had used up most of his sources when collecting funds for the 1990 presidential election and the 1989 general election. He couldn't think where he might get the money. He decided to contact Roy Donovan.

Donovan was a member of the Fianna Fáil fund-raising committee, a director and senior executive with Lisney estate agents, and a director of the Central Bank. He and Kavanagh met in the Shelbourne Hotel for coffee and Kavanagh briefly outlined his difficulty. "The boss," Kavanagh explained, was behind securing the funding for Lenihan's treatment. The public had no idea what a generous heart Haughey had. The bills kept coming in and he, Kavanagh, had used up all his contacts. Could Donovan open any doors for him?

Donovan immediately thought of Monahan, with whom he had a long relationship through their dealings in the property world. Monahan was a very wealthy property developer whose company, Monarch Properties, was involved in developing the Square in Tallaght and the Cherrywood site in south Co. Dublin. He lived in Castleknock, in Lenihan's constituency, another factor which made Donovan think he might make a likely target. Monahan later told the Moriarty Tribunal that Brian Lenihan Jnr lived at the bottom of the drive up to his home and was well known to the Monahan family.

Donovan told the tribunal Monahan was the type of man who would give £50,000 "just like that." He was a tough businessman but personally very generous, Donovan said. He telephoned Monahan, and it was agreed that Monahan and Kavanagh would meet. An entry was made in Monahan's diary in his offices in Harcourt Street. "Paul Kavanagh (snack) (C.J.H.) £25,000." The mention of snack was to remind his secretary that a snack was to be served during the meeting. The two men met and discussed the matter.

Some time in February Kavanagh called out to Monahan's home in Castleknock. He said later he was left waiting in the hall for quite some time before Monahan came downstairs with the cheque. According to Kavanagh it was filled out and signed, but with the payee still blank. Because it was for the Lenihan fund Monahan, Kavanagh said, had not been sure who to make it out to. When Kavanagh said Charles Haughey, party leader's fund, Monahan "foostered around looking for either his glasses or his pen at the time. We were standing in the hallway and he hadn't got whatever he said he wanted and said to me, 'Here, will you fill this in?' and I actually filled it in in his own house in front of him."

Monahan's evidence was that he thought the money was for Fianna Fáil and that he had never been told the money was for Lenihan. "I'm absolutely sure I didn't pay it for the Lenihan fund," he said. It was for this reason that he hadn't brought the matter to the attention of the tribunal, he said. He hadn't believed he'd made any Lenihan payment.

Donovan, for his part, said he had presumed Monahan or Kavanagh would bring the matter to the tribunal's attention, as they had been more directly involved than he had been. For that reason he had not come forward to mention the payment to the tribunal. Kavanagh could not remember if he had managed to collect the complete £50,000 requested by Haughey.

Monahan said people like him would be targetted by party fund-raisers, or "collecting agents," as he called them. "There'd be some of us in the country that would appear to have some wealth," he said.

They seemed to have very strong collectors in the Fianna Fáil party and they'd put the thumb on you, and say you have to contribute. 'The boss says you have to contribute' – a very strong turn of phrase – 'the boss has been with me last night, we've had tea with him last night, I was out in

Abbeville or wherever it was, and he listed you down, he'll write you a personal letter,' that sort of simple pressure.

Collecting agents had the knack of putting on pressure, he said. They'd say such things as "Wouldn't you have a worse time if Fine Gael was in government?"'

12

Financial Services

FROM the early 1980s the Confederation of Irish Industry was pushing the idea of establishing a site for internationally traded services in Dublin. Technological development, and specifically developments in computer and communications technology, meant that such services could be established outside traditional centres, such as London and New York. The confederation thought a site near Dublin Airport would be the most suitable, as it would facilitate people flying in and out of Ireland. A tax regime as set out in earlier industrial development legislation governing internationally traded services could apply.

At some stage the idea was taken up by the stockbroker Dermot Desmond. Desmond, however, wanted to concentrate on financial services and believed the centre should be set up in the Dublin docklands. In the mid-1980s Ruairí Quinn of the Labour Party dined with a number of business figures in the Shelbourne Hotel. He asked the men for ideas which he could take to his coalition Government and which might be helpful to the economy. Desmond spoke about the idea for a financial services centre. Quinn was impressed but didn't manage to sell the idea to his Government colleagues. Desmond, however, who had used a large sum of his own and his firm's money commissioning a consultant's report on the idea, was determined not to let the matter rest. He thought he might take it to Haughey. He needed an introduction.

In the mid-1980s Scruffy Murphy's pub off Lower Mount Street in Dublin was a popular Friday evening venue for some people involved in politics, journalism, and business. Among those who frequented the pub were employees of Desmond's stockbroking firm, National City Brokers (NCB), and Paul Kavanagh, the Fianna Fáil fund-raiser. One Friday evening Desmond approached Kavanagh in the pub and told him he had an idea which he would like to bring to Haughey's attention. Kavanagh recognised Desmond because of his distinctive handlebar moustache, a feature which had led to his being dubbed the Kaiser, but had not met the stockbroker before. Kavanagh asked what the idea was. The two men began talking.

Desmond met Kavanagh the following week to hand him the report he had commissioned and paid for. When Kavanagh learned Desmond had spent his own money looking into the idea, he decided the young stockbroker deserved a hearing. On Friday afternoons he had end-of-week meetings with Haughey, and during the next such meeting he mentioned the approach by the stockbroker. Haughey, after chiding Kavanagh for drinking in a pub which journalists frequented, took the report which Kavanagh handed him.

He read it over the weekend and liked what he read. On Sunday afternoon he telephoned Kavanagh and said he wanted to speak to Desmond. Kavanagh, who didn't have a number for Desmond, went to Scruffy Murphy's, where he was told what street Desmond lived in in Stillorgan but not the number of the house. Kavanagh went to the street and knocked on a few doors. Eventually he found the young stockbroker. Haughey wants to see you, he said. Now. Desmond rushed to shave and change his clothes.

After discussing the financial services centre idea with Desmond, Haughey was interested but still feeling cautious. He was scheduled to address a luncheon in New York three weeks later, and he discussed with Kavanagh the idea of using the occasion to float the proposal for a financial services area with special tax designation in the Dublin docks. His audience was to be made up of senior bankers, stockbrokers, and industrialists. Haughey got Kavanagh to ask Desmond if he'd accompany them on the trip, and Desmond readily agreed. The three men travelled together to New York.

The luncheon was being held in a very up-market venue, and the idea was that Haughey would address his audience at the end of lunch, after which everyone would be driven back to their various work-places. Haughey's speech caused such excitement among the assembled luminaries, however, that many of them delayed their return to work in order to discuss the matter further with Haughey. Ideas and suggestions shot around the room. On his way back over the Atlantic with Kavanagh and Desmond, Haughey felt sure he was on to a winner.

Haughey told the Moriarty Tribunal he may have first met Desmond in 1986 or early 1987, through P. J. Mara, Haughey's press secretary during his later Governments.

> Dermot Desmond arranged a meeting with myself and two
> or three or four of my colleagues on the Fianna Fáil front

bench and he arranged to bring along four of the leading economists in Ireland at the time, well certainly in Dublin, and at his own expense. Mr Dermot Desmond did this at his own expense.

The economists explained to the politicians

the disastrous situation of the finances of the country and outlined what would be necessary for us as an incoming Government to do, an absolutely essential analysis of the situation and pointing out ... what was absolutely vitally necessary in regard to the public finances to sort them out and as a basis of economic recovery ... I just mention that he did that as a public-spirited person who was, because of his own financial knowledge, was very, very keenly aware of the seriousness of our national finances position.

Haughey also said Desmond was very much the "initiator" of the IFSC idea.

I mean, as we all know, success has many fathers, but the real father of the IFSC was Dermot Desmond, whose concept and idea it was and he, as I think I explained before here, he put the proposal to us as an opposition party and we accepted it and ran with it and subsequently implemented it.

Haughey and Desmond became good friends. The two north-siders, ambitious and able men from relatively humble back-grounds, seemed to genuinely like each other. The closeness of the relationship between them was to become a huge political issue in the period of Haughey's last two Governments, and was eventually to be one of the seeds of Haughey's political demise.

Desmond grew up in Marino, not too far from Haughey's childhood home. He left school in 1968, got a job with Citibank, and worked there for seven years before leaving to take up employment with the Investment Bank of Ireland. Some time later again he got a job with the World Bank and was posted to Afghanistan. In December 1979, when the Soviet Union invaded, he came home.

In 1981, aged thirty-one, he established NCB, a money brokering business. Three years later NCB acquired Dillon and Waldrom, thereby breaking into the exclusive Dublin stockbroking sector. NCB prospered, taking on and passing out most of its rivals. Desmond's formula for success was not abstruse. He explained it in an interview once: "Greed is a great motivator of people."

However, he also said he was motivated by a desire to help. In the late 1980s he invested more than £2 million in *NCB Ireland*, a yacht which was entered in the Whitbread round-the-world race in an attempt to raise morale in the recession-mired Republic. "I do have the national interest at heart and I believe in investing in the country," he said. He said a similar motivation lay behind his involvement in the Irish Financial Services Centre.

Despite his dislike of the media, Desmond performed well in its spotlight. When called to give evidence before both the Flood and Moriarty Tribunals he showed his steeliness and capability. When he gave evidence to the Moriarty Tribunal he at times burst forth with Byzantine and rapidly delivered explanations of how money spent on the Haughey family yacht was subsequently treated in the books of his personal companies. At one stage he mentioned that he hadn't written more than four or five personal cheques for all of the 1980s, with even charitable donations coming from the accounts of his personal company Dedeir.

He was driven to Dublin Castle in a Daimler, which was parked in the Upper Yard while he gave evidence. In the back seat there was one of those small balls people squeeze to relieve stress, and tapes of best-selling books concerning "Celtic spirituality" and how to cope with affluence and success. He looked fit and well. A golf player who reportedly has a personal gym in his penthouse offices in Dublin, Desmond was said to be loyal to old friends but quick to take offence. He had reportedly fallen out with a number of former colleagues and was known to respond robustly to adverse or incorrect media comment. A statement issued on his behalf in January 1998, following the publication of a story concerning Desmond and Haughey, included the statement:

> There has been comment with regard to the litigation which Mr Desmond has pursued against sections of the media in recent years. Mr Desmond confirms that he has pursued actions where there have been inaccurate or defamatory statements made against him or his businesses. In 12 such cases Mr Desmond has agreed financial settlements totalling more than a six-figures sum, all proceeds of which have been donated to charities in Ireland. The time and cost involved in pursuing these cases has been borne by Mr Desmond.

Desmond's view by then was that Haughey was an old man, had done the State significant service, and that his private financial affairs were just that, private affairs. Whether he (Desmond) was giving money to Haughey was, in Desmond's view, not a matter of legitimate public interest.

The idea for an Irish financial services centre was included in Fianna Fáil's 1987 election manifesto, and within days of being returned to power Haughey set about making the proposal happen.

As part of the project the Dublin docklands, which had suffered decades of neglect, were to be redeveloped. The coalition Government had established a Custom House Dock Development Authority (CHDDA) just one year earlier. The members of the board were Frank Benson (executive chairman); Ciarán Corrigan; P. V. Doyle; Patrick Herlihy; and Dermot O'Rourke. In August 1987 Haughey, once again Taoiseach, appointed three new board members: Noel Fox, Michael Buckley, and the secretary of the Department of the Taoiseach, Pádraig Ó hUiginn.

Buckley was then a senior executive with Desmond's NCB and was later to become a senior executive with AIB. Fox had already begun, or within months of his appointment would begin, acting as a contact point for Des Traynor when Traynor wanted money from Ben Dunne. Some payments had already been made by Dunne. P. V. Doyle at this time was still responsible for a loan account in Guinness & Mahon which was used for Haughey's benefit.

Haughey, who was known and admired for his ability to cut through red tape when he put his mind to it, ensured that the various Government departments which were involved in the project were not allowed slow it down with unnecessary bureaucratic complexity. The authority established a competition for the contract to develop a 27-acre site between Connolly Station in Amiens Street and the Liffey. The essence of the deal was that the authority would supply the lands and the successful tenderer would develop the site, raising its own finance and taking the commercial risk. The profits would be divided between the two parties, the authority using the funds to develop the docks further.

Eight applications were made, with the applicants spending hundreds of thousands of pounds each in their efforts to win the potentially lucrative contract. The various consortia included major property and development companies from Britain and the United States. Some people made desperate attempts to become members of one or other of the consortia, believing that winning the contract would bring great returns. Tensions were high, and the lobbying from some of the applicants was often intense.

Edmund Farrell told the Moriarty Tribunal that one of his visits to Abbeville was around this time and followed a seemingly dramatic visit to Haughey's home by a builder associated with the Irish Permanent. The builder, who remained unnamed and who it is believed never became involved with any of the consortia, was of the view that Haughey had some influence in relation to who won the contract for the development of the IFSC. He wished to co-develop the site of the proposed centre with the Irish Permanent. The man, Farrell said, "had taken it upon himself … to call upon Mr Haughey without notice and caused disruption and distress" to the then Taoiseach. At the time the CHDDA was "coming to the stage where the consortium would be chosen." Farrell said he did not know the nature of the embarrassment caused but that he and another member of the society's board called to Abbeville on a Sunday following the incident as they were "very anxious that an apology should be tendered." Farrell or the society were never part of any of the consortia which bid for the job.

One of the consortia seeking the contract was led by Mark Kavanagh. Kavanagh had been born into a rich property development family but had spent some years working at odd jobs in London and Dublin before settling back into the family business. He had married a woman from the United States whom he'd met when she was studying in Trinity College, and the young couple lived for a time in a flat in Merrion Square while running Dublin's first hamburger restaurant, Captain America's, in Grafton Street. The singer Chris de Burgh did some of his earliest performances in the restaurant, singing in return for a few pounds and free wine.

Kavanagh's wife, Lynda, was to die tragically in 1988 along with the family nanny, Priscilla Clarke, when the two women were out riding on the family estate in Co. Wicklow. They drowned trying to cross the Dargle River, which was in flood. It was feared at one stage that the two women might have been kidnapped, and Kavanagh was later to say Haughey was hugely helpful to him during his trauma.

Kavanagh worked day and night on his consortium's application for the IFSC contract. His family company, Hardwickes, was the leading member of the consortium, and the partners were McInerney's, the Irish building company, and British Land, a huge UK property concern. The application included a long list of measures which were going to bring life to the docklands area after dark, such as restaurants, marinas and theatres, none of which were ever built.

The Kavanagh application was recommended to the Government by the authority in October 1987, and accepted. The development was scheduled to be completed in five years, but a slump in the property market and in business generally after the outbreak of the Gulf War brought progress to a halt. At times the entire project seemed endangered. The retail and cultural end of the mix which was to have been built on the site was sacrificed to increased office space. Deadlines were missed and a tense relationship developed between the authority and Kavanagh's consortium.

In May 1989, when Paul Kavanagh was drawing up his list for Haughey of persons who might contribute towards a fund for Brian Lenihan, he included Mark Kavanagh's name as well as that of Dan McInerney. Paul Kavanagh said the list was of persons who were supporters of the party, but Mark Kavanagh had only previously made the reasonably modest contribution of £5,000. Questioned about this, Paul Kavanagh said that Mark Kavanagh was on the list because he knew he was doing well.

When the fund-raiser telephoned the property developer and told him he was looking for a contribution for Fianna Fáil, the two men agreed to meet in Kavanagh's offices in Wellington Road. Kavanagh said he was looking for a substantial "dig-out" as the party had huge debts and was facing another general election. He was also looking for money for Brian Lenihan, he explained. He suggested that Kavanagh give £25,000 towards the Lenihan fund and £100,000 towards the party. The figures requested were enormous, even in relation to the amounts of money rich businessmen gave Fianna Fáil. The largest contribution the party was to receive during the 1989 fund-raising effort was £100,000. That contributor was not named during the proceedings of the Moriarty Tribunal.

Kavanagh's consortium had set up a company, Custom House Dock Development Company Ltd, and Kavanagh consulted his fellow-directors about the request which he had received. It was decided that the company would give £100,000 in total. When questioned about it years later Kavanagh could not remember exactly what happened next. It is clear that someone told Kavanagh what form to deliver the money in. However, Kavanagh could not remember who this person was.

The point is important because the contribution was handed over by way of four instruments for £25,000 each. One was a company cheque, made out to Fianna Fáil, the other three were bank drafts made out to cash. Kavanagh had to get permission from his fellow-directors to draw down the needed cheques, and they were aware of the form in which the money was being paid over. Despite the highly unusual nature of the request, no-one was perturbed. The only concern expressed, according to Kavanagh, was that the drafts made out to cash might be lost or stolen, and he gave a personal commitment to his fellow-directors to ensure their safe delivery. Kavanagh, for his part, said later he had no reason to worry about what happened to the funds after the instruments had been delivered, as they were intended for Fianna Fáil and were being delivered to the leader of that party.

According to Kavanagh, the £100,000 was delivered by him to Haughey in Haughey's home at 9.30 on the morning of the 1989 general election. Kavanagh told the Moriarty Tribunal that he had to get up early in his estate and mansion outside Enniskerry, Co. Wicklow, to travel across Dublin to Haughey's estate and mansion in Kinsealy. The meeting was short, Kavanagh said. The cheque and drafts were in an envelope, and when he handed the envelope to Haughey he was asked if he wanted to know how the money would be used. He took it from Haughey's question that Haughey knew the form in which the money had been delivered.

Haughey, he said, told him the money was to be used in the following way: a quarter for Lenihan; half for Fianna Fáil; a quarter for particular Fianna Fáil candidates in need of help with their personal campaign funds, the candidates to be selected by Haughey. Kavanagh said he agreed to such use of the funds, and that was that.

Haughey denied that any such meeting ever took place. He said it most definitely didn't happen on the morning of the general election.

> I had a very strict routine for thirty years of election-eering. I went down always endeavouring to be the first person to vote in our little school in Kinsealy. I went down at one minute past nine to vote with my wife, talked to the election workers there, probably got photos taken. I left my wife back to the house and went off on my rounds.

Haughey said he had no recollection of anyone else handing him three drafts and a cheque for a total of £100,000.

When asked later why he made such a huge contribution, Kavanagh said his company had by May 1989 raised and spent more than £100 million on the initial phase of the financial services centre. He'd had lunch some months earlier with Michael Noonan and Alan Dukes of Fine Gael and had come away feeling they were very lukewarm in their support for the whole project. He was, therefore, concerned that there would be a change of Government after the election and the commercial risk his company had taken would be hugely increased. Hence his support for Haughey and Fianna Fáil.

Haughey brought the cheque made out to Fianna Fáil to party headquarters and handed it to the party accountant, Seán Fleming, a chartered accountant who worked for the party until elected a TD in the 1997 election. Contributions for the party were entered into a cash receipts book, with a carbon copy being kept of each numbered receipt issued. This carbon copy record then constituted the backbone of the party books, providing the basis for checking who gave what and the total received. Every so often a lodgment to the bank would be made and the copy receipt of the last contribution prior to the lodgment marked "lodged". In this way someone reviewing the books could count the contributions recorded between two receipts marked "lodged" and tally this with the entries on bank statements of the party account.

During the 1989 fund-raising campaign Haughey made an unprecedented request to Fleming. He told him to send the receipts for certain donations he delivered to his (Haughey's) office rather than to the contributor, as was the normal practice. Fleming thought this might be so that the contributors could be flattered by receiving their receipt from Haughey rather than party headquarters. Some of the amounts for which this request was made were quite small. One was an amount given by a parish priest whom Fleming thought probably wanted to make sure his housekeeper didn't come across the receipt in the post. However, others were for very large sums. One was for the £100,000 donation which was to be the largest received during that fund-raising drive.

Fleming did as requested but, being a meticulous accountant, he also took a note of those contributions the receipts for which had been sent to Haughey. By the time the books were closed there were nineteen entries on this list. Some of the receipts issued to Haughey were made out to "anonymous", again at Haughey's request and even though Haughey told Fleming who the contributor was. Fleming kept supporting documents in relation to these payments which included notes recording who Haughey had told him had made the "anonymous" donation.

When Haughey handed Fleming the cheque for £25,000 made out to Fianna Fáil, he told him to make out a receipt to "anonymous" and to forward the receipt to his office. The money, he said, came from Mark Kavanagh. This was obvious to Fleming anyway, as it was a cheque on an account of the Custom House Dock Development Company Ltd. Fleming did as he was told, but he also noted the donation as one of those for which the receipt had been sent to Haughey and photocopied the cheque for his backing documents files. Haughey had no recall of giving £25,000 to Fleming and telling him it was from Kavanagh.

Thre three bank drafts given to Haughey by Kavanagh were lodged to Guinness & Mahon bank, presumably by Traynor. Haughey denied he'd given Traynor the drafts.

> I didn't go round toting bank drafts around the place. You know I had other things on my mind to do. I wasn't hanging on to bank drafts and putting them here or giving them to this person or that person. They rarely came my way at all.

One draft was lodged to an Amiens Securities account and subsequently withdrawn, in two tranches, in cash. The other two drafts were lodged to the Guinness & Mahon drafts account, that is, to one of the bank's own accounts as against an account of one of its customers. The money was then used to pay for a £50,000 Guinness & Mahon draft, made out to cash. Again this was most probably Traynor's work, and the point would be so that the draft could not in any way be linked to Kavanagh's company. The two £25,000 drafts had come from the AIB branch where that company had its accounts, and tracing the payment backwards would be reasonably straightforward. By washing the money through Guinness & Mahon, the link with Kavanagh was that much harder to reconstruct. Kavanagh knew nothing of these secretive financial transactions.

Haughey brought the £50,000 draft into Fianna Fáil head-quarters and handed it to Fleming. It was, he said, a contribution from Michael Smurfit, and he asked that the receipt be made out to "anonymous" and sent to his office. Fleming did as told but also made his usual backing notes.

Michael Smurfit was in fact making a payment. Smurfit was a hugely wealthy Irish businessman who developed the Smurfit print and packaging group he took over from his father into a global enterprise. He had been in business at a high level all his adult life and was one of the State's most experienced and knowledgable executives. As well as being at the helm of one of the State's largest industrial companies, he was also in 1989 chairman of Telecom Éireann and actively involved in overseeing the transformation of that company.

Smurfit was involved in the establishment of the exclusive K Club, a golf club used by senior members of corporate Ireland and the State's upper classes generally. In the period 1989 to 1991 when he was canvassing for memberships Smurfit contacted Traynor and asked if he would join. ("God save us all," said Haughey when this bit of evidence was being recounted to him.) Traynor declined the invitation but took the opportunity to say, misleadingly, that Haughey was short of cash and could use a contribution. Smurfit declined. Haughey said later he'd known nothing about the approach.

Smurfit was a tax exile, a resident of Monaco, where he was the Irish republic's honorary consul. He told the Moriarty Tribunal that at some stage around the time of the 1989 general election Haughey contacted him and asked him for money. Smurfit agreed to make a payment and, according to Smurfit, Haughey told him Traynor would be in contact with the details of where the money should be sent. Traynor, of course, had nothing to do with Fianna Fáil money other than sometimes assisting Haughey in stealing some of it. Smurfit was to say later that this was the only time he was ever requested by Haughey to deal on a personal basis with Traynor in relation to payments. "He just said Des is going to handle this one for me," Smurfit said. Asked if he thought Traynor had some official role in Fianna Fáil, Smurfit said: "No, I regarded Mr Traynor very highly."

Traynor got in contact with the late David Austin in the Smurfit Group and gave the details of an account in London to which the money should be sent. Smurfit told the Moriarty Tribunal that he had no reason to distrust Traynor. "I was dealing with somebody who was, in my opinion, a close personal friend, a man of total probity." The transaction details were conveyed. The actual instruction for the sending of the money went out from the head office of the Smurfit Group in Clonskeagh, Dublin. An executive there told AIB in St Helier to have the money sent to an account with Henry Ansbacher Bank, London. The account was a Guinness Mahon Cayman Trust account. Smurfit authorised the sending of the sterling equivalent of £60,000, and Traynor subsequently confirmed its arrival. Smurfit was not himself personally involved in the convoluted routing of the money. It was never forwarded to Fianna Fáil. Told this by the tribunal, Smurfit said: "Well, that's very sad."

Haughey, when asked about the matter, said he was "very doubtful if I ever approached Dr Smurfit." He added that "on that score, I am categoric, as far as I'd like to be, that Des Traynor did not ever involve himself in the financial affairs of Fianna Fáil." If Traynor was involved, said Haughey, the money wasn't for the party.

Smurfit returned to the tribunal to give his response to Haughey. He said he had been requested personally by Haughey to make a donation. He said it was not the case that the payment was intended as a personal donation to Haughey. "My conversation with Mr Haughey was on the basis that a general election was looming, I believe, and they were looking for party funds." He rejected the suggestion that he might be mixed up, and that the £60,000 was money sent on foot of the request he'd received from Traynor at the time he'd approached him in relation to joining the K Club.

The net result of the Smurfit and Kavanagh donations was that Fianna Fáil received £75,000 of the £160,000 total and Haughey took the rest. The extent to which the whole affair was planned is not clear. Haughey, or Traynor, could just as easily have asked Kavanagh for a cheque for £25,000 and a draft to cash for £75,000. They could have asked for a draft for £60,000, being the amount coming from Smurfit, and another for £15,000. In general it would seem the idea to link the two payments might have been made at some stage during the transfer of the money rather than before. The Smurfit money was in sterling and so could be sent straight to the Ansbacher deposits without any foreign exchange transaction.

Kavanagh never received a receipt for his £100,000, and this annoyed him. More importantly from his point of view, he felt he did not get sufficient recognition from the party for his huge donation. Kavanagh was still unhappy about the matter in 1996 when Eoin Ryan Snr, a long-standing and highly regarded member of Fianna Fáil, approached Kavanagh for a contribution. Kavanagh responded by saying that he felt aggrieved that he hadn't received sufficient recognition for his previous donation. Both men were later to say that no figure was mentioned during this conversation, though Ryan was given to understand that the donation was substantial. Fearing the loss of a potential supporter, he sought a meeting with the then party leader, Bertie Ahern, and explained to him what had happened. Ahern said he would look into the matter, and Ryan reported this back to Kavanagh.

Ahern contacted Fleming and asked him two questions: had a donation been received from Kavanagh, and was a receipt issued? Fleming replied positively to both questions and, both men were to say later, probably told Ahern the amount – £25,000. He may also have told Ahern that the receipt was sent to Haughey's office. Ahern soon afterwards met Kavanagh at a lunch in Kavanagh's Wellington Road offices. Kavanagh complained to Ahern and Ahern apologised for the "shoddy" way in which Kavanagh had been treated. Both men were later to say no amount was mentioned during the conversation. Kavanagh was obviously placated. He gave Ahern a cheque for Fianna Fáil for £50,000.

In 1990, a year after the £60,000 payment to Fianna Fáil which the party never received, Smurfit "literally on the spur of the moment" decided to give Haughey a present of a Jack Yeats painting. The painting, *The Forge*, was then valued at £55,000. Haughey was president of the European Union, and the Smurfit Group was presenting the State with a painting, *The Flag*, by Sir John Lavery, to mark the occasion. This painting was about to be delivered in person by Smurfit to Haughey in Haughey's office in the Department of the Taoiseach, when Smurfit decided to throw in the Yeats painting as a gift to Haughey personally.

Asked by a barrister for the Moriarty Tribunal, Jerry Healy, if he thought it inappropriate to be giving an expensive painting to the Taoiseach, Smurfit said no.

But I did put in the caveat that I didn't expect it to be sold the next day. I said I expected him to hold on to it for a long time. I had it in the back of my mind that it would look very bad if you gave a painting like that to somebody and they cashed it in the next day. It would look like a cash gift. I wasn't into that situation and I requested that he would hold it for a considerable period of time. I hoped it would become what is known as a family heirloom.

The paintings were handed over at a private meeting at which no-one else was present. "I thought it was a nice gesture," Smurfit told the Moriarty Tribunal.

By 1996 the IFSC was an established success and one of the elements in the economic boom then gathering pace. By 1999 Kavanagh's company had all but finished its involvement in building the centre. It shared profits of some £69 million with the CHDDA, made from the sale of offices and apartments built on the site. Half the consortium's profits went to Hardwicke, which is essentially owned by Kavanagh. Hardwicke also received over £1 million in fees during the course of the development. A measure of the success of the IFSC is that companies registered there paid corporation tax totalling £430 million in 1999 alone.

So the project that Desmond convinced Haughey to support in the 1980s was not only a huge commercial success but a huge national success. Desmond bought one of the office blocks built on the site and worked from a penthouse office suite there which had a view out over the River Liffey. The glass in his office windows iced over when touched and became clear again when touched again.

The 1998 statement to the media issued on Desmond's behalf stated:

In relation to the International Financial Services Centre, Mr Desmond made no money from the centre nor from the building which he bought in the development. In fact audited accounts show that Mr Desmond made a loss of £6.2 million in the purchase and sale of that building. Mr Desmond did not receive any favourable treatment from anyone in relation to his involvement in the IFSC; indeed he is not aware of having received any political favours from any party on any matter.

While the whole IFSC project was being established and developed Desmond was involved in a myriad other business activities. His relationship with Haughey flourished. Because of the perceived level of contact between them in the late 1980s there were grumbles from opposition TDs about the amount of Government work being received by Desmond's firm, NCB, though Desmond was later to reject claims that his company had received any favourable treatment.

However, the suspicions which existed about favourable treat-ment were partly Desmond's own fault. In 1988 NCB assisted Pernod Ricard in its controversial takeover of Irish Distillers. Desmond later wrote to the company in an effort to justify a fee of £2 million.

We orchestrated entirely the successful campaign to get a positive tax opinion from the Revenue Commissioners, which involved using personal contacts at the highest level, including the Minister for Finance and the secretaries of the departments of the Taoiseach and Industry and Commerce.

He also said: "We used up a large proportion of the favours we can call upon from our political contacts – and no doubt we will pay a price on the other side."

Pernod Ricard eventually paid £1.25 million of the £2 million sought. When Desmond's letter was disclosed in the course of a court hearing, Haughey described the stockbroker's claims as "absurd".

It was not the only time Desmond made such claims. In April 1988 Hill Samuel Bank, in London, gave a loan of £8 million sterling to a company Desmond had connections with called Freezone Investments Ltd. It was later reported by the inspector appointed under the Companies Acts, John Glackin, that the bank sought "detailed information from Mr Desmond relating to his personal affairs" and that Desmond "explained to the bank in considerable detail his personal finances, his political contacts, his personal plans for the expansion of his business interests and, where relevant, the disposal of such interests."

A central figure in Desmond's business activities was a man called Colin Probets, a former director of one of the largest money brokerage firms in the world, Tullett & Tokyo, of London. Probets lived in Guernsey and did not give media interviews. Little is known about how the two men met. Desmond and Probets had been friends since the early 1980s, at least, and Probets invested in NCB when it was being established. Desmond said that Freezone Investments, a company which had substantial assets, belonged to Probets even though he, Desmond, had complete control over the use of those assets. Freezone played a central role in the dealings surrounding the Johnston, Mooney & O'Brien site in Ballsbridge.

Money for dealings in the site came from a Freezone account

in the TSB branch in Grafton Street, Dublin, and £1.3 million from the profits of the sale were lodged back in the account. During late July 1990 Desmond made two cash withdrawals from the Grafton Street bank totalling £500,000. He later told Glackin he kept the money in a tennis hold-all before passing it on to his friend in the Channel Islands, Probets.

The Telecom scandal broke in the media in September 1991, creating huge difficulties for Haughey and, according to some, marked the beginning of the end of his political career. His position wasn't helped when the following month it emerged that information held by NCB on the Aer Lingus subsidiary, Irish Helicopters, was posted to Celtic Helicopters. The brokers said that the document had been inadvertently sent to the wrong company. Feeling the pressure at a Fianna Fáil parliamentary party meeting, Haughey said Desmond was a "business friend" rather than a personal friend, which prompted a spokesman to clarify later that Haughey had never had "any relationship in a personal business capacity" with Desmond.

It was not known at the time that Haughey had directly benefited from money transferred from the Freezone account. Had it been known then, no doubt Haughey's political demise would have been more swift than it was.

Haughey had bought a yacht in Spain in 1988, with £120,000 sterling. The yacht had been spotted for sale in Spain, and Liam McGonigal, a friend of Haughey's who was in Palma at the time, had a look at it. It was subsequently bought through a broker, and again McGonigal was involved. A previous boat owned by Haughey had sunk off Mizen Head. The yacht was brought back to Ireland by Conor, Ciarán and Seán Haughey, with a friend acting as skipper. Haughey personally paid the insurance premium. The yacht was renamed *Celtic Mist*.

Some time early in 1990 Conor Haughey and Desmond were having a conversation about sailing and the progress of NCB *Ireland*. Desmond mentioned the great job Ron Holland, the Cork craftsman, had done on the yacht, and Haughey mentioned the fact that he needed to have refurbishment work carried out on the *Celtic Mist*. Desmond recommended that he use Holland, but Haughey said the family couldn't afford him. Desmond told Haughey not to worry, to have the work carried out by Holland and the bills sent to his office at Ferry House, the NCB head office. Haughey was later to speculate that Desmond did what he did because "the boat used by the Taoiseach of the day should reflect the country in a good light."

The work on the boat, which it had been thought would cost approximately £30,000, eventually cost £75,546. The bulk of it was paid over in April and May 1990. Money given to Holland for the work on the *Celtic Mist* came from the Freezone account in the TSB branch in Grafton Street. Conor Haughey was interviewed about this fact by Glackin in 1992, but the matter was not mentioned in the inspector's report. The payments were later absorbed by a Desmond company called Dedeir as part of a settlement between it and Freezone. Haughey, in his evidence, could not say whether he'd known at the time that the family yacht was being refurbished with money loaned by Desmond. "At this stage I can't say that. I mean, I can't say that I wasn't aware, but on the other hand, I can't say that I was aware at the time."

In a second statement issued to the media on Desmond's behalf in January 1998 it was stated that the "loans" advanced for the refurbishment of the *Celtic Mist* had been "settled". Desmond later agreed that what he meant by this was not that the money had been repaid but simply that he and Conor Haughey had come to a verbal agreement about how the money might some time in the future be repaid. The deal, he said, was that if the boat was ever sold, the interest-free loan would be repaid.

There were other dealings going on involving Desmond and Haughey which were not known to the public. Despite his numerous dealings with Haughey, Desmond was later to say he didn't know Des Traynor very well in the late 1980s. He met him sometimes in relation to banking business, but these meetings were infrequent. He did know that Traynor was a good friend of Haughey's.

According to Desmond, Traynor came to his office some time in late 1987, probably after the October 1987 stock market crash, "Black Monday", and said he was forming a syndicate of five or six people whom he hoped would advance money to repay "our friend's borrowings". Desmond knew who he was talking about, and Traynor indicated that the amount involved was in excess of £1 million.

"That's my best understanding," Desmond told the Moriarty Tribunal. "Best recollection, came to my office and said he is forming a syndicate, five or six-man syndicate to repay borrowings that had been generated by a friend which, you know, the other reference, it was quite obvious who he was talking about."

Desmond said he would give the matter some consideration and, having done so, telephoned Traynor and informed him he was "unable to help at this time." November 1987, as Desmond put it, "wasn't a very good period for stockbrokers." He never received any other request from Traynor to help Haughey, he said, nor did Traynor ever tell him if the matter had been resolved.

However, Desmond found out anyway. Some time shortly afterwards, within a week or two, he was in a golf club and he met Ben Dunne. According to Desmond, Dunne said:

I know that you've been approached. I knew you wouldn't be able to help because you've got no money. I'm making a payment myself for confidential reasons so that Mr Haughey won't be subjected to any pressure from any source.

Haughey was asked later if the approach in 1987 by Traynor to Desmond would have occurred because at that stage Traynor would have known that the two men, Haughey and Desmond, were reasonably friendly. Haughey said he wouldn't have put it in that context.

At that stage, Dermot Desmond certainly became a supporter of mine politically, very much so, because of, well, I suppose, in a way, we had adopted, the incoming Government had adopted two of his proposals, as it were. One, the dealing with the public finances and what was needed to be done and had to be done and the other was the proposal for the financial services centre. So I think that would certainly have persuaded him to support us as a Government and me as Taoiseach.

In 1988 Traynor, who had parted with Guinness & Mahon in 1986 and was subsequently appointed chairman of Cement Roadstone, again called to Desmond's office in NCB. He had some investment accounts he managed placed with Guinness & Mahon and he wanted to transfer them to NCB, he said. The two men discussed the matter, and it was agreed that the business would be transferred to Desmond's firm. In all, six or seven accounts were transferred, with the total involved being a few million pounds. This was money held for Ansbacher account-holders which was being used to invest in the Dublin and London stock markets. The accounts were all in the name of Overseas Nominees, a nominee company belonging to Ansbacher Cayman, formerly Guinness Mahon Cayman Trust. There was, of course, nothing improper in this from Desmond's point of view, as he would not have known about the secretive Ansbacher deposit system run by Traynor. Haughey said in evidence that Traynor never told him he had an investment account.

Desmond said later he did not know the identity of the beneficiary of the first account transferred. This account was opened in July 1988 with a lodgment of £105,586. A month later there was a lodgment of £149,432, and the following month again a further lodgment of £98,504. Desmond was the contact man for the running of the account, and Traynor and Desmond would discuss where best to invest the money. Desmond said the mix of investments made on the account was not dissimilar to the average NCB investment account, and that the final decision on where to invest was always Traynor's.

On 8 May 1990, £206,613 was withdrawn from the account by way of a draft. Just over a year later a further £95,000 was withdrawn, again by way of a draft. This left an overdraft of £23,461 on the account. An overdraft on an investment account is, of course, a highly unusual situation. Desmond said he had no memory of the circumstances surrounding how the account was permitted to become overdrawn.

On 8 February 1994, just three months before he died, Traynor wrote to NCB asking that the stocks associated with the account be sold. At that stage Desmond was no longer operationally involved with NCB, and Traynor corresponded with officials of the company. NCB wrote back to Traynor in March telling him the stocks were being sold. On 11 May Traynor died.

On 12 September 1995 Pádraig Collery wrote to the stock-broking firm in relation to the account and asked that the balance on the account be transferred to an account of a Cayman company in Irish Intercontinental Bank. The Ansbacher deposits had been transferred from Guinness & Mahon bank to Irish Intercontinental Bank during the period 1989–1991. Correspondence indicated that NCB was willing to take instructions from Collery, and also that it knew of a link between John Furze and the accounts, though how this came about is not clear. The NCB account was closed in September 1995, more than a year after Traynor's death, and £169,036 sterling transferred to Haughey's account in the Ansbacher deposits. The transaction was overseen by Collery. For £353,500 invested in 1988, Haughey got £470,600 in return, making a profit of £117,000, despite the fact that more than half the original amount invested was withdrawn after two years and about a third again one year later. Whatever else can be said about Traynor, there was no doubting his genuine skill at managing Haughey's investment account.

In the mid-1990s Desmond made some payments to Haughey, which will be described in a later chapter and which were examined by the Moriarty Tribunal. Desmond gave evidence to the tribunal during which he said he would still gladly give support to Haughey.

> If he needs money now on the back of his assets, I would gladly make it available to him. I am quite happy to make money available on a basis . . . without any documentation, without any interest rate, without any terms of repayment, to Mr Haughey. I was prepared then and I am

prepared to do it now until such time as he resolves his difficulties.

A tribunal barrister, John Coughlan, asked if this was because he admired Haughey. Desmond said: "I am a friend."

Coughlan said: "You are a friend and you are proud of that fact and there is no reason why you shouldn't be."

Desmond said: "I am very pleased with all my interactions and dealings with Mr Haughey."

13

Taxing the Taoiseach

THE scandals and the whiff of money and secret dealings which surrounded Haughey's last years in power were so strong that they prompted a senior official in the Revenue Commissioners to look into the Taoiseach's affairs. The Revenue Commissioners had had their suspicions about Haughey for decades. A file of newspaper clippings existed in the service which went back to the 1970s and contained articles noting elements of Haughey's life-style, such as horse sales and property purchases, as well as speculative and sceptical pieces about the source of his wealth by journalists such as Frank McDonald and Dick Walsh.

One of the Revenue officials who had had most dealings with Haughey's affairs was Christopher Clayton. He was in charge of the capital gains tax section when, in 1984, the Revenue was contacted by Laurence Crowley, the receiver to the Gallagher Group, and told about the £300,000 "deposit" which Gallagher had given Haughey in the immediate wake of his election as Taoiseach in December 1979. Crowley contacted the then chairman of the Revenue Commissioners, Séamus Páircéir. Legal advice was sought. The barrister concerned said that given Patrick Gallagher's unorthodox methods of doing business it would be difficult to prove to a court's satisfaction that the deal was not as laid out in the contract. Páircéir decided he would not risk the funds which would be required to take court action and informed Crowley of this. He then contacted Clayton and told him what had happened. He did not instigate any general re-assessment of Haughey's affairs. "It never came to my mind that I should send it to the Investigation Branch, and even if I had, I don't see what the Investigation Branch could have done," Páircéir later told the Moriarty Tribunal.

Clayton's function was to raise capital gains tax on the £300,000. He first wrote to Haughey's then tax agent, Pat Kenny of Haughey Boland, indicating that he knew Haughey owed money but not mentioning the Gallagher deal. This was done in the hope that Haughey might admit to some other windfall. When Kenny asked Haughey if he had some outstanding capital gain tax issue, Haughey said none that he could think of. He subsequently remembered the Gallagher deposit, and later again produced a copy of the contract.

About a year after sending his letter Clayton, not having received a satisfactory response, decided to raise an assessment against Haughey. He kept Páircéir informed of what he was doing. The assessment was issued in January 1986 and in July the Revenue was given £50,000. Some of this, £12,480, was tax due from the sale of Rath Stud in 1977. Haughey still owed £52,330 on the Gallagher deal.

When the remaining tax had not been received by October 1986, Clayton contacted David Fitzpatrick, an inspector of taxes in Hawkins House, Dublin, and instructed him to set in train the process which would have the money from Haughey secured through the courts. On 20 February 1987, Clayton was contacted by the Collector-General's office and asked to contact Haughey Boland once more about the matter. It was the week after the general election and Haughey was about to be made Taoiseach. Clayton was dealing with a very sensitive matter. Before telephoning Kenny he wrote a note of what he should say. It read in part:

> As you know the tax liability in question has been handled sensitively and as quietly as possible on our side. We have no wish to change that position. However, it is the case that despite the ordinary process of collection . . . the balance does not to date appear to have been paid and the next stage in the collection process is enforcement through the courts . . . I am phoning now because the enforcement stage is imminent . . . I am conscious of the fact that your client has been very busy for quite some time and is not likely to be less busy after 10/3/87.

The date was a reference to when Haughey was to be elected Taoiseach.

Within days Clayton was assured that Haughey had said he would pay. The final payment was made in January 1988. No interest or penalty was charged.

Three years later Clayton had been promoted to a more senior position. He told the Moriarty Tribunal:

> In later 1991 certain things came to my attention and entered into the public domain which caused me to institute a review of compliance in certain matters. I remember in particular the semi-state sector. There were

problems with Telecom Éireann, Greencore, the beef tribunal, all those were happening in late 1991. So I would have been conscious that there was non-compliance by persons from whom I would have expected compliance.

As part of this review Clayton remembered Haughey. As far as the Revenue Commissioners were concerned, Haughey was a PAYE worker, with the bulk of his earnings coming from his position as TD and Taoiseach. Like most PAYE workers he had not submitted a tax return in years. Clayton decided this was not good enough. "It seemed quite inappropriate and perhaps even scandalous that a Taoiseach should be so much in arrears as regards tax compliance."

Haughey was not quick to respond to the demand from the Revenue Commissioners. He hadn't sent in returns since 1985. By the time the first one arrived, Haughey had been ousted as Taoiseach and his career in politics was over. When they came the returns declared Haughey's income from politics, some deer farming, and some rental income. There was no mention of offshore accounts, donations from supporters, or money in the Ansbacher deposits. Clayton's view was that Haughey had been forced to make his returns, and if it subsequently transpired that the returns were incorrect, Haughey would be in trouble. In fact Haughey would never be penalised for having misled the Revenue Commissioners.

Part Three

1992–

14

Bowing Out Gracefully

IF Charles Haughey was one of the greatest chancers to have walked the stage of Irish politics in the twentieth century, then, up until he left power, he was also one of the most successful. He survived as leader of Fianna Fáil for just over thirteen years and spent more than half of that time as Taoiseach. The end came when Seán Doherty, Haughey's controversial Minister for Justice in his GUBU Government, announced in January 1992 that Haughey had known during that Government that the phones of the journalists Geraldine Kennedy and Bruce Arnold were being tapped. Haughey said that what Doherty was alleging was untrue. He called a press conference to counter the claim.

It was held in Government Buildings, which had been wonderfully restored at Haughey's instigation. There was a tiered room in the basement with permanent seating facing a podium, such as you might see in a modern university building. Haughey was on his own, sitting behind a table draped with green felt, a heavy dark curtain covering the wall behind him. His press officer, P. J. Mara, was sitting on a plastic chair to one side of the room. A lot of journalists turned up, including most of the more serious, experienced and respected journalists then on the Dublin scene. Haughey seemed isolated and brave. Dignified. The journalists fired their questions at him and he answered, not giving anything on his stated position. All the time his fingers played, first with a piece of paper he continually folded and unfolded, and then with a paper clip, twisting it this way and that, crumpling it. When he had said his piece and the journalists had tired of him, he went away.

His career was over. The Progressive Democrats, founded by those unwilling to accept Haughey's leadership of Fianna Fáil, announced it would leave the coalition Government if he was not replaced. On 30 January 1992, Haughey told the Fianna Fáil parliamentary party that he was going to resign. He did so with an emotional speech delivered to the Dáil on Tuesday 11 February 1992. It was an occasion of some emotion for him, and opposition politicians were generous in their comments. Haughey himself quoted Othello. "I have done the State some service; and they know't: No more of that." He didn't continue the quotation, which goes:

"I pray you, in your letters,
When you shall these unlucky deeds relate,
Speak of me as I am. Nothing extenuate,
Nor set down aught in malice."

However, as was so often the case with Haughey, the surface dignity was hiding murky dealings. On the day he was preparing to leave office he telephoned Dr John O'Connell and asked him to come to his office. When he arrived, O'Connell said, Haughey "was very upset about … his position that day." Haughey said "we" wanted to buy back the Celtic Helicopter shares O'Connell had bought seven years earlier. O'Connell was surprised, as he had considered the payment to be a contribution rather than an investment. Why Haughey wanted the shares is not clear. O'Connell decided on the spur of the moment he should make a return on his £5,000 investment. He asked for £15,000. Haughey agreed, and the two men shook hands.

However, the money never arrived, and O'Connell resorted to sending a solicitor's letter. The money was eventually handed over during a Fianna Fáil convention in Donnycarney in October 1992 where Seán Haughey was being nominated. Haughey senior handed O'Connell a cheque for the agreed amount. The cheque was drawn on an account in the name of Irish Intercontinental Bank, the bank then holding the Ansbacher deposits. O'Connell became one of the few investors in Celtic Helicopters to make a profit.

Many were impressed by Haughey's dignity in retirement. He withdrew to Kinsealy with the intention of having nothing more to do with public life. As was the practice up to then for former Taoisigh, there was no attendance on the lecture circuit, no appointments to the boardrooms of international capitalism, few public appearances. He continued to open the Dingle regatta every summer. Once or twice he publicly supported a charitable cause. Most of the time he conducted his life out of the public gaze.

When he finished giving evidence to the Beef Tribunal he asked the chairman's permission to return to his "bucolic pursuits". He seemed in good health. It was known he rode out every morning on Portmarnock beach. In many people's eyes his early retirement years were the best role he'd ever played, and it made them think more highly of him than hitherto. By the mid-1990s, when it became known that Mary Robinson would not be seeking a second term as President, there was talk of Haughey being put forward as the Fianna Fáil candidate. And again there was no comment.

He had a few million pounds in his Ansbacher account. Traynor was still making his regular weekend visits to Kinsealy to discuss business matters, and he would supply Haughey with statements of how his affairs stood. The Ansbacher deposits system had undergone a number of changes over the years, but it was still very much in operation. In 1985 the Cayman bank had been bought by a consortium which included Traynor, Furze, Collins, and a Jamaican national and former Jamaican Minister for Tourism called Hugh Hart. The consortium then sold the bank to the Henry Ansbacher Group. The bank's assets at the time were £114 million. Not all of this but certainly much of it was Irish money.

Peter Greenhalgh of Henry Ansbacher told the McCracken Tribunal during a closed hearing in London: "I think initially we had bought, effectively, an Irish operation . . . A significant amount of business was emanating from the Irish Republic as a result of ongoing relationships that had been built up." The name of the bank was changed to Ansbacher Cayman Ltd.

In May 1986 Traynor parted with Guinness & Mahon and soon afterwards became chairman of Cement Roadstone. After he left the merchant bank, structures were established whereby he could continue to operate his secret banking service. He moved to premises in Trinity Street owned by the bank, and Joan Williams moved with him. Both he and Williams were paid by their former employers for their first year. In Traynor's case the salary was £12,500, with a similar amount being paid to him by the Cayman bank. Collery, by then an associate director of

Guinness & Mahon, continued to take instructions from Traynor and to operate the memorandum accounts on the bureau system.

When Traynor was appointed to his full-time job with Cement Roadstone, he and Williams moved to that company's offices in Fitzwilliam Square. Faxes and hand-delivered memos concerning Haughey's and others' affairs started to make their way back and forth around Dublin.

In 1989 an internal Guinness & Mahon report expressed concern about the whole system. At the time the deposits from the Cayman Islands, £38 million, constituted 35 per cent of the bank's total deposits. There were also rumblings back in the Cayman Islands.

Traynor began negotiations with Irish Intercontinental Bank which eventually led to the deposits being moved to it. Irish Intercontinental Bank did not have a cash service, so Traynor opened accounts with the Bank of Ireland in the name of Kentford Securities, a company he controlled. These accounts were then used when large cash withdrawals were needed, the withdrawals being funded with Irish Intercontinental Bank cheques or drafts.

Large bundles of cash would make their way from the Bank of Ireland to the Cement Roadstone offices in Fitzwilliam Square. In 1993, the Fianna Fáil TD for Kerry North, Denis Foley, collected £10,000 in cash from Traynor in this way. The memorandum accounts were moved to a computer in the Cement Roadstone offices after Collery left Guinness & Mahon in 1989. He had a key and would let himself in on Saturday mornings to enter details of the transactions which had occurred during the week. The High Court was to be told ten years later that by 1989 half the Cement Roadstone board was in some way connected with the Ansbacher deposits.

In 1991 Haughey Boland became part of the much larger firm Deloitte & Touche. Before this happened Traynor met Paul Carty, who was to become a partner in the new merged entity, and over lunch the two men discussed Haughey's bill-paying service. Traynor was concerned about the service being operated by a very large firm. Some time after the meeting he contacted Carty and told him Jack Stakelum, the former Haughey Boland accountant who had left and set up his own business, Business Enterprises Ltd, would be taking over the job. This is what happened. Stakelum initially kept a monthly analysis of the payments he was making, but Haughey showed no interest, and Stakelum soon ceased to do so. When he needed money he sought it from Traynor.

15

Helicopters Again

BEHIND the scenes Haughey and Traynor were still busy and still capable of exerting influence. As already noted, Haughey had Ben Dunne to dinner in his home in late 1992 and soon afterwards received £80,000 from a total of £180,000 somehow conveyed from Dunne to Traynor. The other £100,000 had gone to Ciarán Haughey's helicopter company.

Celtic Helicopters was successful in its original aim of providing employment to Barnicle and Ciarán Haughey. As well as providing transport to business people it also had the contract for the "Eye in the Sky" reports on the illegal radio station Q102. Business was good. In the early 1990s the two pilots decided an opening existed in helicopter maintenance. They decided to build a hangar out near Dublin Airport.

In March 1991 a loan of £100,000 was secured from Guinness & Mahon. This was originally meant to be a bridging loan, with ultimate finance coming from the Irish Permanent Building Society. On the books the Guinness & Mahon loan was secured by personal guarantees from Ciarán Haughey and Barnicle, but secretly it was secured by a deposit of £100,000 sterling taken from the Ansbacher deposits. Ciarán Haughey was later to deny any knowledge of this. He and his partner built a 20,000 square foot building with office accommodation and a modern hangar.

The Irish Permanent funding was slow in coming. In May 1991 Traynor negotiated a loan of £150,000 from Irish Intercontinental Bank for Celtic Helicopters, using the money to pay off the debt to Guinness & Mahon, with the balance going into the helicopter company's general account. Again letters of guarantee were signed and again the loan was really backed by funds from the Ansbacher deposits. In this instance it is known that the money came from Charles Haughey's S8 account. Again Ciarán Haughey denied any knowledge of the secret backing.

In February 1992, on Traynor's instruction, the loan was repaid with money from the general Ansbacher account, and the backing deposit which had been used as security was returned to Charles Haughey's S8 account. Ciarán Haughey was later to deny, in evidence to the McCracken Tribunal, any knowledge of the fact that a £150,000 loan taken out by his company had been settled with third-party funds. Mr Justice McCracken chose not to believe him.

A month after this transaction use was again made of the Ansbacher deposits to assist Celtic Helicopters. The company's working account with Bank of Ireland, Dublin Airport, was £100,000 overdrawn and the bank required security. Traynor organised a guarantee from Irish Intercontinental Bank, which was paid a 1 per cent per annum fee. A sum of £100,000 sterling from Haughey's S8 account was deposited with Irish Intercontinental Bank to secure the guarantee.

A second wave of investment requests was made by Traynor and Haughey on behalf of Celtic Helicopters in 1992. The company had spent heavily on its new hangar and was in financial difficulties. This time £290,329 was raised. Those who invested included John Byrne (£47,532); the Kerry businessman Xavier McAuliffe (£50,000); Pat Butler of Butler Engineering, Portarlington (£25,000); and the American businessman Guy Snowdon (£67,000). Michael Murphy, an insurance broker with a business in Trinity Street, Dublin, was involved in the invest-ment of £100,000.

McAuliffe, who invested £52,500 sterling on 5 October 1992, was friendly with the Haughey family. They sometimes used the grounds of his hotel in Dingle as a departure point for Innishvickillane. McAuliffe was interested in helicopters and had once owned one. He and Ciarán Haughey sometimes discussed helicopters, and McAuliffe knew of the younger Haughey's idea of expanding Celtic Helicopters, building a new hangar, develop-ing a maintenance service, and buying a long-range helicopter.

In September 1992 Traynor contacted McAuliffe and asked him if he would make an investment in Celtic Helicopters. Traynor said he knew McAuliffe had spoken with the Haugheys over the years about the helicopter company, and that they were trying to raise £600,000 from various people, and would he invest £50,000? McAuliffe said he would. The money was trans-ferred from an account with AIB, Jersey, to an account with Credit Suisse, London, in the name of Ansbacher, Zürich. The details were given to McAuliffe by an employee of Deloitte & Touche whom Traynor told McAuliffe would be calling him. Deloitte & Touche, which by then had absorbed Haughey Boland, provided services to Celtic Helicopters. Paul Carty, a partner with Deloitte & Touche, was a director of Celtic Helicopters from its incorporation up to 1992 and after that date acted as an adviser to the firm.

McAuliffe never received any financial information about the company, never received any shares, and never heard anything more about the transaction until contacted about it by the Moriarty Tribunal eight years later. He told the tribunal he made the payment only because it was the Haugheys who asked him. The money, £52,500 sterling, was transferred out of his Jersey account so that he wouldn't have to apply for exchange control permission.

Guy Snowdon is an American businessman who ran G-Tech, an American corporation specialising in the lottery industry. G-Tech was awarded a multi-million-pound contract to install and run the Irish National Lottery on-line system in 1987. In 1998 Snowdon resigned from G-Tech after a British jury found he had tried to bribe the businessman Richard Branson to withdraw his rival bid to run the British national lottery. In 1997 G-Tech was accused of improper lobbying and giving gifts in relation to the Texas lottery. Snowdon did not give evidence to the Moriarty Tribunal. Haughey, in his evidence, said that he had never heard of Snowdon until his name was brought to his attention by the tribunal.

Pat Butler ran an engineering company in Portarlington, Co. Laois, which provided steel used in the building of the Celtic Helicopters hangar in Dublin Airport in the early 1990s. He was deceased by the time of the Moriarty Tribunal, and the details of how his investment came about are not known.

John Byrne gave evidence to the Moriarty Tribunal about his contribution to Celtic Helicopters. A month or two before making the investment, he said, he had been contacted by Barnicle and told the company was in need of funds. Around the same time Traynor told him he was in the process of raising capital for Celtic Helicopters. Without presenting Byrne with any documents about the helicopter company's finances, Traynor persuaded him to invest £50,000. The money came from a family trust Byrne had of which Ansbacher Cayman was the trustee.

According to Byrne, when he was asked by Traynor to invest approximately £50,000 he responded that it would be impossible for him to make that sort of investment; that his companies were not investment companies, or they were investment companies concentrating on property. Traynor, of course, was a director and financial adviser to these companies. Traynor then, according to Byrne, asked Byrne if he'd mind if Traynor approached the trustees of the Byrne family trust in relation to the investment. In other words, would he mind if he, the chairman of Ansbacher Cayman, which managed the Byrne trust, asked the trustees to make the investment he was seeking.

"And that's what he did, and that's what happened. It was some time afterwards, a good while afterwards, that he informed me that he had and that I was the proud possessor of shares."

Byrne never saw any share certificates or anything else to do with the company he'd invested in. When Celtic Helicopters was eventually investigated by the Moriarty Tribunal, it was discovered, in books kept by Deloitte & Touche, that Byrne's November 1992 investment was recorded as being held by Management Investment Services on behalf of Larchfield Securities, which was holding them in trust for Byrne. Management Investment Services is the company owned by Sam Field-Corbett.

The most mysterious of all the investments in Celtic Helicopters was one for £100,000 made through Mike Murphy. Even though the details of this investment were extensively inquired into by the Moriarty Tribunal, it is still not clear what happened.

What is clear is this. In November 1992, around the time a second series of requests were being made by Haughey for "investments" in his son's troubled helicopter company, a cheque for £100,000 from Murphy's insurance company was sent to Credit Suisse, London, with instructions that the money be lodged to an account in Zürich in the name of Ansbacher Cayman. Traynor advised Furze, in the Cayman Islands, that the money was on its way to Zürich. He asked to be told by Furze when it had arrived. Later the £100,000 was lodged to the Ansbacher account with Irish Intercontinental Bank in Merrion Square. A memo from the Celtic Helicopters file kept by Traynor and Collery noted that the amount was lodged to the S8 account – Haughey's Ansbacher account – on 30 November 1992.

It was a roundabout way for Murphy to make an investment in a company based in Dublin Airport, but he says he was only doing what he was told to do with the cheque. One of the effects of the roundabout route was that funds were placed in Haughey's sterling "offshore" account without Traynor having to worry about exchange control issues. Murphy's business was involved in a large number of international transactions, and his company was regularly given permission to make payments outside the State. So the cheque might have been used in one of the switches Traynor was in the practice of making.

Murphy says the money belonged to David Gresty, an Englishman who runs an insurance business in Monaco, DB Agencies. Murphy placed £2 million worth of business with Gresty in the years up to 1992. Murphy says the cheque was stamped with exchange control permission, because he intended to give it to Gresty at a meeting they had in Paris to discuss their affairs. However, the two men got to discussing Celtic Helicopters. Gresty decided to invest in the company, and so the cheque, which still didn't have the payee written on it, was brought back to Dublin. It was purely by coincidence, Murphy said, that his instructions in relation to the investment in Celtic Helicopters, which he later received, were to send the money to Zürich. The instructions about where to send the money were given to Murphy by someone in Deloitte & Touche, who had earlier been given the details by Traynor. Gresty travelled to Dublin and gave evidence to the Moriarty Tribunal stating he had made the investment on Murphy's advice.

A cheque for £100,000 was lodged to the Celtic Helicopters account in Bank of Ireland, Dublin Airport, at around this time, but it didn't come from Gresty or Murphy. It came from Carlisle Trust, the company owned by John Byrne. The money came originally from Dunnes Stores and was part of the £180,000 mentioned earlier.

The net effect of all this was that the funds from Murphy, which had exchange control approval, were lodged in Haughey's offshore account, while the funds from Dunne, intended for Haughey, were given to Celtic Helicopters.

Gresty said Murphy offered to guarantee his investment in Celtic Helicopters and to hold the shares for him. No share certificates were ever issued, and no dividend was ever paid. Gresty, when he gave evidence to the Moriarty Tribunal, seemed not at all perturbed by this.

Around the time all this was happening the helicopter company was facing disaster because it couldn't pay its insurance bill. If the company was not covered to fly its helicopters it would quickly go out of business. Murphy was the company's insurance broker. He raised a loan of £100,000 for Celtic Helicopters to allow it pay for the insurance he was selling to it, and then proceeded to pay off the loan in monthly £10,000 instalments. In other words, he paid for the insurance he was supposedly selling to Celtic Helicopters. Murphy said the assistance he gave the company was being repaid by Celtic Helicopters in both money and flying hours granted to his company.

Murphy said his motivation was to avoid bringing down Celtic Helicopters. "Under no circumstances did I want it to be known, did I want to be known as the person responsible for the collapse of Celtic Helicopters, due to its obvious association with Charles J. Haughey," he told the Moriarty Tribunal. Such a development, he said, would have been bad for business. Haughey, of course, was no longer Taoiseach at this time.

Murphy said he particularly feared the loss of his beef business if he was seen to be associated with the collapse of Celtic Helicopters. Gresty said he never mentioned this to him. During the late 1980s and early 1990s Murphy's firm was conducting significant amounts of business with the beef and food industries. Larry Goodman's Goodman International was its biggest customer. Murphy had been involved in negotiating Goodman's export credit insurance for Iraq and was also insurance broker to the Department of Agriculture in relation to intervention beef. Much of the Goodman insurance business with Murphy was placed by Murphy with Gresty's firm in Monaco. Gresty said his business really took off over the four-year period during which Goodman's beef empire was profiting from its use of the state-allocated export credit insurance.

This connection with the Goodman Group was mentioned by counsel for the Moriarty Tribunal, John Coughlan, during his questioning of Murphy. At the time Murphy was convincing Gresty to invest in Celtic Helicopters the Beef Tribunal was under way in Dublin Castle, prying into the Goodman Group and its relationship with senior politicians. The money for

Murphy's investment in Celtic Helicopters came from a running account linked to business which included that from the Goodman Group, and the investment was made one month before Haughey gave evidence to the Beef Tribunal.

"This was a very sensitive matter," Coughlan suggested to Murphy. Murphy said the point never crossed his mind. He said it would have been "very unwise" for a man in his position to make an enemy "of the son of the most powerful man in the State." If he had not helped Celtic Helicopters, he said, he might have lost "substantial customers in the beef business."

Goodman, when he later appeared at the Moriarty Tribunal, took the opportunity to hotly object to his having been mentioned during Murphy's evidence and to criticise Coughlan. "I am very concerned at what was stated at the tribunal on that day and it led to twenty-eight media articles, all of which were incorrect," he said.

I want to make it clear to the tribunal that I believe that was misleading. If we were his largest customer at the time, we had no discussion with Mr Murphy and we had no investment … I had no investment with Mr Murphy directly, I had no investment indirectly. I had no investment.

Charles Haughey too, during his evidence, took the opportunity to make a complaint. He could not see why his trying to help his son's company, after he had left the office of Taoiseach, was a matter for public inquiry.

I know very well that Celtic Helicopters would never have figured in any tribunals or anything else were it not for the fact that Ciarán Haughey is my son. And this pernicious doctrine of connected persons throws up this sort of anomalous situation where he is pilloried in newspapers, himself and his partner John Barnicle, day after day, week after week for no other reason, not for anything, the way they fly their helicopters or the way they do anything, but for no other reason than Ciarán Haughey is a son of mine and I really, maybe I am going a bit too far in saying this, but I sort of feel perfectly entitled to resent all that, to resent the way one unfortunate little aviation company, doing their best and indeed providing a very good service, a very, very good service to the tourist industry and otherwise, racing industry, should be dragged before a tribunal the way they have been.

16

An Innocent Bystander

RIGHT from the start Haughey's retirement was troubled by concerns about Ben Dunne and the possibility that the public might learn about the payments Dunne had made to him. Haughey made his retirement speech to the Dáil on 11 February 1992. On 20 February Ben Dunne had his panic attack in a hotel room in Florida, and when the police were called they discovered he was in possession of cocaine.

Dunne was on a golfing holiday in Florida with a number of colleagues and was staying at the Hyatt Regency Grand Cypress Hotel. After he and the others had retired to their rooms for the night Dunne had telephoned "Escorts in a Flash" and asked that a woman come to his room. He had a large amount of cocaine with him, and it seems that he and the woman, Denise Wojcik, took cocaine and at some stage got into the bath together. Dunne took a lot of cocaine and Wojcik became concerned. Dunne began acting strangely, and the young woman got dressed and fled. Down in the hotel lobby she told the security manager that the occupant of suite 1709 had gone crazy. "He's screaming and yelling," she said. When security guards went to the room they found Dunne, a tall, heavy-set man, screaming at the top of his voice. The police were called, and after Dunne was eventually overpowered they found 32.5 gram of cocaine. Because of the amount of cocaine found he was charged both with possession and trafficking. He was in trouble.

Soon the Irish media heard what had happened and Dunne's difficulties became national news. The story received blanket coverage. No doubt Haughey watched these events more closely than most.

One of Dunne's solicitors, Noel Smyth, flew to Florida and took charge. He eventually managed to plea-bargain so that the Florida attorney-general dropped the more serious charge of trafficking. When the matter came to trial Dunne was spared a custodial sentence, though he had to agree to attend a British addiction clinic.

Smyth played a crucial role in influencing the public response to Dunne's predicament. When Dunne returned from the United States he acted on Smyth's advice and made himself available for a series of one-to-one meetings with journalists during which he expressed his regret for all the hurt he had caused to his family. Considering the mess Dunne was in, the approach worked perfectly, transforming any delight people might be taking in the misfortunes of a multi-millionaire into sympathy for a fellow-human going through a difficult time. Smyth was to give similar and similarly successful advice to the Bishop of Ferns, Dr Brendan Comiskey, in 1996, when the bishop returned from having been absent from his diocese for a period without explanation. He had been in an American alcohol treatment centre.

The events in Florida in 1992 and the publicity which surrounded them exacerbated the differences and tensions which already existed within the Dunne family. The disputes between Ben Dunne and his siblings, which were already a feature of their relationship, became both more frequent and more acrimonious. In February 1993 Dunne was removed as chairman of the Dunnes Holding Company, and the following July he was removed as an executive director. It seems his close relationship with Fox may have come to an end at around this time.

Ben Dunne's ousting from his position of power within the Dunnes Group was not amicable, to put it mildly. At first he maintained hopes that he would be able to fight his way back. When that did not work he decided he would take as much money as he could from the group. As part of this strategy he decided he would threaten to destroy the Dunnes trust, a move which could lead to tax bills for tens of millions of pounds being raised against the various trustees. Specifically, he threatened to argue in court that the trust was a sham, something he believed he could illustrate by disclosing how he had taken money out from under the control of the trust, to use as he pleased. He would try to break up the trust if he did not get a satisfactory settlement from his siblings. The best lawyers in the State were engaged by both sides for a court battle which would involve massive financial stakes on both sides. The members of one of the richest families in the State were at war, and a number of third parties were going to get caught in the crossfire.

Margaret Heffernan had moved to replace Ben Dunne as the member of the family running the family group. She had heard rumours that her brother was giving money to Haughey, but when she'd asked him about it he'd denied it. Noel Fox had given her a non-committal answer when she approached him. Now in the bitter atmosphere of the family crisis and with both sides setting out their stalls, Ben Dunne threatened to use the

fact of the Haughey payments as part of his case against the bone
fides of the Dunnes trust. Moreover, while doing so he
threatened to state not only that he had made payments to
Haughey but that they had been made so as to receive political
favours in return.

This emerged during the proceedings of the McCracken
Tribunal. Dunne agreed that at one stage during his falling out
with his siblings, during a telephone call with a member of the
trust, Bernard Uniacke, he claimed that the payments to
Haughey had been to influence Haughey and get changes to the
trust law which would be to the advantage of the Dunnes trust.
The comment was made on the day after a particularly
acrimonious meeting of the Dunnes board.

Dunne told the McCracken Tribunal that it was a "stupid"
comment to make and wasn't true. He was under tremendous
pressure at the time, he told the tribunal counsel, Michael
Collins. Pleas to his family turned to threats, and stupid things
were said, he said. He agreed that the statement was totally at
odds with his evidence to the tribunal that the payments were
not made with any such motive.

Collins said Uniacke had said the comment about seeking to
influence Haughey was just one of twelve points made by Dunne
during this conversation. Collins continued:

> But you had to think up the point nevertheless. It had to
> cross your mind that these payments could be construed as
> being made for the purpose of influencing legislation. And
> it crossed your mind sufficiently that you actually made
> that statement to Mr Uniacke.

"What had put the thought in your mind?" he asked Dunne.

Dunne said he had never attempted to interfere with legislation. "I would say survival, and I was under ferocious pressure to try and get what I felt was mine and I made some very, very stupid allegations." He also said the payments were not made so he would have access to Haughey. "I have been in serious trouble lots of times in the past and neither Mr Haughey nor anybody I know could get me out of that trouble except myself."

With all these allegations and threats circulating in the upper reaches of the Dunnes organisation, Heffernan decided to renew her earlier, unsuccessful attempts to establish whether payments to Haughey had actually been made. She went out to Kinsealy to meet Haughey and demanded the return of the money her brother had given him. Haughey, seemingly completely relaxed, expressed surprise at the request, said he couldn't be responsible for what her brother said, and raised the question of Ben Dunne's mental stability. He neither confirmed nor denied receiving the money. "I can't be responsible for what your brother says," he said.

Heffernan told the McCracken Tribunal: "I have to tell you I left there having doubts about the stability of my brother and whether he [Haughey] ever got payments."

Immediately after Heffernan left, Haughey got on to Traynor to tell him what had happened. About a week after the meeting with Haughey, Heffernan met Traynor to ask him about the same matter. The two met in Traynor's Cement Roadstone offices in Fitzwilliam Square.

I said to him that my brother, Ben, had given Haughey £1 million. I asked him did he know anything about this. He said he knew absolutely nothing about it.

I was very confused. I suppose I was looking for some-one to tell me it wasn't true. I would prefer to think some-

one didn't get £1 million of Dunnes Stores money. I still
feel that way, sir.

Heffernan said the relationship between her brother and
Haughey developed subsequent to her father's death in 1983 and
"certainly would not have happened in my father's time." He
would not agree, she said, with being over-friendly with politicians
"and certainly not with Mr Haughey." Asked why this was so, she
said: "I don't want to go into it, but there was something between
my father and Mr Haughey." This is understood to have been a
reference to an incident at a trade show in New York in the late
1960s. Haughey, then Minister for Finance, was there hoping to
show off the best Ireland had to offer and took exception to
produce Ben Snr had on display. He had him thrown out of the
show, shouting: "What do you think this is? The fucking Iveagh
Market?"

Traynor died from a heart attack in May 1994, just a month after
his sixty-third birthday. He had been suffering from cancer. A
twelve-paragraph report in *The Irish Times* noted his passing, his
association with John Byrne and the involvement he'd had in
financial dealings with the disgraced former premier of western
Australia, Brian Burke, before mentioning the positions he held
at the time of his death. A few days later a letter from John Gore-
Grimes was published saying the report "grossly misrepresented
the real character and talent of the late J. D. Traynor. To write
off the achievements of this man in such a negative way does not
reflect the many genuine contributions which Des made to the
Irish business community."

Gore-Grimes complained that the report had caused distress
to Traynor's family and friends and expressed the hope that a "fair

and balanced" assessment might be published in the future. The same page of the same edition carried an appreciation of Traynor by J.P.C. The writer attributed Traynor's non-existent public profile to the fact that he "detested the cult of personality."

> He had rare natural talents and his financial acumen and shrewd judgment were such that he was frequently consulted by the highest in the land. He had many fine qualities and was a good listener. He took everything in, and when he spoke you listened.
>
> Des was the person you went to if you were in trouble and he took great pride in helping you resolve your difficulties. His dry wit was legendary; one-liners were his speciality.

Haughey attended the funeral, as did a large number of the most senior business people in the country. Furze flew in from the Cayman Islands and had a brief conversation with Haughey. So too did Collery, who informed Haughey that he would be taking over Traynor's role in relation to his Ansbacher account. Furze, meanwhile, asked Collery to help him deal with the secret files which were still in the computer in Traynor's former office in Fitzwilliam Square.

Collery had a key. The two men let themselves in to the Cement Roadstone offices on a Saturday morning and removed the computer records as well as papers kept in a filing cabinet. They moved the material to the offices of the former Haughey Boland employee and close friend of Traynor's, Sam Field-Corbett, in Winetavern Street. Field-Corbett gave them the use of a desk and a filing cabinet. Near the end of 1994 Furze returned to Dublin and went through the files. He selected some which he would bring back with him to the Cayman Islands. Others he left with Collery, and others still he destroyed. In 1995, after Furze had parted company with Ansbacher Cayman and returned to Dublin for another visit, Collery, with the Cayman bank's permission, destroyed more of the Dublin files.

By this stage Haughey's money was in the control of a company called Hamilton Ross Co. Ltd, which was controlled by Furze. Collery continued to keep the memorandum accounts for Hamilton Ross and to issue money to Stakelum when asked to do so.

In early 1994, when it looked as if the Dunnes dispute was going to reach the courts, Ben Dunne's solicitor, Noel Smyth, suggested Haughey should be informed of what was being alleged. This development was to become a central element in the later destruction of Haughey's reputation, in which Smyth was to play a leading role.

Smyth had a successful legal practice in Dublin, but as the 1990s progressed he all but gave up practising law to concentrate on property development. The property developer Pat Doherty once said of Smyth that he was the sort of solicitor "to whom you went for advice only to come away with a business partner." Doherty told the inquiry into the Telecom scandal: "Mr Smyth was the sort of person who would have ten balls in the air at any one time and you wouldn't know whether you were in or out of a deal." Smyth acted as Dermot Desmond's representative during some of the negotiations surrounding the Telecom site. He never got a slice of the action but he did receive fees.

In 1994, having discussed the matter with Dunne, Smyth called Haughey on the telephone and told him there was something they needed to discuss. Haughey suggested they meet in Kinsealy. Haughey met Smyth alone in a room at Abbeville and listened while the solicitor outlined the background to the litigation which was heading towards the courts. When Smyth said he was satisfied the research he'd carried out while preparing for the case would support the allegations, Haughey's response was that he had never received the money. Despite all that was involved, Smyth wasn't alarmed by this reaction from Haughey. He didn't believe him. The meeting between the two men lasted twenty minutes.

A short time later Haughey telephoned Smyth in his office and said he wanted to talk to him "as a matter of urgency." He told Smyth he was going to Cheltenham the following day (his horse Flashing Steel was running) and asked if he could meet Smyth in Abbeville early in the morning, at 7 a.m. We could have breakfast, Haughey suggested.

The two men met. Haughey seemed to Smyth to be very agitated. He said he had considered the first meeting they'd had and that he thought that this was an attempt to destroy him. Smyth told him it was nothing of the sort, that there was nothing personal involved but they were "stuck in a situation whereby these events had occurred." Haughey began to tell Smyth about how long he'd been in public life and that these allegations, if they became publicly known, would be "devastating" for him. When Smyth explained that Dunne had no particular desire to see the matter go all the way to the courts, and that they should wait and see what happened, Haughey took some comfort from the suggestion. However, he remained very concerned that the matter would go all the way to court, and also that the details of what was being alleged were in the hands of third parties, solicitors and barristers. He was afraid of a leak even if the matter was settled.

The matter rumbled on, and Haughey continued to worry. He invited Margaret Heffernan out to Kinsealy and urged her to settle. She listened to what he was saying but she was aware her brother was in contact with him and was very wary. Haughey's concern about the whole matter was such that at one stage he visited Dunne when he was in hospital and urged him to drop his case against the trust. To no avail.

As if all this worry concerning the Dunne family was not enough, Haughey was now also in the position of having to make direct approaches around this time concerning his financial situation, rather than going through Traynor. One man who offered to help out was Dermot Desmond. The matter was broached a few months after Traynor's death. According to Desmond, he was talking with his old friend when Haughey mentioned the fact that he might have to take up a non-executive position on the board of a German bank in the IFSC. Desmond asked whether he was considering taking up the position because he wanted to or because he needed the money. Haughey said it was the latter. In evidence Haughey said he did not know "specifically" what his financial position was at the time. "Let me put it this way: it was such that an additional source of income would have been welcome." In fact his balance in the Ansbacher deposits was such that it earned him £84,000 in interest in 1994. On the other hand, his outgoings were such that he needed more than the £1 million plus he had in the bank, if he wasn't going to have to tighten his belt. In September 1992 his balance in the Ansbacher deposits was £1.2 million. During the following four-and-a-half years, Jack Stakelum paid bills for Haughey totalling £1.47 million.

Desmond told Haughey not to bother joining the German

bank and that he would help him out. "I suggested he look at restructuring his assets and that if money was needed, I would make it available to him." The offer was to be open-ended.

On 20 September 1994 Desmond had £100,000 sterling sent from the account of an entity owned by Desmond, Anesia Établissement, at Banque Scandinave en Suisse in Geneva, to the Royal Bank of Scotland, London, to the account of Henry Ansbacher. The money was subsequently transferred to Dublin and lodged to Haughey's Ansbacher account, from which it was used to defray his personal expenses. Jack Stakelum was told by Haughey that Desmond was making a payment. Stakelum got details of where the money should be sent from Collery before passing those details on to Desmond.

Meanwhile the Dunne dispute rumbled on. In November the two sides had to swap what are called notices of particulars; documents which set out the allegations being made. Haughey was contacted by Smyth again, who told him the matter was becoming known to a widening band of legal people. Haughey said he understood and that the matter was outside the control of Smyth or Dunne. All he could do was sit and wait, hoping for a settlement. On 19 November 1994, as the matter was very close to going to trial, a settlement was finally agreed. The fact was published in the newspapers and read with relief in Kinsealy. Dunne had reportedly managed to squeeze £125 million from his siblings, the money to be paid over in tranches. When Smyth telephoned Haughey a few days later to assure him everything had been resolved, Haughey suggested he call out to Kinsealy some time for a drink.

But it was too early for celebrations. Within a month Haughey received a letter from Dunnes' solicitors, Matheson Ormsby

Prentice, demanding the return of the money which had been "improperly diverted" to him. Haughey wrote back: "As no such monies have been received there is no question of repayment . . . I take great exception to the phrase 'improperly applied'." Before doing so he telephoned Smyth and asked for another meeting. Smyth made another trip to Kinsealy, and the two men met privately. Haughey told him what was happening and showed him the solicitor's letter he'd received. What he wanted to know was what Ben Dunne's stance would be if he (Haughey) was brought to court by Dunnes Stores. Smyth said Ben Dunne had no stomach for more litigation. Haughey said he was going to write back indicating that he hadn't received the money. He watched Smyth's face while he said this, but Smyth didn't react.

Within weeks Haughey was on to Smyth again. He'd received another letter from Dunnes Stores' solicitors and didn't know what to do. Get yourself a solicitor, said Smyth. Haughey decided not to respond. There the matter rested.

Unbeknownst to Haughey, something else had happened. Smyth's staff kept a log of all calls to the office, and the calls from Haughey to Smyth had all been entered. Haughey's actions, prompted by his fretting about whether or not the fact of the Dunne payments would come to light, would themselves in time contribute to his difficulties.

Life went on. In 1995 one of Desmond's companies made a commercial advance to Celtic Helicopters for flying hours. The transaction was mentioned in a statement issued to the media in 1998. "In 1995 IIU Ltd, of which Mr Desmond was chairman, made a commercial advance of £100,000 to Celtic Helicopters to cover flying hours for executives ... To date, hours to the value of £56,150 have been used."

A year later Haughey himself got another dig-out from Desmond. This time the amount was £25,000 sterling and it came from the Isle of Man account of a company Desmond owned called Bottin International Investments Ltd. Again the transfer occurred after Haughey had mentioned a shortage of funds. After Desmond offered to help, Haughey told Stakelum to contact the financier, which he did. Stakelum went to see Desmond in his IFSC penthouse offices and gave him the details about where the money should be sent. Stakelum told the Moriarty Tribunal that there was no particular shortfall in the funds available to Haughey at the time, so the money was more by way of a general donation.

When questioned about the payments later Desmond insisted they were loans and not gifts and said that he had so advised Haughey's tax agents. Because the Moriarty Tribunal's terms of reference end at 31 December 1996, it had no powers to investigate whether further payments had been made to Haughey by Desmond after that date.

17

Disclosure

A close associate of Haughey's said that Haughey always feared that his financial secrets would be disclosed, and always believed this dreaded event would one day come to pass. Certainly it must have seemed a distinct possibility during 1993 and 1994, with the visits to Kinsealy by Heffernan and the updates Haughey was receiving from Smyth. When the immediate crisis had passed, Haughey, an old operator, had identified the danger created by the fact that so many third parties now knew of the allegations which had been made by Dunne. As Dunne himself had said in 1987, Christ had only twelve apostles, and one of them betrayed him.

In November 1996 Haughey awoke to discover that the nightmare was continuing. The journalist Sam Smyth had a story on the front page of the *Irish Independent*: Ben Dunne had paid more than £300,000 on the extension and renovation of the Co. Tipperary home of the Fine Gael minister Michael Lowry; the bills had been paid by Dunnes Stores and invoiced to the group as work carried out on the Dunnes outlet in the ILAC Centre, Dublin. On the face of it it had nothing to do with Haughey, but reading the story he knew that someone was talking.

He was correct. The day the story appeared sources said the payments made by Dunne to Lowry were detailed in a confidential report, the Price Waterhouse report, and that payments to Haughey were also listed. The report was one which had been commissioned by Heffernan after the ousting of her brother from executive positions in the Dunnes Group. It was an attempt to list irregular payments which had been made during his stewardship. The report included information that Haughey had received more than one million pounds, the sources said. The race began in the journalism world to see who would first land the story.

Lowry resigned on 2 December. On 3 December Cliff Taylor of *The Irish Times* reported that a senior figure in Fianna Fáil had received £1 million from Ben Dunne. Haughey wasn't named, but everyone in the political establishment knew who the story was referring to. An inquiry into the matter was initiated. The Dáil Committee on Procedure and Privileges appointed a retired judge, Judge Buchanan, to report to it in relation to the Price Waterhouse report and any payments to politicians documented in it. Dunnes Stores agreed to give a copy of the confidential report to the judge on the understanding that anything not relevant to the committee's inquiry would remain strictly confidential.

Smyth's office in Fitzwilliam Square began to log more calls from Haughey. In the period from 2 December 1996 to 13 February 1997, Haughey made seventeen phone calls to Smyth's offices, and all of them were logged. Smyth's calls to Haughey from the office were not logged, but other calls he made on an Eircell phone were later identified from the phone bills.

The first contact from Haughey was a phone call in the wake of Lowry's resignation. Haughey wanted to discuss with Smyth the fact that the issue of payments from Dunne was now in the public domain. The media were reporting that an affidavit was in existence which outlined these payments. Smyth said there was no affidavit but there was a notice of particulars. Haughey suggested that they meet.

Smyth later told the McCracken Tribunal: "I was conscious at that time that I didn't know where these allegations were going and I was concerned that while my client was Mr Dunne, I was still talking with Mr Haughey, and I suggested we try and meet in what I termed as a neutral venue." Smyth informed Dunne of what was happening, and Dunne said he had no objections.

Haughey and Smyth met in the home of a man called Corcoran, a friend of Smyth's and a neighbour of Haughey's. The meeting took place on 4 or 7 December. Corcoran was concerned about facilitating the meeting, but Smyth assured him it would remain confidential. Haughey arrived first and on time and was waiting in the house when Smyth arrived, a few minutes late. The two men went together to Corcoran's office and began to discuss what was for Haughey an enormous personal crisis.

They discussed the setting up of the Dáil committee inquiry. Haughey asked what Dunne's attitude would be to such an inquiry, and Smyth said that if called to give evidence, Dunne would be obliged to appear. Haughey had brought with him a copy of the Oireachtas Compellability, Privileges and Immunity of Witnesses Bill and he read out a section of it to Smyth concerning who was and was not compellable. The meeting concluded on the note that if Dunne was called, he would have to appear. The two men agreed to stay in touch.

On 14 December Haughey met Smyth again, again in Corcoran's house. Haughey wanted to quiz Smyth about what was in the Price Waterhouse report. Media comment had suggested that the report would include the payments to him, but Smyth, having been asked by Haughey, explained that Haughey wasn't named in the report. The report, he explained, was concerned with payments from within the Dunnes Group, but the payments to Haughey had come from sources outside the group. (They had mostly come from the offshore and Far East structures Dunne had set up and which were outside the control of the Dunnes trust. At the time the report was written the Tripleplan and second Dunnes Bangor cheque had not been identified as payments to Haughey.) Haughey, of course, had never admitted to Smyth he had received money from Dunne. In fact he had claimed the opposite.

Smyth did not bring a copy of the Price Waterhouse report with him to the meeting. Haughey had brought a copy of a report on a Dáil debate which had taken place that week, and pointed out certain sections of it to Smyth. Armed with the information that he was not named in the Price Waterhouse report, Haughey then discussed with Smyth the fact that the Dáil committee, if it called Dunne, would be limited by its inquiry's terms of reference to questioning him about matters contained in the Price Waterhouse report.

Christmas came and went and the net continued to close on Haughey. On 2 January he again contacted Smyth and again requested a meeting. Smyth couldn't manage to contact Corcoran so the two men met in Abbeville. They met on 4 January and Smyth came armed with a copy of the Price Waterhouse report. He showed Haughey the three entries in the report concerning small payments to Maureen Haughey, Ciarán Haughey, and Fr Eoghan Haughey, the former Taoiseach's brother. Haughey listened as Smyth expressed the view that there would be unanswered questions left after Judge Buchanan reported and that his report was unlikely to satisfy the main issue, which was the supposed affidavit. At the McCracken Tribunal Smyth was asked if he thought Haughey was concerned about the possibility of a tribunal of inquiry being established. "He didn't appear to be. I think he felt that once Judge Buchanan's inquiry was completed that that would be the end of the matter, but I took a different view." Asked if he felt a tribunal of inquiry was likely, Smyth said: "I did."

The judge was having meetings with Dunne where he answered questions concerning payments outlined in the report. Haughey discussed the matter over the telephone with Smyth and Smyth assured him that though these payments were "voluminous," they were also "quite innocuous".

Smyth was right about the Buchanan inquiry leaving a sense of dissatisfaction. When the committee received the judge's report on 3 February, it outlined payments to Lowry and to Haughey's wife, son and brother, as well as a payment of £85,000 to Fine Gael, but there was no mention of Haughey. On 7 February the Dáil and Seanad voted to establish the McCracken (Dunnes Payments) Tribunal.

As well as the events which were taking place in public, Haughey was privately aware of another, from his point of view, disastrous development. Up to early February the whole controversy was concerned with payments totalling £1.1 million which were detailed in the statement of particulars drafted during the battle within the Dunne family. These payments had been made from various legal entities and had been lodged to accounts in London and Dublin which had, ostensibly, no link with Haughey. He could simply deny receiving the money or if that didn't work deny ever having knowingly received the money. However, some time in early 1997 Dunne remembered something which created a direct link between him and Haughey: the three bank drafts made out to fictitious names which he'd given to Haughey one morning in Kinsealy.

During the preparation for the litigation over the Dunnes trust, Ben Dunne had believed these three drafts had been given to members of his family, and so had not made any allegation that they had been given to Haughey. Now, in the midst of one of the greatest political controversies in years, if not decades, Dunne was changing his mind and suddenly stating that he had given the drafts directly to Haughey. His credibility in relation to everything he was saying could be called into question. Smyth advised Dunne that they should try to establish what had happened with the drafts before making any new allegations. They knew that the drafts had been lodged to Irish Intercontinental Bank. Dunne suggested that Smyth contact Haughey. That is what he did.

Haughey had already been in contact with Smyth around this time, to ask if they could meet again because he had some questions he wanted to ask. Now Smyth telephoned Haughey and told him he had something else he wanted to discuss. He asked if Haughey knew anything about three drafts which came to a total of £210,000 sterling. Haughey said no.

But the matter bothered him. Haughey was later to claim he could not remember receiving the drafts, but few believed him. He rang Smyth and asked him if he would call out to Abbeville and bring copies of the three drafts with him. He was panicking. The two men met in the study in Kinsealy, where so many other secret and controversial matters had been discussed over the years. Now these three drafts threatened to expose the truth about what lay behind so many of those secret meetings.

The two men exchanged pleasantries and then Smyth handed Haughey copies of the three drafts which, he'd already told

Haughey, had been lodged to an account in Irish Intercontinental Bank. Smyth watched him and registered Haughey's realisation that the documents were "lethal".

"Did you lodge these to your own account?" Smyth asked.

"No," said Haughey. "I didn't."

The two men started to talk about something else but then Haughey said: "But they could be a source of some embarrassment to me."

"Well, if you didn't lodge them to your account, whose account were they lodged to?"

"I think they were lodged to an account in Irish Intercontinental Bank either connected to or belonging to Des Traynor."

Up to now Smyth had not known of any connection between Traynor and the drafts. Haughey's revelation was critical, because it created the connection between the drafts and the other payments: Traynor.

Smyth told the McCracken Tribunal what happened next:

I think I reacted to say, "I think this is very serious because . . ." I think I used the word nexus, that I believed if they were lodged to the Irish Intercontinental Bank, the only person who could have lodged them would be Mr Haughey or somebody on his behalf. On that basis I immediately saw that what he had never admitted or said to me before was now, in my mind, clear; that it created the connection between the earlier payments that had been made by Mr Dunne, and I said that obviously I thought that this was quite serious.

Haughey's initial reaction was to say that this was a disaster. "He immediately recognised I think himself, that the bank drafts were a very lethal, if I can use that word, piece of paper. He was very concerned."

Haughey had still not admitted to Smyth that he'd received money from Dunne. Nevertheless Smyth pointed out to him that the drafts established the link with the earlier payments. He formed the impression that Haughey, there and then in the library, accepted that this was so. For a moment, "a very split second", Haughey panicked. "He was looking for a way out very quickly and I think he said, 'is there any way we can get rid of these?' or 'what can we do?' or ' where are we going with these?'"

Haughey was suggesting they destroy the evidence. Smyth said: "Hold on a second," and Haughey calmed down and regained control of his nerves. Smyth explained to him that the drafts were mentioned in an affidavit which had been sworn before the Master of the High Court, that they were in the public domain and would be given to the tribunal then being established. All this information would be investigated thoroughly. Haughey saw that Smyth was right. The investigative process would continue, and the matter of the drafts would have to be dealt with. Smyth left to report back to his client, Dunne, and Haughey sat in his mansion in Kinsealy and pondered the fact that what he had kept hidden during his entire political career was now likely to be exposed.

When Smyth met Dunne he told him his recollection was correct. He had given the drafts to Haughey.

The tribunal was setting about its work, sending questionnaires to politicians and making initial inquiries. On 24 March Ben Dunne furnished it with a lengthy statement and supporting documents. He outlined the payments which had been made to Haughey, where the money had come from in each case, and precisely who the payee had been. This in turn led the tribunal to make inquiries of the various parties and institutions identified in Dunne's statement. An approach was made to the courts in England to take evidence there. An approach was also made to the Grand Court of the Cayman Islands. The tribunal's legal team were trying to follow the money trail, to see if it would lead them to Haughey.

Meanwhile, despite all the evidence which he now knew existed, Haughey decided he would lie to the tribunal and deny any knowledge of ever having received money from Ben Dunne. This was despite the fact that Smyth had urged him to come clean, and warned him that the tribunal team would discover and disclose the truth irrespective of Haughey's previous positions in Irish society. Times had changed, Smyth said, but Haughey wasn't listening. Perhaps he felt he had nothing to lose.

During one of their meetings in February Smyth asked Haughey if he had availed of the tax amnesty introduced by Bertie Ahern in 1993. Haughey indicated that he hadn't. Smyth thought the tax bill arising from the Dunne payments was the biggest problem facing Haughey. When he reported back to Dunne about the meeting, Dunne asked Smyth what sort of a tax bill Haughey could be facing. Smyth said anything up to or exceeding £1 million, when interest and penalties were included. Dunne told Smyth to tell Haughey he was willing to give him "up to £1 million" to help him deal with his difficulties, if Haughey would make a full disclosure.

It was around the middle of February. Smyth telephoned Haughey, and the two men agreed to meet again in Abbeville. Smyth told Haughey he should come clean and that his biggest problem was his tax bill.

I told him that at a guesstimate that he would need to have at least a million pounds available to him and that he should employ a good tax consultant to make a submission to the Revenue Commissioners, and that as part of that submission if he had, as I put it at the time, if he had a draft for a million pounds with him, he'd make a lot of progress.

Haughey said it was a "very gracious offer" but that he couldn't accept it. It would be impossible for him to accept it, he said. Smyth said the tribunal had very extensive powers and was "likely to get all of the information sooner rather than later." Haughey could do himself a huge favour by making a clean breast of it. "You will get more than a fair hearing if you explain the circumstances in which you found yourself at the time that the payments were made," Smyth said. "If you were in a position to say you had made a substantial payment on account to the Revenue, then a lot of the heat might be taken out of the problem."

Haughey thanked Smyth for his advice but said it would be impossible for him to take such an approach. The two men discussed the pros and cons of Haughey coming clean for about twenty minutes. Though he hadn't managed to convince Haughey to come clean, Smyth left the meeting thinking he would at least give the matter some thought. He had gone to the meeting expecting Haughey to take up the offer, and he and Dunne were disappointed when they later discussed the outcome. Dunne told Smyth to ring Haughey and tell him the offer of financial assistance would be withdrawn if it wasn't taken up.

The next day Smyth phoned Haughey. They used careful language. Smyth asked if there had been any progress. Haughey said no. Smyth said the offer would then be withdrawn.

"Fine," said Haughey. It was the end of the contact between the two men.

On 3 March the tribunal sent a letter to everyone who had been a member of the Oireachtas between January 1986 and December 1996 asking about payments. Haughey replied saying he had received no payment of the nature referred to in the tribunal's terms of reference. On 27 March, having received Dunne's original statement, the tribunal wrote to Haughey again, this time enclosing extracts from Dunne's statement. The tribunal solicitor, John Lawless, asked that Haughey respond to the various transactions outlined by Dunne. No reply was received, and Lawless wrote a reminder on 2 April. On 3 April a response was received from Haughey. It included the statement: "It is suggested that the accompanying documents support the said allegations and with respect to the tribunal I venture to suggest that a careful perusal of these documents on their own does not corroborate the allegations being made against me." On 19 April Lawless again wrote to Haughey seeking answers to certain questions. Haughey replied saying he intended to co-operate with the tribunal, but he did not supply the information requested.

Meanwhile, the tribunal was making progress with its investigative work and also taking evidence from witnesses. Haughey was declining the offer of legal representation before the tribunal, and so the public proceedings when they began took place without the presence of representatives of the main personality involved. Haughey still hoped he would be able to deny receiving the money.

The statement and the documents given by Dunne led the tribunal to Guinness & Mahon bank and Irish Intercontinental Bank and from there to Joan Williams, Pádraig Collery and, following some initial resistance, the whole Ansbacher deposits structure. After more than twenty-five years the secretive financial service operated by Traynor for the Republic's most powerful businessmen had been discovered by the authorities. Most of the depositors still remaining had removed their money just weeks before the tribunal's discovery, but documents still in Collery's possession, coupled with documents held by the two banks, meant they were facing inevitable disclosure and shame if the authorities decided on a public inquiry. More reputations than Haughey's were about to be destroyed by the work of the McCracken Tribunal.

While the discovery of the deposits was a significant development, the documents which were seized from Collery were nevertheless concerned with the memorandum accounts and were therefore in code. This meant the tribunal had discovered the existence of the deposits and could show the Dunne money going into general pooled accounts linked to the deposits, but didn't have documentary evidence showing a link between Haughey and a particular memorandum account. However, when going through the piles of papers it now possessed, which covered lodgments and withdrawals and statements of account, one of the tribunal's legal team spotted a note scribbled by Williams on the corner of an instruction concerning a withdrawal from a particular coded account. "By hand to C.J.H." It had to be Haughey.

The tribunal now had evidence of money going directly from an account to Haughey; it had the Dunne money going into a pooled account; and it got a statement from Collery saying that Haughey had an Ansbacher or memorandum account. He was able to confirm the codes on Haughey's accounts, S8 and S9.

The tribunal team discovered the bill-paying service run for Haughey by Haughey Boland and later by Jack Stakelum. Stakelum was able to tell them that when he wanted money for Haughey he contacted Traynor and, after Traynor's death, contacted Collery. The tribunal team found evidence of money from Haughey's Ansbacher accounts being lodged to his bill-paying accounts. This meant that now they could show the money from Dunne going into general Ansbacher deposit accounts, as well as money coming out of Haughey's coded memorandum accounts to pay for his lavish life-style. The had all but completed the money trail.

The one problem remaining was to show the money from Dunne being allocated to Haughey's account within the Ansbacher deposits. If this could be achieved, then the money trail would be complete and there could be no disputing Haughey's having received the money. No documents existed in the jurisdiction which could prove this, and so the tribunal took a case to the Grand Court of the Cayman Islands, to seek a ruling from the authorities there that Ansbacher should co-operate with the tribunal's inquiries. Without such a ruling the island's strict banking secrecy laws precluded the bank from co-operating.

The approach to the Cayman court, which was heard in May 1997, was opposed by Furze, who had by this stage left Ansbacher Cayman. Furze was closely following developments in Ireland, reading each day's *Irish Times* on the internet. He engaged a barrister in Dublin to quietly keep an eye on the work of the tribunal. The legal costs incurred by Furze while contesting the tribunal's efforts to get information from the Cayman bank were later paid for with money taken from the accounts of Irish customers still with money in the Cayman Islands. Eventually the court ruled against the tribunal, on the grounds that the islands were obliged to co-operate with foreign courts investigating non-revenue crimes but that the tribunal was not a court or tribunal within the meaning of the act which covered such co-operation.

Just prior to the May and June break during which the tribunal made its application to the Cayman court, there had been some dramatic public developments in Dublin Castle. Smyth had become a central witness in the tribunal's proceedings because of the conversations he'd had with Haughey in Kinsealy concerning the Dunne payments. On Friday 25 April Smyth, giving evidence, told how Dunne had earlier that year suddenly changed his mind about the three drafts he'd given Haughey in November 1991. This was three years after he had said, during his assault on the Dunnes trust, that the drafts had been given to members of his family, Smyth explained. He was worried about the effect this change of evidence would have on Dunne's credibility, he added. He and his client decided they should take up the matter with Haughey. Michael Collins, barrister for the tribunal, asked what happened next.

"I telephoned Mr Haughey and told him . . ." Collins stopped him, but the questioning soon returned to the issue of Smyth and Haughey. Smyth said he had met Haughey five times since late 1996. Collins said this was the first the tribunal had heard of this, and that Smyth had not mentioned it in his statement to the tribunal. Smyth explained that when he'd met Haughey the two men had spoken as if their discussions were covered by the professional legal privilege which covers conversations between solicitors and their clients. Because, in his view, Haughey had not distinguished between his being a solicitor and being Haughey's solicitor, Smyth had decided he would not divulge the content of the meetings unless directed to do so by the tribunal. Collins said it was proper and correct for Smyth to have left the matter out of his statement, but he was now applying for a direction that Smyth divulge the content of the meetings.

Haughey had still not taken up the tribunal's offer of legal representation, so there was no-one there to speak on his behalf. Also, because Smyth had not mentioned the conversations he had had with Haughey in his statement, Haughey may have thought their content would not be revealed. Mr Justice McCracken decided it would be best to give Haughey an opportunity to make an argument if he so wished, before he made any direction.

Everyone who had been watching the tribunal's proceedings was on tenterhooks, wondering what the import would be of Smyth's conversations with Haughey. At this stage nothing had been heard from Haughey other than a denial that he had received the money. The judge's ruling meant that an adjournment would be necessary before the direction would be issued, and as it was Friday it now looked as if everyone would have to wait until Monday for the next development.

The excitement and tension were then added to by Smyth. He said he had expected that the matter would arise during the course of his giving evidence and had made some preparations. On the advice of his barrister he had written out a statement covering his meetings with Mr Haughey and posted it to himself. It was now in a sealed envelope, and he would give it to the tribunal if directed to do so. There was, Smyth said, nothing in the envelope which should be new to Haughey.

Mr Justice McCracken directed that the envelope be handed over, that it not be opened, and that it be sent forthwith to Haughey in Kinsealy. The tribunal then adjourned until Monday, when Smyth was to return to the witness box and the judge would decide whether or not he would direct that he should reveal the content of his conversations with Haughey. The tribunal's solicitor, John Lawless, took the sealed envelope and drove out to Kinsealy, where he handed it to Haughey. The nation then settled back to wait for Monday. Not even the tribunal's legal team knew what was inside Smyth's sealed envelope.

As it transpired, the nation had longer than a weekend to wait before discovering what had been discussed between Smyth and Haughey. When the tribunal resumed on Monday, the barrister Eoin McGonigal requested that Haughey be granted limited representation solely in relation to the issue of the admissibility of Smyth's evidence. He also requested an adjournment to consider the legal position, prepare submissions, and advise his client. This request fitted in with the tribunal's own requirement to consider all the evidence it had already gathered, and prepare for hearings pending in London and the Cayman Islands. After hearing evidence from a number of witnesses unconnected with Haughey, the tribunal adjourned. It was not to resume its sittings in Dublin Castle until Monday 30 June.

Significant evidence concerning the Traynor operation was gathered during the London hearings on 1 May and 8 May. All the banks involved co-operated fully. Mr Justice McCracken travelled with his team to the Cayman Islands for hearings there on 22, 23 and 27 May. Judgment, when given on 30 June, was, as already noted, against the tribunal's application.

Nevertheless by mid-June the tribunal had amassed a huge amount of information, enough to show that the Dunne money had been, in all likelihood, lodged to Haughey's accounts in the Ansbacher deposits, and that money from these accounts was used to fund Haughey's life-style. For the period 1988 to 1991 it could be shown that Haughey, in addition to his salary, was spending in the region of £300,000 per year. Haughey was served with whatever information he had not already been given and was informed that the tribunal was going to resume its sittings on Monday 30 June. The tribunal still did not know what was in Smyth's statement in the sealed envelope.

Observers had to withstand further frustration when the tribunal resumed its Dublin sittings. McGonigal rose to his feet on the Monday morning and requested full representation for his client. The request was immediately granted. McGonigal then said Haughey would be furnishing documents to the tribunal on Friday and that the documents would include a statement to the effect that, "as a matter of probability," the £1.3 million alleged by Dunne to have been given to Haughey had been lodged to accounts controlled by Traynor and used for Haughey's benefit. In other words, Haughey would now accept that he had received the money. A huge part of the tribunal's work was completed, but the truth had not yet emerged.

Haughey, McGonigal added, would make it clear that he was not aware of the transfers totalling £1.1 million which came in the wake of the 1987 communication between Traynor and Noel Fox, and would say it was not the case that he had been given three bank drafts for a total of £210,000 sterling by Dunne in Kinsealy in November 1991. In other words, it was because of the work carried out by the tribunal that Haughey now accepted he must have received the money. Up to this he had not known about the payment.

McGonigal sought and was granted an adjournment of one week in the matter of Smyth's evidence. The chairman decided that, considering all the material which Haughey and his team had to work through, the request was a reasonable one.

Haughey's statement failed to arrive on Friday as promised. It did not arrive at the tribunal's offices in Dublin Castle until minutes before the day's hearing was due to begin on Monday. It was a seven-page document and, as anticipated, included an acceptance by Haughey that he had received the money, but a denial that he had known about it. When the tribunal sat, counsel for the tribunal requested a 24-hour adjournment to allow it to consider Haughey's statement. McGonigal said he was not going to argue that the conversations between Haughey and Smyth should remain confidential. He also suggested that Smyth might want to engage his own counsel, a remark that some took to mean that Haughey was going to strongly dispute Smyth's version of what had been said during their conversations. Smyth never took up the suggestion.

The adjournment was granted. What happened next in private led to the exposure of the fact that Haughey was blatantly lying to the tribunal. The tribunal team got a copy of Smyth's statement concerning the conversations he'd had with Haughey. Smyth was given a copy of Haughey's statement delivered that morning. He read it very closely.

Haughey's statement began with a brief summary of his political career and continued with a lengthy synopsis of his relationship with Traynor.

I never had to concern myself about my personal finances as Desmond Traynor took over control of my personal financial affairs from about 1960 onwards. He saw to it as his personal responsibility to ensure that I would be free to devote my time and ability to public life and that I would not be distracted from my political work by financial concerns. Mr Traynor had complete discretion to act on my behalf without reference back to me.

This was to be the bones of Haughey's defence over the coming years.

Haughey said that after Heffernan called to see him in 1993 and mentioned "rumours of a payment to me from Dunnes," he'd said to her that there were all sorts of wild rumours going around and that he could not be responsible for them.

> I subsequently telephoned Desmond Traynor and told him what Margaret Heffernan had said. He replied that he was meeting Margaret Heffernan in a few days' time and would hear what she had to say but that I need not be concerned about these rumours as they were without foundation.

He continued:

> As a result of the evidence adduced before this tribunal and the documentation as furnished to me I now accept that the payments totalling £1.3 million as set out by the tribunal were received for my benefit. I had no knowledge of the circumstances surrounding the payment of such monies but I accept the description offered in evidence to this tribunal by Mr Noel Fox in so far as it touches upon the four payments totalling £1.1 million.

That left the three drafts.

> I dispute the evidence of Mr Bernard Dunne that he called to Abbeville, Kinsealy, Co. Dublin on some date on

or prior to the thirtieth of November 1991 and personally handed me three bank drafts on the account of Tutbury Ltd. I say that no such meeting ever took place and Mr Bernard Dunne is mistaken in his recollection in this regard. I never on any occasion received any of the three bank drafts referred to from Mr Bernard Dunne or from anyone on his behalf. Nor was I aware of their existence until Noel Smyth referred to them on third February 1997.

He then moved on to the issue of the conversations with Smyth. His version of events differed from Smyth's.

Noel Smyth telephoned me around the time the Lowry story broke in the newspapers at the end of November/ early December 1996. He inquired if I had any information as to who was behind the leaking of the Lowry story to the newspapers and said that in his opinion that whoever was responsible was playing a very dangerous game. I informed him that I had no idea whatsoever as to who was behind the story.

Smyth, Haughey said, subsequently telephoned again and sought a meeting. At Smyth's request the venue for the meeting was changed from Abbeville to Corcoran's house.

Haughey said he was shown the Price Waterhouse report at this meeting, and told that he wasn't mentioned in it. He went on to say that a second meeting in Corcoran's house was also at Smyth's request, and that the two men discussed the possibility of a tribunal being established. On 3 February 1997 another meeting took place, this time in Haughey's study in Abbeville. The meeting was at Smyth's request and followed a telephone call from Smyth, Haughey said. Smyth had said he had copies of bank drafts which "Mr Bernard Dunne had recently formed an impression" he might have given to him.

> I said this could not be so as I had never received them. I also indicated that I had no knowledge of any such bank drafts . . . When Mr Smyth arrived in Abbeville, Kinsealy, he produced three copy drafts. I looked at them at his request and I was in a position to confirm that I had never seen them before and I had no knowledge of them. Mr Smyth appeared to accept that this was the position and our meeting concluded.

Haughey denied that he had indicated that he had knowledge of the drafts or that Smyth had asked him if he had lodged them to his (Haughey's) account. These were all direct rebuttals of points made in Smyth's statement concerning the meeting. As Smyth did not ask the question he (Haughey) could not have replied in the negative, nor could he have said the drafts could be a source of embarrassment to him. He went on to say he had not indicated to Smyth that the drafts could have been lodged to an account associated with Traynor. "I deny that I asked Mr Noel Smyth if it was possible to get rid of or destroy the copy bank drafts which he had in question."

Haughey said he remembered a later meeting in Abbeville in February and again said it followed a telephone call from Smyth and a request from him for a meeting.

> At this meeting Noel Smyth advised me very strongly to take the easy way out of all the tension and stress by going to the tribunal and indicating that payments made to

Desmond Traynor from Dunnes sources had in fact been for my benefit. He stated that as there was no impropriety involved and as I had never sought these from or spoken to Bernard Dunne about them or granted any favours to Bernard Dunne or Dunnes Stores that I was in fact in no difficulty in regard to them.

He said Smyth conveyed Dunne's offer to help with any tax bill by providing up to £1 million.

I rejected this offer and suggestion out of hand . . . I have never spoken about my place in history or in the community or anything of that kind to anyone.

Haughey's statement made no reference whatsoever to the meetings he and Smyth had in 1994.

On the face of it Smyth now faced having to enter the witness box to give his version of the meetings with Haughey, and have McGonigal dispute this evidence on Haughey's behalf. Haughey would then give his evidence disputing Smyth's version of events, and the tribunal would have to decide who was telling the truth. At issue was a crucial matter: the receipt of the drafts. If Haughey had received the drafts, then he had been lying to the tribunal since his first communication with it. This in turn raised the spectre that Haughey had known at the time of all the payments from Ben Dunne.

Smyth contacted the tribunal legal team and told them that his version of events was the correct one. He could, he revealed, show that Haughey contacted him in late 1996 and early 1997. His office, he informed the tribunal, logged all calls received, and the logs showing the precise time of the calls from Haughey still existed. The tribunal team was astonished by the revelation. It immediately sought a new statement from Smyth, the logbook recording the calls, and Smyth's diaries. The logbooks and diaries were later described by one source as "the nail in the coffin" for Haughey.

Copies of the new documents received from Smyth were sent to Haughey's solicitors, Ivor Fitzpatrick and Co., late on Monday. On Tuesday morning McGonigal sought a further adjournment for twenty-four hours. Also on Tuesday the tribunal received more documents and a further statement from Smyth. These are understood to have concerned the 1994 contacts which Haughey had failed to mention in his statement. Copies of these were also sent to Haughey's representatives. The information from Smyth had sparked a series of explosive meetings between Haughey and his legal representatives. Haughey's position was now untenable, and it was obvious he had lied to his legal team. Such was their concern that the idea of their resigning from the case may have arisen. On Wednesday morning McGonigal rose and made a short, two-paragraph statement to the public sitting of the tribunal. It was a short statement but for Haughey it was a public admission that he had lied to a tribunal established by the Oireachtas. It was, moreover, a devastating public acceptance that he had received money from a known benefactor while holding the office of Taoiseach. He was a disgrace.

The statement read:

I wish to thank the chairman for yesterday's adjournment. As a result of reviewing the excellent work of the tribunal in considering the very helpful documentation recently received from Mr Ben Dunne's solicitor, I now accept that I received £1.3 million from Mr Ben Dunne and that I became aware that he was the donor to the late Mr Traynor in 1993 and furthermore, I now accept Mr Dunne's evidence that he handed me £210,000 in Abbeville in November 1991.

In making this statement I wish to make it clear that until yesterday I had mistakenly instructed my legal team. They have however agreed to continue acting for me for the duration of the tribunal. I wish to thank them in this regard. I will give evidence to the tribunal when required to do so.

The statement, McGonigal said, was signed Charles J. Haughey.

On the same day that the dramatic two-paragraph statement from Haughey was read out by McGonigal, Smyth finally took the stand and revealed the content of his meetings with Haughey in 1994 and again in 1996–1997. It added to the picture of Haughey as a scheming, dishonest man hiding the shameful truth of his conduct by whatever means he could. His public disgrace preceded his public appearance to give evidence, which came six days later, on Tuesday 15 July. The overall position was now accepted by the parties involved, but it was still considered necessary to hear from Haughey. Public humiliation was required.

There was great build-up to his appearance. Only a limited number of the members of the public who turned up could be accommodated in St George's Hall, where the hearings were being conducted, and a room in the basement was set out with chairs and a large television monitor. People queued in the castle square from before dawn to assure themselves of a seat. Haughey arrived early, before the television cameras and the press photographers, and said hello to some of those who had come out to see him before going inside and awaiting the commencement of the proceedings. He attended with his son Conor and a young woman relative who later sat beside him in St George's Hall with tears in her eyes. When Haughey was called he walked straight-backed up to the witness box and asked the chairman for permission to read a statement. Given the events of the preceding few weeks, the tone was remarkable.

I accept that I have not co-operated with this tribunal in a manner which would have been expected of me. I deeply regret that I have allowed this situation to arise.

When I walked out of Government Buildings on February the eleventh 1992 I was determined to leave public life firmly behind me, to detach myself completely from it and to leave those who followed me free to manage things in their own way without any attempt by me to influence or interfere.

He had difficulty recalling some events because of the way he had cut himself off from public life after his retirement. He "omitted" to instruct his lawyers fully, he said.

I was concerned as to the effect that the publication of these payments would have for me in the public mind and in hindsight I accept that a lot of the problems and embarrassment that I have caused would have been avoided if I had been more forthcoming at each and every relevant period.

He said he accepted that he had received the £1.3 million from Dunne "and that I became aware that he was the donor to the late Mr Des Traynor in late 1993." He said he accepted that he had received the three drafts but

I have absolutely no recollection of the November 1991 meeting, but it is clear from the evidence that the late Mr Des Traynor received the money and that I got the benefit of it. I can offer no other rational explanation to show how the late Mr Des Traynor could have received these drafts other than in the manner outlined by Mr Ben Dunne and I am prepared to accept his evidence in this regard.

It was an unsatisfactory statement. How could he have received such a large amount of money in such circumstances and not remember? He said that in 1993,

subsequent to my departure from office, the late Mr Traynor indicated to me that Mr Ben Dunne had contributed in excess of £1 million to help him manage my finances between 1987 and 1991, but I wish to emphasise that he had not told me this while I was in office.

Traynor had told him in the wake of the visit from Heffernan. His earlier statement in relation to what Traynor had said in 1993 after Heffernan's visit was a lie.

Haughey repeated his statement that Traynor had managed his affairs since about 1960.

He saw it as his personal responsibility to ensure that I would be free to devote my time and ability to public life and that I would not be distracted from my political work by financial considerations. The late Mr Des Traynor had complete discretion to act on my behalf without reference back to me. In hindsight it is clear that I should have involved myself to a greater degree in this regard.

In two sentences he managed to aggrandise himself in the midst of his disgrace, and dump his loyal friend. It was a mean piece of evidence. He finished by saying Dunne had not sought or been granted any favours, and that he apologised

> but wish to emphasise that this serious lapse in the management of my personal affairs did not in any way affect the discharge of my public duty when in office.

At the time, Haughey's appearance seemed as if it was something of a cathartic moment for the State. Here was a sober, methodical exposure of what he and Traynor and their circle had been up to for more than thirty years. What had been surrounded by so much mystique and pomp and pretentiousness was now being laid out in all its relative simplicity. The examination by Denis McCullough, barrister for the tribunal, was short enough. He bore in mind, he said at the outset, that Haughey had indeed "done the State some service."

McCullough got him to admit he had lied, though neither man used the word. Haughey said that at some level he knew all along he was caught.

"Would you accept now, Mr Haughey, that you sat outside the tribunal in Abbeville waiting to see whether or not the tribunal would gather sufficient evidence to make it incumbent upon you to make a statement? Would that be a fair summation?"

"Well, it could be, but I suppose basically I was looking at the fact of the inevitable disclosure."

He broke the back of his humiliation by cracking a joke. McCullough mentioned that Haughey was an accountant and a former Minister for Finance, and Haughey said accountants did not always make good Ministers for Finance. It raised a bit of a laugh. After that the encounter seemed more cosy, as if Haughey was one among equals, or even more than that.

When the examination ended he went with his entourage to private rooms in the castle. The tribunal's proceedings were over, and some of the legal team went across the road to Thomas Read's café and pub and bought champagne. The crowd which had come to see Haughey waited in the Upper Yard of the castle for Haughey to come out. Haughey, mistakenly thinking they wished to express support for him, chose to walk out the main door of the State Apartments towards his waiting Mercedes, rather than waiting or leaving through some back entrance. When he and his son Conor came out one or two people made what sounded like cheers but then, within seconds, the cheers were drowned by a general outbreak of booing. Haughey kept going, walking towards the car while waving past the photographers at the booing crowd. A 78-year-old waiter from the Trocadero restaurant, Frank Harrison, rushed forward; Haughey, unsure of the man's intentions, touched his hands but kept moving towards the car. Harrison wanted to express support, but the handshake never came off. Haughey got into his car and was driven away through the booing crowd.

"He might have made a mistake, but he is still a great man," Harrison said afterwards. "Look at all he did for old people, for instance. I love Charlie. My background is Clann na Poblachta but I canvassed for Charlie in elections." He said he first met Haughey when working in the Coachman's Inn in Cloghran, Co. Dublin, in 1965. "He was there with the late Matt Gallagher and I liked him from the moment we met."

Harrison's admiration for Haughey was not mirrored in the report of the tribunal chairman.

It is quite unacceptable that a member of Dáil Éireann, and in particular a cabinet minister and Taoiseach, should be supported in his personal lifestyle by gifts made to him personally. It is particularly unacceptable that such gifts should emanate from prominent businessmen within the State. The possibility that political or financial favours could be sought in return for such gifts, or even be given without being sought, is very high, and if such gifts are permissible, they would inevitably lead in some cases to bribery and corruption.

The judge did not believe the evidence given by Haughey. Some aspects were "quite unbelievable." Other aspects were "unbelievable', "incomprehensible", "beyond all credibility" and "unlikely".

Because Haughey had at the outset denied he had received any money from Dunne but then accepted that he had, and that he'd known since 1993, the judge referred the papers in the matter to the Director of Public Prosecutions, who later brought criminal charges.

The chairman also noted the following:

When asked by the chairman of the tribunal whether he discussed with Mr Desmond Traynor [in 1993] whether the money from Mr Ben Dunne was all spent or whether some of it was still there, Mr Charles Haughey gave the answer:

"No. I mean he would have been supplying the statements of account in that regard."

The clear implication is, that despite his earlier denials, Mr Charles Haughey had in fact received statements dealing with his accounts which he read and noted, and therefore he did not have to ask about his affairs, because he was already aware of them. The tribunal believes this to be the true state of affairs.

In other words, all along Haughey knew how much he was being given and how much was in his accounts in the Ansbacher deposits.

18

Endgame

WITHIN a month of the McCracken Tribunal report being published the Government appointed a new tribunal, the Moriarty Tribunal. The McCracken Tribunal lasted seven months. The Moriarty Tribunal was to last for multiples of that.

Haughey's retirement years were being devoured by investigations into his past behaviour. In the period since his retirement the State had become more wealthy and more confident. Its agents had become less respectful or fearful of influence and authority. The media had also become more aggressive and intrusive. The Irish Republic, suddenly finding itself as wealthy as most of its western European counterparts, began to conduct a critical examination of the recent past. Matters which in many cases had been known about and accepted in a some vague and general way were now being dragged into the cold light of day, usually as a prerequisite to the allocation of blame. Child abuse; a Catholic Church more concerned with its authority than with the protection of its weakest and most vulnerable members; corruption in the planning process; the arrogance of some members of the medical profession; a golden circle at the heart of big business; secret payments to Charles Haughey. Throughout the period of exposure no individual came in for such passionate and sustained public abuse as did Haughey.

He was booed when he walked into the Upper Yard in Dublin Castle after appearing before the McCracken Tribunal. Two years later, when details of the Moriarty Tribunal's inquiries into the Brian Lenihan fund were disclosed, cartoons appeared in the national press showing him eating liver and alfalfa lettuce and calling for more Chianti, an allusion to the cannibal Hannibal Lector from the film *Silence of the Lambs*. A documentary series on the history of the Irish State, "Seven Ages," broadcast by RTÉ, invited viewers to see that history as a political struggle leading up to Haughey's rise to power and betrayal of all that had gone before. The series included film of Haughey, seated by a window in Abbeville, turning his head to one side and refusing to comment after he was asked about taking money. Perhaps he thought that by holding his head like that the film could not be used, but it was, and it seemed very harsh, the cornering of a man in his seventies, a man who was trying to but couldn't find anywhere to hide.

As the century closed, the Moriarty Tribunal was conducting an examination of his affairs going back twenty years; High Court inspectors were investigating the Ansbacher deposits, in which he'd had substantial sums; and the Revenue Commissioners had accepted a £1 million settlement arising from the payments detailed by the McCracken Tribunal. Some of the land at Kinsealy he'd given to his children years earlier was sold to help foot the bill.

The Revenue Commissioners were also monitoring the Moriarty Tribunal and preparing a new tax assessment based on the evidence being heard. The value of Haughey's home had even been reassessed and the new value backdated for property tax purposes. Property tax, at 1.5 per cent, was a self-assessed tax, where people assessed the value of their own property and answered a few questions on a standard form.

Haughey had made returns over the years in relation to the value of Abbeville. In 1983 he had valued his home at £250,000. Over the years to 1989 he'd said its value remained steady. In 1989 he'd declared a small increase, to £262,500. The value of the property then remained steady until 1995, when it increased to £272,500, according to his returns. The 1996 valuation he submitted was £295,000.

The Revenue Commissioners had had the property checked by people in the Valuation Office. On 6 November 1986 an official had visited Abbeville, and the Revenue Commissioners subsequently advised that the assessment made by Haughey was satisfactory.

In 1997, in the wake of the McCracken Report, the value of Abbeville was reassessed and backdated. The revised figure for 1988 was £300,000, a 20 per cent increase. The percentage increase for other years was of similar magnitude. The revised figure for 1996 was £1.3 million, three times the previously accepted valuation for that year. A new tax bill based on increased valuations for every year up to 1996 was submitted to Haughey. On the face of it the market value of his mansion had been markedly affected by the content of a report into payments from Ben Dunne.

As well as all this a criminal charge arising out of his evidence to the McCracken Tribunal was going round and round in circles in the Four Courts. Almost all his public appearances were for the public sittings of inquiries into his affairs. The State was out to get him.

Through it all he maintained a surly silence, inviting observers to come to the view that he felt himself to be the victim of malicious and ungrateful elements. There was no hint of remorse, no hint that he had reassessed how he'd lived and come to regret it. One friend said he accepted he had a case to answer but would not go so far as to say he had no-one to blame but himself. Another said he put on a show of strength when in company but in private revealed an obsession with the progress of the tribunals. His life's work, instead of winning him acceptance and admiration, had made him a social pariah.

His refusal to engage with the society in which he'd held such important and powerful positions had the effect of increasing the anger and disapproval felt by the public. The mystique which had at one stage surrounded him fell away. The McCracken Tribunal had been packed in June 1997 when he came to give evidence. Three years later, when he appeared before the Moriarty Tribunal, the extra seating which had been put in remained unused.

And all the time he was not only growing older but also suffering from cancer. Friends and supporters alluded to the fact during background briefings but were treated with suspicion by the media. When Haughey returned to Dublin Castle in June 1999 his evidence was similar to that heard two years earlier: Des Traynor knew the details of his financial affairs and never told him; he could be of no assistance. Few people believed him.

Because of his medical condition Haughey gave evidence for only two hours a day, four days a week. On the first day he gave evidence, 21 July, he looked well but appeared prone to bouts of tiredness and loss of concentration. At times he even said he was confused and had difficulty following the proceedings. For the first time he was seen in public wearing reading glasses. In her sketch in the *Irish Independent* Miriam Lord wrote, with feigned horror: "Call Melina Mercouri! The Haughey marbles are missing!"

On subsequent days Haughey did not seem as confused but still occasionally lost concentration. At other times he seemed to know the documents he was being brought through at least as well as the tribunal counsel, John Coughlan. Observers differed about the extent to which they believed Haughey was hamming it up, emphasising his confusion. The truth seemed to be that his attitude to giving evidence to tribunals remained unchanged but that he had weaker mental resources to call on than hitherto, and this troubled him.

Haughey gave evidence for five days in July, and the tribunal then broke for the summer recess. He went on a boating trip in the Mediterranean, but friends say his fretting about the tribunal never ceased. On 21 September he returned to the witness box. Up to this point the focus was on his relationship with AIB in the 1970s. The tribunal counsel, John Coughlan, tried to use Haughey's file in AIB to undermine his evidence that Traynor managed his affairs and that he (Haughey) rarely knew the details. Nothing concrete was proved either way, and the point remained one of credence. At one stage Haughey differed with evidence which had already been heard, from Catherine Butler, concerning the frequency with which he saw Traynor at the weekends. It was much less often than she'd said, Haughey claimed. He met Traynor only five to six times a year. The tribunal later called in Traynor's son, Tony Traynor, who said his father travelled from his home on the Howth Road to see Haughey in Kinsealy "perhaps most Saturdays or at least on two Saturdays per month on average." His father would be away for an hour or two, and the pattern did not change up to the time of his death in 1994. His father would sometimes visit Haughey on Sundays as well, Traynor said. His evidence supported Butler's.

He gave evidence for a further five days, but then the tribunal adjourned again, on 3 October. Haughey was examined by his doctors. During the adjournment the tribunal conducted a hearing at which officials of the Revenue Commissioners were questioned in private. Before the hearing went into private session, however, Haughey's counsel, Eoin McGonigal, stood and made a submission concerning his client's medical condition. The matter, he said, was now one of public interest and for that reason Haughey had decided the details should be revealed to the public. The tribunal was taken by surprise.

McGonigal disclosed that Haughey's main medical adviser, Peter McLean of the Mater Private Hospital, was of the view that Haughey should not give any more evidence to the tribunal because of the effect it was having on him. Haughey's engagement with the tribunal should come to a complete halt, McGonigal said, and there was no possible regime which the tribunal could arrange which the doctor believed would not be equally deleterious to his patient's well-being.

The doctor had furnished the tribunal with a recent medical report, which McGonigal began to read into the record. The assembled journalists scribbled for all they were worth.

Mr Charles Haughey, Abbeville, Kinsealy, was seen by me in October 1995 when a diagnosis of moderately and anaplastic adenocarcinoma of the prostate was established. The lesion was treated with external beam radiation therapy.

At this time the disease has progressed as evidenced by clinical assessment, biochemical testing and radio isotope scanning. This progression has been particularly marked over the past six months. He has now commenced total androgen blockade therapy. This form of treatment is purely palliative and is used together with pain relief in the terminal care of patients with prostatic cancer.

I reviewed this patient on the 28/9/2000 on the afternoon of the day, which coincidentally he had in the morning appeared before the Moriarty Tribunal. He was fatigued, stressed and I felt that he was slightly disorientated. I concluded unequivocally on medical scientific grounds that he should not appear before any such official bodies in the future unless his general medical condition greatly improves.

McLean said he had discussed the matter with Haughey's GP, a colleague in the Mater Private Hospital, and an American professor who had also examined Haughey. The decision was unanimous, the consultant said in his report.

The tribunal was handed a book of medical reports on Haughey, going back at least to October 1995, when he was first diagnosed with prostate cancer. The reports noted that Haughey had suffered a heart attack on 2 January 1997, in the period between the media stories which first disclosed payments from Ben Dunne to a senior member of Fianna Fáil, and the establishment of the McCracken Tribunal. Haughey was also suffering from other medical conditions, McGonigal said. The details were not read out. "It is unfortunate that Mr Haughey has been subjected to so much protracted public pressure and strain in recent years," McGonigal read out from the report. "This has certainly been and continues to be seriously detrimental to his health and general well-being. The elimination or reduction of stress in his daily life would have a major beneficial effect on his life expectancy and in preventing further deterioration in his overall medical condition." When Haughey's counsel sat down Coughlan got to his feet and said the tribunal had not been aware the matter was to be raised. He disclosed that a week earlier the tribunal had met McLean and discussed the situation, and that afterwards the tribunal solicitor, John Davis, had written to Haughey's solicitor, Deirdre Courtney. He read out the letter:

> The sole member [Moriarty] acknowledges the serious nature of Mr Haughey's medical condition and the obvious distress associated with it . . . While the tribunal's public duty to conduct an inquiry must be fulfilled, the sole member recognises, as exemplified by the arrangements put in place to accommodate Mr. Haughey to date, that this also entails a duty to give sympathetic consideration to and to take any reasonable steps and to make every appropriate allowance for a medical condition or any other disability from which a person testifying at the tribunal may be suffering.

Davis wrote that the tribunal was

> relieved that Mr Haughey is not in any pain and is not receiving any treatment by way of pain relief. At the same time, it is also recognised that Mr Haughey has a generalised cancer of the prostate and this is causing symptoms of lethargy, a feeling of being unwell, and a loss of concentration, all of which are likely to affect his preparation for and the actual giving of evidence. The tribunal also recognises that any doctor advising a patient will, as a counsel of perfection, advise against exposure to the upset of the kind associated with the daily demands of,

say, business or in this case appearing before the tribunal's public sittings.

From the correspondence read out it became clear that the previous week Haughey had received the report from McLean and had not afterwards felt in a position to prepare for a scheduled public appearance at the tribunal. That appearance had not gone ahead. Davis noted these facts, then continued:

> However there is no suggestion that in his current state of health, Mr Haughey's mental capacity is impaired. Noting the absence of pain, the absence of treatment for pain and Mr McLean's confirmation that Mr Haughey is a physically strong man and a compliant patient, the tribunal has decided it must continue with its public duty.

Davis informed Courtney that the tribunal wanted to devise a regime for continuing to take evidence from Haughey, whether in oral evidence or by way of questionnaires, and perhaps with a schedule less onerous than the two hours per morning, four days per week, which had originally been arranged for Haughey.

Davis noted that as far back as March 1999 one of Haughey's medical advisers had said it would be best if Haughey's dealings with the tribunal were brought to an end as soon as possible. He continued:

> It is perhaps regrettable that this was not brought to the attention of the tribunal at the time, as it might have been easier at that time to make the appropriate arrangements to expedite the taking of evidence from Mr Haughey.

The matter was adjourned, and soon afterwards the tribunal took up McGonigal's suggestion that it engage its own medical experts. A London urologist, Gordon Williams, examined Haughey's cancer of the prostate gland. He developed concerns about other aspects of Haughey's health and recommended that he be seen by a neurologist. The tribunal engaged Martin Rossor from London, an expert in Alzheimer's disease, Pick's disease, Creutzfeldt-Jakob disease and conditions affecting the memory. Rossor found that Haughey was "cognitively impaired" to an extent which had implications for the tribunal. The reports made by the two men for the tribunal were not released to the public. The judge studied the documents in conjunction with the reports he'd had from Haughey's medical team, and came to a decision.

In December Mr Justice Moriarty announced his decision that Haughey would be ordered to give evidence "on commission", meaning that he would be examined in a private room for one hour a day, four days a week, the transcripts later to be read into the public record. The judge said the questioning would be short and to the point, in an effort to expedite matters as much as possible and thereby reduce the strain on Haughey. In the new year the process of questioning Haughey in private began. As with most matters involving lawyers and tribunals, the taking of evidence from Haughey was to last much longer than originally anticipated.

He gave evidence in private on twenty days between Thursday 18 January and Thursday 15 March 2001. Not much was learned as a result of the twenty hours of engagement between himself and the tribunal counsel, John Coughlan. Haughey found it trying and wearisome. On the first day, his first comment was to request to be allowed make a statement. By all means, said Mr Justice Moriarty. Haughey then said:

I have come here to this tribunal today not voluntarily but solely because the tribunal, in the exercise of its powers, has compelled me to be here. I do so against the wishes and the advice of my doctors and also in the knowledge that they are of the opinion that this procedure which we are about to embark upon will both worsen my medical condition and shorten my life expectancy. I am presently on medication to relieve my pain and discomfort. I am increasingly forgetful and I say, with absolute sincerity, that I am quite mentally and physically incapable of dealing in any satisfactory way with the vast amount of documentation that I am expected to.

I want to say, chairman, that I believe that in all these circumstances, in compelling my appearance here and subjecting me to the trials and trauma of this tribunal, that the tribunal is infringing on my fundamental human rights and I look forward to the period immediately ahead greatly perturbed. Thank you.

Documents were being supplied to Haughey so that he could prepare for each following morning's session. During the evidence heard on Wednesday 14 February, Coughlan referred Haughey to some documents. Haughey turned to Mr Justice Moriarty (called the commissioner during the taking of evidence on commission).

Mr Commissioner, I would just like to explain to you that when I leave these sessions and return home, I am not really – I suppose what you might – colloquially know as a downer. I am not really – in the afternoons, I am not really in a position to handle material and I got a book of documents yesterday or the day before dealing with Celtic

Helicopters and a lot of it I recall and so on, but I am not able to read from these documents in the afternoons.

Mr Justice Moriarty said there were days when all the documents depressed him also and that he could appreciate something of what Haughey felt. "Thank you, commissioner," said Haughey. "Abbeville is a big house, commissioner, and it's nearly full already."

On Wednesday 21 February, the twelfth day of the taking of evidence on commission, Mr Justice Moriarty asked Haughey how he was bearing up.

Thank you very much, commissioner, and may I say that, through you perhaps also, to Mr Coughlan, that if I appear irascible from time to time, it's not deliberate on my part. I find it very stressful indeed. I shudder when these things arrive from my solicitor, because I can't handle them. I just can't bring myself to go through all the – which I should be doing if I am to serve, help the tribunal. But I have deep feelings of apprehension and anxiety coming in here every day. I do not sleep at night time. I am increasingly resorting to medication and I long, long deeply for the whole thing to come to an end.

The agony was to last another three weeks. On occasion his doctor, Mr McLean, would call out to see him in Abbeville in the afternoons. McLean expressed the view that the questioning sessions were taking a heavy toll. On Thursday 15 March, Haughey completed his final session and headed home for the St Patrick's Day weekend. McLean saw him that afternoon and sent a letter to the tribunal outlining his view that the tribunal was taking a heavy toll on his patient's health and should trouble Haughey no more. That weekend Haughey, at home, suffered a heart crisis during which his heart stopped on two occasions. He was rushed to Beaumont Hospital. McLean later said Haughey would have died but for the excellent work of Mrs Haughey, the ambulance crew, and the hospital staff. He said the attack proved that he was right, that Haughey should not have been made continue answer questions to the tribunal. Friends subsequently said Haughey decided afterwards he would never again attend the tribunal. If the tribunal wanted him back, it would have to go to the High Court and argue its right to drag an old and sick man in for more questioning.

19

The Case for the Defence

DURING the course of the Moriarty Tribunal I wrote to Charles Haughey, pointing out that I was covering the tribunal for my newspaper and working on this book. I felt it was unfortunate to be writing so much about a man I'd never spoken to, a man I'd never had the opportunity to form an opinion of on the basis of a one-to-one conversation. I asked if he would be prepared to meet me. I was hoping for an invitation to Kinsealy, or that he might agree to meet for lunch and I would manage to persuade him to share a bottle of Bordeaux with me. After so much time watching the tribunal's proceedings I was anxious to have a more personal interaction with him and, also, an exclusive one. I wanted my own personal Charlie Haughey story. All through his life people must have felt like that about him, even friends.

We could have an entirely off-the-record meeting, I suggested. We didn't have to discuss the details of what had been discovered by the tribunal. I got no response. A friend of his I bumped into some days later told me he'd seen the letter and that Haughey was not ill-disposed towards me but that he wouldn't be taking up the suggestion. He gets a lot of requests for meetings, the friend said.

He said Haughey wasn't well. He had to take medication and it got him down. On occasion he had to take boosters, and these really knocked him back. When he took them his vision was affected and he couldn't read, and that made him depressed. But he was still drinking wine. The friend had been up in Kinsealy with him recently and he and Haughey had done some work together and then some other cronies – his word – had arrived and at Haughey's suggestion they'd opened a few bottles of wine. They'd started drinking at noon, the friend said, laughing. Another Charlie Haughey story.

I thought that if I met him we might discuss generalities but inevitably come to the topic of his accepting money, that even a few sentences would provide me with a key, an entry point into understanding his view of himself and how he fitted the fact of his receiving money with his overall self-image which, I presumed, was flattering. I wondered if he was a likable rogue or was he venal and self-satisfied and cruel?

I could tell his friends liked him. They said he was entertaining, smart, lacking in real malice, that he was very close to his wife and children, that he was, despite Keane, a family man. His friends were never candid but did seem to want to be helpful if they could. They were likable enough, despite being cautious, suspicious, partisan. What Haughey had done was something which in general made them shake their heads while smiling. He was some operator, Haughey, seemed to be their view. He had a case to answer but his enemies were trying to make capital out of it. There was more a sense of a contest than agreement that what

had been done was wrong. There was no contrition, no acceptance of the corrosive effect Haughey's ambition and greed had
had on the body politic.

Most said they'd never known he was getting quite so much
money. They were neither upright nor righteous, and gave the
impression they disliked such people. The law and society's
institutions were matters to be negotiated, a sort of opposition.
The law and authority were threats to achievement, and anyone
worthy of respect recognised them as such. Morality was a private
matter, particularly when it came to money. It was a seductive
world view. Get what you can from the world, from life. Become
rich, play for high stakes, live close to or at the centre of power
and influence. Have a bit of craic.

And yet the people who held these views, friends and
supporters of Haughey, were for so long the heart of the political
establishment, the locus of authority and power. It seemed the
paradox was explained by feelings of moral or general superiority.
Entrepreneurs and self-made men, they could cheat on their
taxes or condone such action at a time when the State was close
to bankruptcy, and yet feel patriotic, because they felt that by
running their business affairs so successfully they made an above-
average contribution to the affairs of the nation. This superiority
absolved them from the obligations which applied to less
wealthy and, therefore, less able people. Or so it seemed.

During the questioning of Haughey in public in September 2000
concerning his dealings with AIB, the barrister John Coughlan
strayed from the immediate topic to ask more general questions
about politicians accepting money. The following are a number
of extracts. They constitute, most probably, the most sustained
on-the-record questioning of Haughey concerning the general

issue of accepting financial gifts that we are ever likely to have. How credible they are remains a matter for the reader.

Coughlan asked if Traynor had what he called Haughey's "implied authority" to ask people for money. Yes, said Haughey, "donations". He said that whatever Traynor might have done in this regard was done of his own volition.

"If Mr Traynor approached individuals, and you say he had that implied authority from you if necessary, can I take it that it would be individuals who would be supporters of yours, would that be a fair way of putting it?"

"That's a likelihood but I am – I cannot say whether it's a definitive position or not."

"He'd hardly approach your political enemies?"

"Well, they might be neutral."

"And if he approached people to make what appear to be substantial contributions for or on your behalf, would you accept that that was by reason of the office you held at the time?"

"No."

"Would you have had a concern if you had known at the time that Mr Traynor had approached somebody, had solicited funds of this size on your behalf?"

"I cannot say at this stage what my position would have been at that time."

"But looking at it now – well perhaps I will go back to that time. I take it that as the holder of the office of head of government, you would not have wanted to be beholden to anybody, wouldn't that be correct?"

"Well, the main purpose of the exercise at that stage was not to be beholden to AIB or not to be subject to public pressure by them."

"I think we can take it as a given that it would be inappropriate for a Taoiseach to be beholden to anybody financially, would you agree with that?"

"Yes."

"And I am not even talking in the context now of some vulgar or crude way or somebody paying money to get an actual job done. I am talking in its broadest context, it would be inappropriate for a Taoiseach to be beholden financially to anybody, would you agree?"

"Well, it all depends on beholden, the meaning of the word beholden. I would think that it would be valid for individuals or institutions to support a political person, because they believed in him or her or what they were doing, for absolutely totally disinvolved motives."

"I just want to be clear about that. There are two levels of support, and for the assistance of the tribunal, because your view is important on this, Mr Haughey, you being the professional politician; there is support which is normal political support, which is contributions which are made to politicians to enable them to fight election campaigns or perhaps to service their clinics or something like that; isn't that correct?"

"Yes."

"There is support then which is of – and I take it that we probably don't have any great issue to join on that concept of support?"

"No."

"Now, is that the type of support you are talking about?"

"Both."

"So you are talking about support over and above that which would be to fund the living expenses of a Taoiseach?"

"No, to alleviate the financial difficulties of a particular politician. I am quite sure in modern political history it's happened time and time again. I am thinking of the sort of situation where a group of friends would come together and out of purely altruistic motives, assist a particular politician in a particular spot of difficulty."

"Should that be made public?"

"Not necessarily, because the circumstances of the politician's difficulties, he might not wish to have them made public, or the fact that he had difficulties."

"I understand that the politician may not wish to have them made public, but a public man's affairs, if he is being supported by individuals, surely you must agree is a public matter?"

"Well, there is very little – I don't see there is any great difference between that sort of support, assisting a politician with a particular difficulty, and a group of friends and supporters assisting the same politician in the discharge of his public duties or fighting election campaigns or running a constituency office. I can't see there is any big line of differentiation."

"Well, can I ask you this: If a politician is supported by – if a public person is supported by individuals or a group in respect of his own personal financial affairs, is there not a risk that, first of all, the public person may behave even subconsciously more benignly to the interests of such people? Isn't there the risk that the person who makes the contribution would feel that they were in some way entitled to preferential treatment?"

"No, that does not follow."

"That does not follow?"

"No."

"That there is such a risk?"

"There are many public-spirited people who subscribe to political parties and to individual politicians and who have no anticipation of anything other than the political success of the individual."

"The political success of the party of the individual because that's giving rise to a policy which somebody favours and wishes to support?"

"No, no, no, because they are doing a good job."

"I see."

"Because they are running a country well, because they are engaging in initiatives which are beneficial to everybody, as I think I continually did."

"So as far as – and I am inviting your view on this, Mr Haughey. You see no distinction between political contributions, say, for the purpose of fighting elections and personal contributions to support the public person whilst he is in public office? You see no distinction?"

"Supporting his public career, yes."

"I see. To whatever standard that person may aspire to, for example – I am being serious – to whatever standard that person may aspire to himself even, that that is appropriate, in your view?"

"I am not quite sure of the thrust of that question."

There was discussion of the Gallagher deal, and then Coughlan returned to the general matter of accepting money.

"Is it your view that to support a public person in their private life is appropriate; that's your view?"

"Not quite. The public life. I mean, a politician could get into financial difficulties inadvertently or as a result of accumulation of election campaigns, which has happened very much in our recent history, and a group of supporters and friends come together and, as I say, without any ulterior motive whatsoever except to support the politician in his political activities to help out those difficulties."

When Coughlan said that this seemed like normal political support, Haughey said they were getting into very "nebulous" areas. "You have asked me for my view about these matters and I have given it to you as best I can."

Coughlan asked if Haughey believed it was appropriate for individuals or a group to support a politician who decided he wanted to live in a bigger and better house than the one he was in.

"Not in that particular situation of moving from one house to another, a bigger, better house, no."

"Or if he had run into financial difficulties by attempting to maintain a position?"

"Well, I don't know that the nature of the origin of the financial difficulties would be all that relevant, but what I am saying is that if a particular politician who people – whose work people value and whose policies they support was in particular financial difficulties at any stage – and there are many reasons apart from the one you mentioned which would give rise to such financial difficulties – then I cannot see that it would not be legitimate for a group of supporters or friends with no motive whatsoever, no ulterior motive whatsoever, to come to the aid of that politician."

Coughlan made the point that no financial support seemed to be coming Haughey's way during the 1970s, when his overdraft with AIB was growing and growing. "And you became Taoiseach on the eleventh of December 1979 and on that same day, all of the money began to become available to deal with the Allied Irish Bank indebtedness; isn't that correct?"

"Well, I think that's putting an entirely false coincidental aspect. The point was, as I was becoming Taoiseach, I decided that it was, for two reasons it was necessary to settle the AIB situation: one was, as I say, for the public perception of it; and the second was for the pressure being exercised by AIB. And, therefore, I asked Des Traynor to enter into discussions with AIB to resolve the matter so that I could go ahead – go into the office of Taoiseach with a clear sheet from that point of view, as it were."

"So it was – "

"That's the way I look at it."

Coughlan put it to Haughey that it was wholly incredible that Haughey, knowing that £300,000 had come from Gallagher and that another £450,000 was found elsewhere to settle the AIB debt, did not ask Traynor where the money came from. Haughey rejected this. He also said he would not necessarily have expected Traynor to tell him where the money had come from if it had been given by supporters.

"Because he may have respected, if there were people who were making the contributions in confidence, he would have respected that confidence."

"But . . ."

"And, in fact, I will go further. I would say that he would probably regard it as a protection of me that I would not know who had subscribed."

He was asked if the acceptance of money in this way did not make him "hostage" to whoever had made the donations. "If somebody knew that they had given it to you, that they may have said it, they may have publicised it, they may have spoken to Traynor and said, look, I gave £150,000, I am not looking for Mr Haughey to hand me a licence or something or anything like that, but I want my view on some particular matter taken into account. Wasn't there that risk?"

"I can assure you that Mr Traynor would never ever do anything like that. He was totally removed from any form of political activity of that kind."

He said he didn't discuss confidentiality in relation to donations with Traynor but that it was implicit in the whole situation. Going back to the AIB situation, Coughlan asked whether it was not because of the office he took on in December 1979 that Traynor was able to raise money for him. Haughey said this was not the case. It was because "as incoming Taoiseach there was a situation which could be of embarrassment to me which had to be dealt with. Not because of the office I held . . . It was because of the difficulty in which I was, rather than because of the office. There is a distinction."

Later Coughlan said: "And on many occasions in the course of your life, you received very large donations from individuals; isn't that right?"

"On occasions."

"Yes, and you knew that, Mr Haughey, didn't you?"

"I don't understand what you mean, I knew that."

"But you knew that when you became Taoiseach, that if Mr Traynor wasn't going to raise money by way of a loan, that he had your implied authority to solicit funds from individuals or groups on your behalf by way of donation, didn't he?"

"He had implied authority at any time to deal with my affairs as he thought best."

"But you knew that that was one of the possibilities; isn't that right?"

"It was always a possibility, yes."

At the end of that day's evidence the tribunal chairman, Mr Justice Moriarty, asked Haughey if he didn't need to know who Traynor was approaching for money so as to be sure they were not political rivals.

"I don't think so, chairman, because Mr Traynor would certainly have been wise enough and experienced enough to know not to go to somebody who might be politically hostile to me."

"In other words, your implicit remit to him would have been wide enough to trust him to get somebody who would have been acceptable?"

"Absolutely."

When the tribunal returned to this theme a few days later, Coughlan asked if Traynor ever had an involvement in Haughey's political affairs.

> Oh, no, certainly not, no. He was always very insistent that he was not a political person and that in so far as he would make any sort of contribution to our country's affairs, it would be through relieving me of financial responsibilities and handling them himself. He felt that that was the best way he could contribute to his country's well-being.

Later Coughlan asked where Haughey thought the money for his bill-paying service came from.

"I don't suppose I gave it very much thought. As I said, it was his [Traynor's] responsibility to keep the show on the road, as it were, and I was always satisfied that he could do that, and I got on with my political life."

Later again:

"But bearing in mind, Mr Haughey, that you found nothing wrong, and I use that in its broadest possible context, in a person holding public office being supported, if they got into financial

311

difficulties, by an individual or by a group, if they supported the man or woman's policies, or if they just thought he or she was doing a good job, you saw nothing wrong with that?"

"Public-spirited people, disinterested people – I think I used the word altruistic people."

And on another day, in what seemed to be in hope that if he summed up the whole matter he might be spared any further questions:

> I accept that Des Traynor and others did succeed in approaching people and interesting them in my financial problems and raising funds which were subsequently disbursed for my benefit and, secondly, that Judge McCracken found that there was no question of any favours or concessions given in return by me, and really, as far as I am concerned, Mr Coughlan, I don't know that I can take it any further at this very minute.